# Responsive Web De HTML5 and CSS

Fourth Edition

Build future-proof responsive websites using the latest HTML5 and CSS techniques

**Ben Frain**

BIRMINGHAM—MUMBAI

# Responsive Web Design with HTML5 and CSS
## Fourth Edition

**Senior Publishing Product Manager:** Suman Sen

**Acquisition Editor – Peer Reviews:** Gaurav Gavas

**Project Editor:** Parvathy Nair

**Content Development Editor:** Lucy Wan

**Copy Editor:** Safis Editing

**Technical Editor:** Tejas Mhasvekar

**Proofreader:** Safis Editing

**Indexer:** Pratik Shirodkar

**Presentation Designer:** Rajesh Shirsath

First published: April 2012
Second edition: August 2015
Third edition: April 2020
Fourth edition: September 2022

Production reference: 3170223

Published by Packt Publishing Ltd.
Livery Place
35 Livery Street
Birmingham
B3 2PB, UK.

ISBN 978-1-80324-271-2

www.packt.com

# Contributors

## About the author

**Ben Frain** has been a web designer/developer since 1996. He is currently employed as a UI/UX Technical Lead at bet365. Before the web, he worked as an underrated (and modest) TV actor and technology journalist, having graduated from Salford University with a degree in Media and Performance. He has written four equally underrated (his opinion) screenplays and still harbors the (fading) belief he might sell one.

He likes to pretend he isn't a nerd but spends an inordinate amount of time building keyboards and talking about them, text editors, and the web on his blog and YouTube channel. Outside of geekery, he enjoys simple pleasures. Playing indoor football while his body and wife still allow it, and trying to keep up with his two sons.

*I told the team at Packt it would take me a short age to write this book. I was true to my word! Their patience and understanding throughout was appreciated.*

*The team of reviewers did a sterling job; I'd like to take the chance to thank them here for giving up their time to improve this title. I'll also extend thanks here to my editor, Lucy Wan. She shepherded everything along with efficiency, and made smart and effective amendments throughout.*

*Finally, thanks to my family. I was told as a child that the most important thing you can give someone is your time. I'm looking forward to having more of that to give you, whether you like it or not!*

# About the reviewers

**J. Pedro Ribeiro** is a Brazilian software engineer based in London. He has been working on the web since the mid-90s, back when dial-up connections, GeoCities, and Netscape Navigator were a thing.

His work is focused on building performant, accessible websites and apps that deliver great user experience. Alongside web development, Pedro has worked as a technical reviewer for other publications like *Mastering Responsive Web Design* and *Responsive Web Design Patterns*, both at Packt Publishing.

He is also the author of Baseliner, a Chrome extension with over 6,000 weekly users.

- Blog – jpedroribeiro.com
- Twitter – https://twitter.com/jpedroribeiro
- GitHub – https://github.com/jpedroribeiro

**Michelle Manemann** was raised by—and with—the internet (long before it became the norm). She spent her formative years exploring the web as it evolved from simple text-only sites, to sites with pages formatted as tables within tables like so many nesting dolls, through the rise and fall of Flash, to the (relatively) standardized modern web of today. Influenced by the scrolling marquees and animated GIFs of the mid-90s, it's perhaps fortunate that her earliest efforts in web design are lost to the sands of time (R.I.P. GeoCities).

While finalizing her degree in Anthropology from Grinnell College, Michelle rediscovered the allure of web design. Anthro B.A. in-hand, she accepted an internship that allowed her to hone her HTML and CSS in real time; her formative love of web design and its possibilities reignited immediately. Originally the sole designer in her organization, Michelle built a full-fledged Web Design Department from the ground up; a decade later, she manages a small but mighty team of fellow designers and together they create beautiful websites for educators across North America.

While this is Michelle's first turn as a technical reviewer, she is a veteran of the publishing industry, having created hundreds of print cover designs and online web experiences for her company and its partners over the course of a decade. When business hours are over, Michelle is on the move. If she's not exploring the natural beauty along her native Mississippi River, she's traveling the world to uncover new founts of inspiration and creativity.

*I would like to thank Packt Senior Project Editor, Parvathy, for her patient handling of my questions and comments over the better half of a year.*

*Any success I enjoy is due to the unconditional love and support of my parents and my youngest brother, Chase, whose humor and strength far surpass my own. I strive to be his equal in kindness every day.*

# Join our book's Discord space

Join the book's Discord workspace to discuss all your responsive web design concerns directly with the author and interact with other readers:

https://packt.link/RWD4e

# Table of Contents

## Chapter 2: Writing HTML Markup 27

# Section II: Core Skills for Effective Front-End Web Development                                      167

## Chapter 6: CSS Selectors, Typography, and More                          169

# Preface

When I wrote the first edition of this book in 2011 and 2012, it was by no means certain that responsive web design would become the *de facto* approach for web design for the foreseeable future. Here we are, 10 years and three further editions later, and its popularity and utility show no sign of abating.

There's a saying that is apt for the authors of technical books, "When one person teaches, two people learn." That's certainly been the case each time I write a new edition. I've learned so much more covering these topics than I imagined I would. In my day-to-day work, I already find myself coming back to certain chapters and sections when trying to refresh my memory on how to do one thing or another that I have subsequently forgotten. I hope these pages prove as resourceful for you!

Thinking back on the contents of the first edition, it's also struck me just how capable the technologies we have at our disposal have become. If you are an old hand at the web development game, feel free to jump right in to some of the newest topics such as CSS color or cascade layers – I'd be shocked if you didn't come away the least bit excited. Many of the things now trivial would have blown my mind a decade ago.

I won't waste any more of your precious time here. Thank you for taking the time to read this book. I hope you enjoy this latest edition and take plenty from it. Please reach out to me via my website at benfrain.com with your thoughts, both good and bad, and any questions that arise. They will naturally inform the content of any future editions.

Finally, while the publishers mention it again in a moment, if you do enjoy it, please consider adding a review on Amazon or your book store of choice. From a commercial point of view, it really does help with sales. From a personal perspective, it's really lovely to read them and know people around the world are making use of something you spent so long working on.

It should go without saying here that if you don't enjoy it, please keep your opinions to yourself!

# Who this book is for

Are you a full stack or backend developer who needs to improve their frontend skills? Perhaps you work on the frontend and you need a definitive overview of all modern HTML and CSS has to offer? Maybe you have done a little website building but you need a deep understanding of responsive web designs and how to achieve them? This is the book for you!

All you need to take advantage of this book is a working understanding of HTML and CSS. No JavaScript knowledge is needed.

# What this book covers

## Section I: The Fundamentals of Responsive Web Design

*Chapter 1, The Essentials of Responsive Web Design*, is a whistle-stop tour of the key ingredients in coding a responsive web design.

*Chapter 2, Writing HTML Markup*, covers all the semantic elements of HTML5, text-level semantics, and considerations of accessibility. We also cover how to insert media such as video into our pages and how to use the new `dialog` element.

*Chapter 3, Media Queries and Container Queries*, covers everything you need to know about CSS media queries: their capabilities, the syntax, and the various ways you can wield them. There is also an overview of container queries.

*Chapter 4, Fluid Layout and Flexbox*, covers how to convert designs into proportional layouts and provides a thorough exploration of Flexbox layouts.

*Chapter 5, Layout with CSS Grid*, is a deep dive into the two-dimensional layout system of CSS grid, with an explainer of how to make use of the new subgrid property.

## Section II: Core Skills for Effective Front-End Web Development

*Chapter 6, CSS Selectors, Typography, and More*, gets us to grips with the endless possibilities of CSS selectors, feature queries, and web typography, including variable fonts, viewport relative units, and a whole lot more.

*Chapter 7, CSS Color*, covers the latest developments in expressing colors and color manipulation, including Lab/LCH, P3 color, and new color functions like `color-contrast` and `color-mix`.

*Chapter 8, Stunning Aesthetics with CSS*, covers CSS filters, box shadows, linear and radial gradients, multiple backgrounds, and how to target background images to high-resolution devices.

*Chapter 9, Responsive Images*, covers how to make use of new image formats like AVIF and WebP, and how to make the most relevant version of an image available to the browser.

*Chapter 10, SVG*, teaches us everything we need to use SVG graphics inside documents and as background images, as well as how to interact with them using JavaScript.

*Chapter 11, Transitions, Transformations, and Animations*, gets our CSS moving as we explore how to make interactions and animations using CSS.

*Chapter 12, Custom Properties and CSS Functions*, covers the many benefits of custom properties, then moves on to the utility of new CSS functions like `min()`, `max()`, and `clamp()`.

*Chapter 13, Forms*, shows us how the latest HTML5 and CSS features make interacting with forms easier than ever before. Many HTML input types give you easy access to the relevant software keyboard on mobile devices.

## Section III: Latest Platform Features and Parting Advice

*Chapter 14, Cutting-Edge CSS Features*, covers how to use CSS layers to better organize your code and how to write nested CSS, hopefully coming to your browser in the near future.

*Chapter 15, Bonus Techniques and Parting Advice*, explores the essential considerations before embarking on a responsive web design and also provides a few last-minute nuggets of wisdom to aid you in your responsive quest.

# To get the most out of this book

- You need a text editor such as Sublime Text, Neovim, or VS Code.
- You'll need a modern browser such as Firefox, Edge, Safari, or Chrome.
- You'll need an appreciation of mediocre jokes and obscure references to popular culture.

# Download the example code files

The code bundle for the book is hosted at the book's dedicated website at `https://rwd.education/`, as well as on GitHub at `https://github.com/benfrain/rwd4`. We also have other code bundles from our rich catalog of books and videos available at `https://github.com/PacktPublishing/`. Check them out!

## Conventions used

There are a number of text conventions used throughout this book.

CodeInText: Indicates code words in text, database table names, folder names, filenames, file extensions, pathnames, dummy URLs, user input, and Twitter handles. For example: "We can fix that prior problem easily by adding this snippet in the <head>."

A block of code is set as follows:

```
img {
    max-width: 100%;
}
```

When we wish to draw your attention to a particular part of a code block, the relevant lines or items are set in bold:

```
img {
    max-width: 100%;
    display: inline-flex;
}
```

**Bold**: Indicates a new term, an important word, or words that you see on the screen, for example, in menus or dialog boxes. For example: "When writing HTML, you will typically be **marking up** or writing content inside a series of **tags** or **elements**."

 Warnings or important notes appear like this.

 Tips and tricks appear like this.

# Get in touch

Feedback from our readers is always welcome.

**General feedback**: Email feedback@packtpub.com, and mention the book's title in the subject of your message. If you have questions about any aspect of this book, please email us at questions@packtpub.com.

**Errata**: Although we have taken every care to ensure the accuracy of our content, mistakes do happen. If you have found a mistake in this book, we would be grateful if you would report this to us. Please visit http://www.packtpub.com/submit-errata, selecting your book, clicking on the **Submit New Errata** link, and entering the details.

**Piracy**: If you come across any illegal copies of our works in any form on the Internet, we would be grateful if you would provide us with the location address or website name. Please contact us at copyright@packtpub.com with a link to the material.

**If you are interested in becoming an author**: If there is a topic that you have expertise in and you are interested in either writing or contributing to a book, please visit http://authors.packtpub.com.

# Share your thoughts

Once you've read *Responsive Web Design with HTML5 and CSS, Fourth Edition*, we'd love to hear your thoughts! Scan the QR code below to go straight to the Amazon review page for this book and share your feedback.

*https://packt.link/r/180324271X*

Your review is important to us and the tech community and will help us make sure we're delivering excellent quality content.

# Download a free PDF copy of this book

Thanks for purchasing this book!

Do you like to read on the go but are unable to carry your print books everywhere?

Is your eBook purchase not compatible with the device of your choice?

Don't worry, now with every Packt book you get a DRM-free PDF version of that book at no cost.

Read anywhere, any place, on any device. Search, copy, and paste code from your favorite technical books directly into your application.

The perks don't stop there, you can get exclusive access to discounts, newsletters, and great free content in your inbox daily

Follow these simple steps to get the benefits:

1.  Scan the QR code or visit the link below

https://packt.link/free-ebook/9781803242712

2.  Submit your proof of purchase
3.  That's it! We'll send your free PDF and other benefits to your email directly

# Section I

# The Fundamentals of Responsive Web Design

This first section is described as fundamental, as it is the section on which the other two build. In *Chapter 1, The Essentials of Responsive Web Design*, we will create our first fully responsive website. In *Chapter 2, Writing HTML Markup,* we are going to understand how to express meaning through markup. Avoid understanding HTML elements at your peril! Many problems in web development, even among seasoned developers, can be avoided simply by using structured and semantic markup. Finally, in *Chapter 3, Media Queries and Container Queries*, we will learn how to encapsulate styles that only apply in certain eventualities, functionality that's a cornerstone of responsive web design. The final two chapters, *Fluid Layout and Flexbox*, and *Layout with CSS Grid*, conclude this first section, covering the two most powerful layout methods available to us in modern web design, Flexbox and Grid.

If you feel these are topics you already have a strong grasp of, go right ahead and skip to the next section. Otherwise, take the time to deeply understand these fundamentals before moving on. With the fundamentals understood, everything that comes later – in this book, and in your web adventures – will be so much easier to achieve.

# 1

# The Essentials of Responsive Web Design

When the first edition of this book came out in 2012, responsive web design was a new and exciting possibility to address the needs of the ever-growing list of devices that could access the internet. A decade later, as I write this in 2022, it's simply the *de facto* standard. If you're building a website or web application and it isn't responsive, you're probably doing it wrong!

This first chapter serves as a quick and basic refresher on building out an extremely simple web design, responsively. By the end, we will have covered everything needed to author a fully responsive web page.

You might be wondering, why do we need the other chapters then? By the end of this chapter, that should be apparent too.

Here's what we will cover in this first chapter:

- The ever-evolving browser and device landscape
- Defining responsive web design
- Setting browser support levels
- A brief discussion on development tools and text editors
- Our first responsive example: a simple HTML5 page
- The viewport `meta` tag
- Fluid images

- Writing CSS3 media queries to make pages adapt
- The shortfalls in our basic example
- Why our journey has only just begun

Are you sitting comfortably? Then we will begin!

# The browser and device landscape

A little over a decade ago, it was reasonable to build websites with fixed widths. The device landscape was a whole lot more limited, so the expectation was that all end users would get a fairly consistent experience. This fixed width (typically 960 px wide or thereabouts) wasn't too wide for laptop screens, and users with large-resolution monitors merely had an abundance of space on either side.

But in 2007, Apple's iPhone ushered in the first truly usable phone browsing experience, and the way people accessed and interacted with the web changed forever.

In the first edition of this book, published in early 2012, the following was noted about the percentage of total browser usage by device type recorded at gs.statcounter.com:

> *...in the 12 months from July 2010 to July 2011, global mobile browser use had risen from 2.86 to 7.02 percent...*

By September 2019, writing the third edition, using StatCounter, mobile was a whopping 51.11%, desktop was 45.18%, and tablet was 3.71%.

As I write this latest edition, the latest data at gs.statcounter.com for July 2022 shows an even more pronounced change with mobile at 60.73%, desktop at 37% and tablet at 2.27%..

The indisputable fact is that the number of people using smaller-screen devices to view the internet is growing at an ever-increasing rate, while at the other end of the scale, 40-inch ultrawide displays are now also commonplace (along with various tablet and console devices). There is now more difference between the smallest screens browsing the web and the largest than ever before.

Thankfully, there is a solution to this ever-expanding browser and device landscape. A responsive web design, built with HTML and CSS, allows a website to "just work" across multiple devices and screens. It enables the layout and capabilities of a website to respond to their environment (screen size, input type, device/browser capabilities).

# Defining responsive web design

The term **responsive web design** was coined by Ethan Marcotte in 2010. In his seminal *A List Apart* article, http://www.alistapart.com/articles/responsive-web-design, he consolidated three existing techniques (flexible grid layout, flexible images/media, and media queries) into one unified approach and named it responsive web design.

## Responsive web design in a nutshell

To attempt to put the philosophy of responsive web design in a "nutshell," I would say it's the presentation of web content in the most relevant format for the viewport and device accessing it.

In its infancy, it was typical for responsive design to be implemented by starting with a fixed-width desktop design before trying to scale the design down as needed for smaller screens. However, processes evolved and it became apparent there was a better way. Namely, that everything from design to content management and development worked better when starting with the smallest screens first, and then "progressively enhancing" the design and content for larger screens and/ or more capable devices. If the term "progressive enhancement" makes no sense right now, fear not. We'll be talking about that again in a moment.

Before we get into things fully, there are a few subjects I'd like to address and get squared away before we continue: browser support, text editors, and tooling.

## Browser support

The sheer volume of disparate devices that access the web means most people understand the need for technical solutions that cater to most devices.

The popularity and ubiquity of responsive web design usually make the approach an easy sell to clients and stakeholders. Nowadays, most people have some idea what responsive web design is about, even if that understanding amounts to little more than "a website that looks good and works on phones as well as computers."

However, one question that almost always comes up when starting a responsive design project is that of browser support. With so many browser and device variants, it's not always pragmatic to support every single browser permutation fully. Perhaps time is a limiting factor, perhaps money. Perhaps both.

Typically, the older the browser, the greater the work and code required to achieve feature or aesthetic parity with modern, evergreen browsers such as Firefox or Chrome. Be as pragmatic as possible.

By the same token, we are going to practice progressive enhancement, in essence, starting with a functional and accessible website for the most basic browsers, which will get progressively enhanced with features for more capable browsers. It should be a very rare occasion indeed that you are forced to create a website that isn't at least functional on an old browser or device.

Ultimately, the only browser statistics that really matter are yours.

 If you are working on a greenfield project, where there is no existing browser usage data, you can at least think about the demographics of your target audience and make some broad assumptions about likely devices/browsers based on those demographics.

Before considering any web project it makes sense to decide, in advance, what platforms you need to fully support and which you are happy to concede visual/functional anomalies to.

For example, if you're unlucky enough to have 25% of your website visitors stuck using old versions of iOS (for example), you'll need to consider what features that browser supports and tailor your solution accordingly.

To this end, if you aren't already, become familiar with websites such as `http://caniuse.com`. *Can I Use* provides a simple interface for establishing the browser support for each web platform feature.

Generally speaking, when starting a project, as a simple and broad way to determine what browsers to support, I apply the following crude piece of logic: if the cost of developing and supporting browser X is more than the revenue/benefit created by the users on browser X, don't develop specific solutions for browser X.

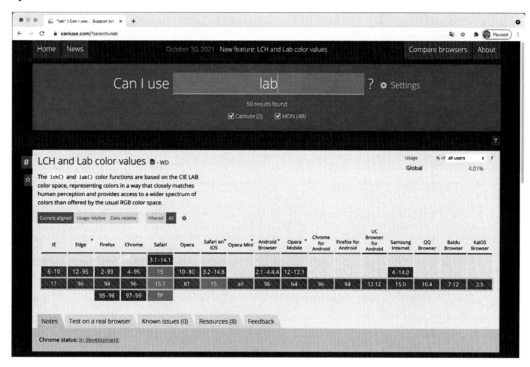

*Figure 1.1: Can I Use provides browser support data for every web platform feature*

## Text editors

It makes no difference what tool you use to write your code. All you actually need is something that enables you to type HTML, CSS, and JavaScript. Whether your preference is Sublime Text, Vim, Emacs, Nova, Visual Studio Code, or Notepad – it matters little. Just use what works best for you.

## Tools for software development

Similarly, there are no requisite tools that are essential to get responsive web design out of the door. That said, you should be aware that there are many freely available tools to negate many of the manual and time-intensive tasks of building websites.

CSS post-processors such as PostCSS can automate horrible and thankless jobs like CSS vendor prefixing, an old requirement that necessitated writing multiple versions of a property for each browser engine, and poly-filling new CSS features, where newer syntaxes can be made to work on older browsers. Linting and validation tools can check your HTML, JavaScript, and CSS code as you work, eliminating many time-wasting typos or syntax-induced errors. More recently, code formatters have become popular. Tools like Prettier, for example, automatically format your code with indentation and spacing when you save. None of these tools are essential but they may afford you some benefits.

New tools come out constantly and they are continually evolving. Therefore, while some relevant and beneficial tools will be mentioned by name as we go, be aware that something better may be just around the corner. Hence, we won't be relying on anything other than standards-based HTML and CSS in our examples. You should, however, use whatever tools you can bring to bear to produce your front-end code as quickly and reliably as possible.

With that out of the way, without further ado, let's get our first responsive web design made!

# Our first responsive example

In the introduction, I promised that by the end of this chapter you would know all you needed to build a fully responsive web page. So far, I've just been talking around the issue at hand. It's time to walk the walk.

**Code samples**

You can download all the code samples from this book by visiting `https://github.com/benfrain/rwd4` or the book's dedicated website, `rwd.education`. It's worth knowing that where individual examples are built up throughout a chapter, there will typically be a "start" and "end" version for each. The start contains just the essentials to start following along. The end contains the completed exercise/example.

# Our basic HTML file

We will start with a simple HTML5 structure. Don't worry at this point about what each of the lines does, especially the content of the `<head>`, as we will cover that in detail in *Chapter 2, Writing HTML Markup*.

For now, concentrate on the elements inside the <body> tag. There we have a few divs, a graphic for a logo, some text, and a list of items. Although you can see more of that content in the screen-grabs, below is a shorter version of the code. For brevity I have removed the paragraphs of text, as we only need to concern ourselves with the core structure.

However, what you should know is that the text is a recipe and description of how to make scones: a quintessentially British dessert.

Remember, if you want to get your hands on the full HTML file, you can download the example code from https://github.com/benfrain/rwd4 or the rwd.education website.

```html
<!DOCTYPE html>
<html class="no-js" lang="en">
    <head>
        <meta charset="utf-8" />
        <title>Our first responsive web page with HTML5 and CSS3</title>
        <meta
            name="description"
            content="A basic responsive web page - an example from Chapter
            1"
        />
        <link rel="stylesheet" href="css/styles.css" />
    </head>
    <body>
        <div class="Header">
            <a href="/" class="LogoWrapper"
                ><img src="img/SOC-Logo.png" alt="Scone O'Clock logo"
            /></a>
            <h1 class="Strap">Scones: the most resplendent of snacks</h1>
        </div>
```

```
        <div class="IntroWrapper">
            <h2 class="IntroText">
                Occasionally maligned and misunderstood; the scone is a
                quintessentially British classic.
            </h2>
            <div class="MoneyShot">
                <p class="ImageCaption">
                    Incredible scones, picture from Wikipedia
                </p>
            </div>
        </div>
        <p>Recipe and serving suggestions follow.</p>
        <div class="Ingredients">
            <h3 class="SubHeader">Ingredients</h3>
            <ul></ul>
        </div>
        <div class="HowToMake">
            <h3 class="SubHeader">Method</h3>
            <ol class="MethodWrapper"></ol>
        </div>
    </body>
</html>
```

By default, web pages are inherently flexible. If I open the example page, even as it is at this point, with no special work done to make it responsive, and resize the browser window, the text re-flows as needed.

What about on different devices? Again, with no CSS whatsoever added to the page, this is how that renders on an iPhone 13:

*Figure 1.2: Not pretty, but by default all web pages are inherently flexible*

As you can see, it's rendering, but like a desktop page shrunken down to fit the space available. The reason for that is that iOS renders web pages at 980 px wide by default and shrinks them down into the **viewport.**

Before responsive design was "a thing," it was commonplace to see websites render like that on an iPhone. Nowadays, thanks to the ubiquity of responsive web design, they are as rare as rocking horse droppings!

 The area of a browser window that a web page is allowed to be viewed in is known technically as the **viewport.** To be clear, the viewport area excludes the browser toolbars and URL bar etc. From now on, we will generally use this more accurate term.

We can make the page more mobile friendly by adding this snippet in the `<head>`:

```
<meta name="viewport" content="width=device-width,initial-scale=1.0" />
```

This viewport `meta` tag is the non-standard but *de facto* way of telling the browser how to render the page. Although introduced to the web by Apple, rather than a standard process, it remains essential for responsive web design. We will cover the `meta` tag and its various settings and permutations in *Chapter 3, Media Queries and Container Queries.*

For now, you just need to know that in this case, our viewport `meta` tag is effectively saying "make the content render at the width of the device."

In fact, it's probably easier to just show you the effect this line has on applicable devices:

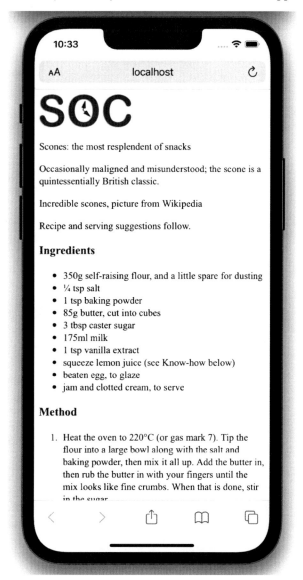

*Figure 1.3: With just one line added, already things are improving dramatically*

Great! Another snag fixed; the text is now rendering and flowing at a more "native" size. Let's move on to images.

## Taming images

They say a picture speaks a thousand words. All this writing about scones in our sample page and there's no image of the beauties! I'm going to add in an image of a scone near the top of the page; a sort of "hero" image to entice users to read the page.

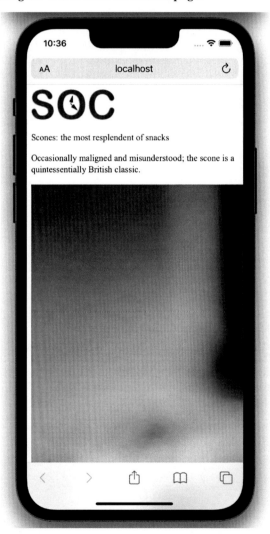

*Figure 1.4: There is a line or two of CSS that's always needed to make images appear a sensible size*

Oh! That nice big image (2000px wide) is forcing our page to render more than a little wonky. We clearly need to fix that.

Ideas? Well, we could add a fixed width to the image via CSS, but the problem there is that we want the image to scale to different screen sizes. For example, in CSS, our iPhone XR is 414 px wide by 896 px high. If we set a width of 414 px to that image, what happens if a user rotates the screen? On this device, the 414 px-wide viewport is now 896 px wide. Thankfully, it's pretty easy to achieve fluid images with a single line of CSS.

I'm going to create the css/styles.css CSS file now that's already linked in the head of the HTML page.

In our blank styles.css file, here is the first thing I'm adding. Ordinarily I'd be setting a few other defaults, and we'll discuss those defaults in later chapters, but for our purposes I'm happy to open with just this:

```
img {
    max-width: 100%;
}
```

With that file saved and the page refreshed, we see something more akin to what we might expect:

*Figure 1.5: With a little CSS, our images will never exceed their bounds*

All this max width-based rule does is stipulate that all images should grow to be a maximum of 100% of their size. Where a containing element (such as the body or a `div` it sits within) is less than the full intrinsic width of the image, the image will simply scale up to display as large as it can within that constraint.

## A brief tangent on width/max-width for images

To make images fluid, you could also use the more widely used `width` property, for example, `width:100%`, but this has a different effect. When a property of `width` is used then the image will be displayed at that width, relative to its container if using percentages, regardless of its own inherent size. The result in our example would be that the logo (also an image) would stretch beyond its intrinsic size to fill 100% of its container. With a container far wider than the image, as is the case with our logo, this leads to a massively oversized image.

Excellent. Everything is now laid out as expected. No matter the viewport size, nothing is overflowing the page horizontally.

However, if we look at the page in larger viewports, the basic styles start to get both literally and figuratively stretched. Take a look at the example page at a size around 1400 px:

*Figure 1.6: We clearly need to fix the size of this image for larger viewports*

Oh dear! In fact, at even around 800 px wide it's starting to suffer. Around this point, it would be handy if we could rearrange a few things. Maybe resize the image and position it off to one side. Perhaps alter some font sizes and background colors of elements.

Thankfully, we can achieve all this functionality quite easily by employing CSS media queries to bend things to our will.

## Enter media queries

As we have established, somewhere beyond the 800 px-wide point, our current layout starts to look stretched. We'll use CSS media queries at this point to adjust the layout depending upon the screen width. We will cover media queries in great depth in *Chapter 3*, but for now, all you need to appreciate is that media queries are directives in CSS that allow us to isolate CSS rules to certain environment conditions; size of screen, in this instance.

## Breakpoints

Before we proceed, it's worth familiarizing you with the term "breakpoint."

The term **breakpoint** is web developer vernacular to define a viewport width or height at which a responsive design should change significantly.

When people first started making use of media queries, it was common to see designs built with specific breakpoints to cater to the popular devices of the day. At the time it was typically iPhone (320 px x 480 px) and iPad (768 px x 1024 px) devices.

That practice was a bad decision then, and it would be an even worse one now. The problem is that doing that means a design caters to specific screen sizes. We want a responsive design – something that is agnostic of the screen size viewing it, responding to any size viewport it finds itself in, not something that only looks its best at specific sizes.

Use a breakpoint if your design, visually, needs to change at a certain point, but not to cater to a specific device!

For the purpose of whipping our basic example into shape, we will concentrate on just one type of media query: a minimum-width media query. CSS rules within this type of media query only get applied if the viewport is or exceeds a certain width.

The exact minimum width can be specified using a raft of different-length units including percent, em, rem, and px. In CSS, a minimum-width media query is written like this:

```
@media screen and (min-width: 800px) {
    /* styles /*
}
```

The @media directive tells the browser we are starting a media query, the screen part (declaring screen is technically not needed in this situation, but we will deal with that in detail in *Chapter 3*) tells the browser these rules should be applied to all screen types, and we then have the and keyword, which chains together another set of conditionals, which in this case is the (min-width: 800px). That tells the browser that the rules should also be limited to all viewports at least 800 px wide.

I believe it was Bryan Rieger, http://www.slideshare.net/bryanrieger/rethinking-the-mobile-web-by-yiibu, who first wrote that:

> *The absence of support for media queries is in fact the first media query.*

What he meant by that is that the first rules we write, outside of a media query, should be our starter, or "base," rules for the most basic devices, which we then enhance for more capable devices and larger screens.

That is what we are doing in this example. The basic styles are written first. It is only when we need to do something different that we introduce a media query.

This approach also facilitates a "smallest screen first" mentality and allows us to progressively layer on detail as and when the design needs to change for bigger screens.

## Amending the example for a larger screen

We've already established that our design is starting to suffer at around 800 px width. Therefore, let's mix things up a little by way of a simple example of how we can lay things out differently at different viewport sizes.

First off, we will stop that main "hero" image from getting too big and keep it over on the right. Then the intro text can sit to the left.

We will then have the main portion of text (the "method" that describes how to make the scones) on the left below, with a small boxed-out section detailing the ingredients over on the right.

All these changes can be achieved relatively simply by encapsulating these specific styles within a media query.

There are some further visual embellishments that don't add to the understanding of what's happening responsively, hence I have omitted them here, but if you'd like to view the relevant code, download the chapter code at http://rwd.education.

Here are the layout styles that were added:

```css
@media screen and (min-width: 800px) {
    body {
        border-left: 4px solid #f9f9f9;
        border-right: 4px solid #f9f9f9;
        padding: 1rem 2rem;
    }

    .IntroWrapper {
        display: flex;
        gap: 0 20px;
        flex: 1 1 auto;
        align-items: center;
    }

    .MoneyShot,
    .IntroText {
        margin: 0;
        flex: 1 1 50%;
    }

    .MoneyShotImg {
        filter: drop-shadow(0 0 20px #0008);
        border: 0;
    }
```

```css
    .IntroText {
        padding: 0.5rem;
        font-size: 2.5rem;
        text-align: left;
        position: relative;
    }
    .Ingredients {
        font-size: 0.9rem;
        float: right;
        padding: 1rem;
        margin: 0 0 0.5rem 1rem;
        border-radius: 3px;
        background-color: #ffffdf;
        border: 9px solid #debb71;
    }

    .Ingredients h3 {
        margin: 0;
    }
}
```

That wasn't too bad, was it? With only minimal code, we have built a page that responds to the viewport size and offers a preferable layout as needed. By adding just a few more styles, things look even easier on the eye.

With those in place, our basic responsive page now looks like this on an iPhone:

*Figure 1.7: A few more styles added and our basic page is palatable*

And like this when the viewport is 800 px or wider:

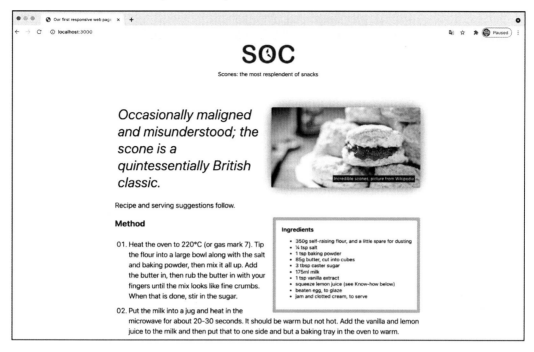

*Figure 1.8: The same HTML and CSS provides a different layout for larger viewports*

 The code samples provided throughout this book do not include "vendor prefix" styles. Vendor prefixes have been employed historically to prefix experimental CSS properties in different browsers. For example: `-webkit-backface-visibility`. Including vendor prefixes in CSS is often essential to achieve support for certain properties in older browsers. There are now tools to automate this prefixing and, as you might imagine, the tools perform the task faster and more accurately than we can.

Therefore, I'm refraining from including any vendor-prefixed code in the samples, in the hope you will adopt a similar painless approach.

This has been a very basic example but it has encapsulated the essential methodology of building out responsive web design.

Let's just go over the important points we have covered in this chapter and our basic example:

- Use whatever text editor you like

- Tools exist to make writing code easier, but don't get hung up on what to use

- Responsive designs are made possible with a flexible layout, fluid images, and media queries

- A `meta` tag is needed in the head of your HTML so a browser knows how to render the page

- You'll want all images to be set with a max width of 100% in the CSS by default

- A breakpoint is just a point, typically a screen width, at which we use a media query to alter the design

- When you write CSS for responsive design, start with base styles that can work on any device, typically the smallest screen, and then use media queries to adapt for larger screens

- Scones with clotted cream and jam are really tasty

 You can find the full specifications for CSS Media Queries (Level 3) here: `https://www.w3.org/TR/mediaqueries-3/`.

There is also a working draft for CSS Media Queries (Level 4) here: `https://drafts.csswg.org/mediaqueries-4/`.

## The shortcomings of our example

In this chapter, we've covered all the essential parts of building a basic responsive web page with HTML and CSS. Granted, it's not what I'd call a real looker. I'll forgive you for using words like "infantile," "lazy," and "ugly," but just do it quietly amongst yourselves; I have feelings, you know!

The point here is you and I both know that this basic responsive example is far from the limit of what we will likely be tasked with building day to day. Nor should it reflect the limit of what we are capable of building.

We need to cover typography, color, shadows, hover styles, semantic markup, accessibility concerns, animation, scalable graphics, forms, and so much more!

You get the picture; the truth is we have barely scratched the surface. But don't worry. That's what the rest of the book is for.

# Summary

Well done, you now know and understand the essential elements needed to create a fully responsive web page. However, as we have just discovered, there are plenty of places where things could be improved.

But that's fine. We don't just want the ability to make competent responsive web designs, we want to be able to create "best-of-breed" experiences. And as you're here, investing your time for the betterment of websites everywhere, I know you're up to the challenge. So let's press on.

In the next chapter, *Chapter 2, Writing HTML Markup*, we are going to take a deep dive into HTML5 markup. HTML is the very skeleton of any web page or application, the bedrock on which to build anything meaningful, the oxygen a website breathes, the... OK, I'm out of analogies – suffice it to say, HTML is pretty important, so let's press on and get stuck in.

# Join our book's Discord space

Got any burning questions? Join the book's Discord workspace to discuss all your responsive web design concerns directly with the author and interact with other readers:

`https://packt.link/RWD4e`

# 2

# Writing HTML Markup

HTML stands for *HyperText Markup Language*. It is a language that allows content to be marked up in a manner that makes it more understandable to technology, and then, in turn, humans. You can have content on the web without CSS or without JavaScript. But you can't have human-friendly content without HTML.

It's a common misconception that HTML is the "easy" part of authoring web pages and applications. Writing the HTML is often dismissed out of hand as something anyone can do easily. My experience tells me otherwise. Also consider that for users who require the use of assistive technology to browse the web, the way you author HTML can mean the difference between a confusing unusable mess and a meaningful, useful, and delightful experience. Writing good quality HTML is not a specific need of responsive web design. It's far more important than that. It's a prerequisite of anything that you want to be accessible to all users of the web.

This chapter is therefore going to be about writing HTML markup. We will be considering the "vocabulary" of HTML; its semantics. More succinctly, the way we can use the elements of HTML to describe the content we place in markup. HTML is what's known as a **living** standard. A few years back, the latest version was typically referred to as **HTML5**, a buzzword that helped identify modern web techniques and approaches. It's the reason this book was originally named *Responsive Web Design with HTML5 and CSS3* instead of simply *Responsive Web Design with HTML and CSS*. Back in 2012, you could more easily highlight that your techniques were modern by using "HTML5" and "CSS3". As I write this in 2022, this distinction is less important. To read the living standard of HTML, head over here: https://html.spec.whatwg.org/multipage/.

The topics we will cover in this chapter are:

- Starting HTML pages correctly
- Possible economies from using HTML that you should avoid
- Sectioning, grouping, and text-level HTML elements
- Putting HTML elements to use
- WCAG accessibility conformance and WAI-ARIA for more accessible web applications
- Embedding media
- Responsive video and iframes
- Creating pop-ups with the dialog element

 HTML also provides specific tools for handling forms and user input. This set of features takes much of the burden away from more resource-heavy scripting for form validation. However, we're going to look at HTML forms separately in *Chapter 13, Forms.*

The basic structure of an HTML page looks like this:

```
<!DOCTYPE html>
<html lang="en">
    <head>
        <meta charset="utf-8" />
        <title>Web Page Structure</title>
    </head>
    <body></body>
</html>
```

When writing HTML, you will typically be **marking up** or writing content inside a series of **tags** or **elements**. Tags are defined by the "less than" (<), and "greater than" angle brackets (>) around the tag name. The majority of elements in HTML have an opening and closing tag, with the closing tag differentiated by the forward slash before the element name. To exemplify the opening and closing nature of HTML tags, a paragraph of text would be most suitably marked up with an opening <p> at the beginning and a closing <p> at the end. A few elements, like the meta tag in the example above, are known as **void** elements, these don't wrap around anything, and hence are **self-closing** – notice the closing forward slash at the end with no element name.

There's only a limited number of self-closing, or void, elements, which are listed here: `https://html.spec.whatwg.org/multipage/syntax.html#void-elements`. Presently, the void tags are `area`, `base`, `br`, `col`, `embed`, `hr`, `img`, `input`, `link`, `meta`, `param`, `source`, `track`, and `wbr`.

Although we are about to start our understanding of HTML by covering the head section, which is the content between the opening `<head>` and closing `</head>` tags, be aware that the lion's share of HTML authoring is done in the body section.

However, as ever, the best place to start is at the beginning.

# Getting the start of HTML pages right

Let's consider the opening elements of an HTML page and ensure we fully understand all the essential component parts.

Like so many things with the web, remembering the exact syntax of each thing inside the head section is not particularly important. Understanding what each thing is for, is. I generally copy and paste the opening code each time, or have it saved in a text snippet, and I would recommend you do too. The first few lines in an HTML page should look something like this:

```
<!DOCTYPE html>
<html lang="en">
    <head>
        <meta charset="utf-8" />
```

## The doctype

So, what do we actually have there? First of all, we opened our document with the HTML5 Doctype declaration:

```
<!DOCTYPE html>
```

If you're a fan of lowercase, then `<!doctype html>` is just as good. It makes no difference.

## The HTML tag and lang attribute

After the Doctype declaration, we open the HTML tag; the first, and therefore **root** tag for our document. We also use the `lang` attribute to specify the language for the document, and then we open the head section:

```
<html lang="en">
    <head>
```

**Specifying alternate languages**

 According to the specifications (`https://html.spec.whatwg.org/multipage/dom.html#the-lang-and-xml:lang-attributes`), the `lang` attribute specifies the primary language for the element's contents and for any of the element's attributes that contain text. You can imagine how useful this will be to assistive technology such as screen readers. If you're not writing pages in English, you'd best specify the correct language code. For example, for Japanese, the HTML tag would be:

```
<html lang="ja">
```

For a full list of languages, take a look at `https://www.iana.org/assignments/language-subtag-registry/language-subtag-registry`.

# Character encoding

Finally, we specify the character encoding which, in simple terms, tells the browser how to parse the information contained within. As the `meta` tag is a void element, it doesn't require a closing tag:

```
<meta charset="utf-8" />
```

Unless you have a specific reason not to, the value for the charset should always be `utf-8`.

# The forgiving nature of HTML5 markup

If you're conscientious about how you write HTML markup, you'll typically use lowercase for the most part, wrap attribute values in straight quotation marks (not curly ones!), and declare a type for scripts and style sheets you link to. For example, perhaps you link to a style sheet like this:

```
<link href="CSS/main.css" rel="stylesheet" type="text/css" />
```

The fact is that HTML5 doesn't require such precision; it's just as happy to see this:

```
<link href=CSS/main.css rel=stylesheet >
```

Did you notice that? There's no end forward slash at the end of the tag, there are no quotation marks around the attribute values, and there is no type declaration. However, easy-going HTML5 doesn't care. The second example is just as valid as the first.

This more lax syntax applies across the whole document, not just linked assets. For example, specify a div like this if you like:

```
<div id=wrapper>
```

That's perfectly valid HTML5. The same goes for inserting an image:

```
<img SRc=frontCarousel.png alt="front Carousel">
```

That's also valid HTML5. No end tag/slash, no quotes (although you still need quotes where the value has whitespace in, like in the alt tag of the example), and a mix of capitalization and lowercase characters. You can even omit things such as the opening <head> tag and the page still validates!

 Want a shortcut to great HTML5 code? Consider the HTML5 Boilerplate (https:// html5boilerplate.com). It's a pre-made "best practice" HTML5 file. You can also custom-build the template to match your specific needs.

So, given the loose rules, what's the "right" way to be writing your markup?

## A sensible approach to HTML markup

Personally, I like writing my markup quite strictly. That means closing tags, quoting attribute values, and adhering to a consistent letter case. One could argue that ditching some of these practices would save a few bytes of data, but that's what minification tools are for (any unnecessary characters/data could be stripped if needed). I want my markup to be as legible as possible and I would encourage others to do the same. I'm of the opinion that clarity in authoring code should trump brevity. When writing HTML documents, therefore, you can write clean and legible code while still embracing the economies afforded by HTML5. To exemplify, for a CSS link, I'd go with the following:

```
<link href="CSS/main.css" rel="stylesheet" />
```

I've kept the closing forward slash at the end of the element and the quotation marks, but omitted the type attribute. The point to make here is that you can find a level you're happy with yourself. HTML5 won't be shouting at you, flagging up your markup in front of the class, and standing you in a corner for not validating. However you want to write your markup is just fine...

No. Who am I kidding? I can't let it go – I want you to know that if you're writing your code without quoting attribute values and closing your tags, I am silently judging you!

Despite HTML5's looser syntax, it's always worth checking whether your markup is valid. Checking that markup validates catches basic human errors like missing or mismatched tags, missing `alt` attributes on images, incorrectly nested elements, and so on. The W3C validator was created for just this reason: `https://validator.w3.org/`.

Enough of me berating writers of "slacker" markup. Let's look at some genuinely useful economies of HTML5.

# All hail the mighty <a> element

The a tag (short for anchor tag) is arguably the most important and defining tag of HTML. The anchor tag is the tag used to link from the document a user is on to another document elsewhere on the internet, or another point in the same document.

 You can read the specification for the `<a>` element here: `https://html.spec.whatwg.org/#the-a-element`.

A welcome benefit of HTML5 is that we can wrap multiple elements in an a tag. In prior versions of HTML, if you wanted your markup to validate, it was necessary to wrap each element in its own a tag. For example, look at the following code:

```
<h2><a href-"index.html">The home page</a></h2>
<p><a href="index.html">This paragraph also links to the home page</a></p>
<a href="index.html">
    <img src="home-image.png" alt="A rendering of the home page" />
</a>
```

Nowadays, we can ditch all the individual a tags and instead wrap the group, as demonstrated in the following code:

```
<a href="index.html">
    <h2>The home page</h2>
    <p>This paragraph also links to the home page</p>
    <img src="home-image.png" alt="A rendering of the home page" />
</a>
```

The only limitations to keep in mind with a tags are that, understandably, you can't wrap one a tag within another a tag or other interactive element (such as a button) and you can't wrap a form in an a tag either.

That's not to say you can't physically do it; I doubt your text editor is going to start a fight with you about it, but don't be surprised if things don't work as expected in the browser if you do!

# New semantic elements in HTML5

My dictionary defines semantics as "the branch of linguistics and logic concerned with meaning." For our purposes, semantics is the process of giving our markup meaning. Why is this important?

Most websites follow fairly standard structural conventions; typical areas include a header, a footer, a sidebar, a navigation bar, and so on. As web authors, we will often name the divs we use to more clearly designate these areas (for example, `<div class="Header">`). However, as far as the code itself goes, any user agent parsing that content – and that includes a web browser, screen reader, search engine crawler, and so on – couldn't say for sure what the purpose of each of these div elements is. HTML5 solves that problem with new semantic elements.

 For the full list of HTML5 elements, get yourself (very) comfy and point your browser here: `https://html.spec.whatwg.org/#semantics`.

We won't cover every one of the new elements here, merely those I feel are the most beneficial or interesting in day-to-day responsive web design use. After we have gone through the elements and got an understanding of their intended use, we will look at some content examples and consider how they might be best marked up. Then, to end the chapter, I'm going to set you a bigger challenge!

In terms of the HTML specification, the elements we will be looking at fall into one of three groups:

- **Sectioning elements**, for the broadest strokes in an HTML page. These are the kind of elements to use for header, footer, and sidebar areas.
- **Grouping elements**, which are used to wrap associated elements. Think of paragraphs, blockquotes, and content of that nature.
- **Text-level semantics**, which are the elements we use to designate particulars, like a section of bold or italic text or code.

We will now look at the most commonly used from each of these sections in turn. The aim here is to acquaint you with the varied vocabulary of HTML. Knowing that elements exist to convey certain meaning is a huge part of making accessible websites and applications.

First up, let's consider the various sectioning elements.

## The <main> element

For a long time, HTML5 had no element to demarcate the main content of a page. It was argued that the content that wasn't inside one of the other new semantic HTML5 elements would, by negation, be the main content. Thankfully, we now have a more declarative way to group the main content: the aptly named main tag. Whether you're wrapping the main content of a page or the main section of a web-based application, the main element is what you should be grouping it all with. Here's a particularly useful line from the specification:

*The main content area of a document includes content that is unique to that document and excludes content that is repeated across a set of documents such as site navigation links, copyright information, site logos and banners, and search forms (unless the document or application's main function is that of a search form).*

It's also worth noting that there shouldn't be more than one main on each page (after all, you can't have two main pieces of content) and it shouldn't be used as a descendent child element of some of the other semantic HTML5 elements, such as article, aside, header, footer, or nav.

 Read the official line on the main element at https://html.spec.whatwg. org/#the-main-element.

## The <section> element

The section element is used to define a generic section of a document or application. For example, you may choose to create sections around your content; one section for contact information, another section for news feeds, and so on. It's important to understand that this element isn't intended for styling purposes; if you need to wrap an element merely to style it, you should continue to use a div as you would have before.

When working on web-based applications, I tend to use section as the wrapping element for visual components. It provides a simple way to see the beginning and end of components in the markup.

You can also qualify for yourself whether you should be using a section element based on whether the content you are sectioning has a natural heading within it (for example, an h1-h6). If it doesn't, it's likely you'd be better off opting for a div.

 To find out what the specification says about the section element, go to the following URL: https://html.spec.whatwg.org/#the-section-element.

## The <nav> element

The nav element is used to wrap major navigational links to other pages or parts within the same page. As it is for use in major navigational blocks, it isn't strictly intended for use in footers (although it can be) and the like, where groups of links to other pages are common. If you usually mark up your navigational elements with an unordered list (ul) and a bunch of list tags (li), you may be better served with a nav and a number of nested a tags instead.

 To find out what the specification says about the nav element, go to the following URL: https://html.spec.whatwg.org/multipage/sections.html#the-nav-element.

## The <article> element

The article element, alongside section, can easily lead to confusion. I certainly had to read and re-read the specifications of each before it sank in. Here's my re-iteration of the specification.

The article element is used to wrap a self-contained piece of content. When structuring a page, ask whether the content you're intending to use within an article tag could be taken as a whole lump and pasted onto a different site and still make complete sense. Another way to think about it is, would the content that you are considering wrapping in an article actually constitute a separate article in an RSS feed? Obvious examples of content that should be wrapped with an article element would be blog posts or news stories. Be aware that if nesting article elements, it is presumed that the nested article elements are principally related to the outer article.

 You can read the specification for the article element here: https://html.spec.whatwg.org/multipage/sections.html#the-article-element.

## The <aside> element

The aside element is used for content that is tangentially related to the content around it. In practical terms, I often use it for sidebars, or content in a little tip about a related subject in a blog post. It's also considered suitable for pull quotes, advertising, and groups of navigation elements. Basically, anything not directly related to the main content would work well in an aside. If it was an e-commerce site, I'd consider areas like *Customers who bought this also bought* as prime candidates for an aside.

 For more on what the specification says about aside, visit https://html.spec. whatwg.org/multipage/sections.html#the-aside-element.

## The <header> element

Practically, the header can be used for the "masthead" area of a site's header but also as an introduction to other content, such as an introduction section within an article element. You can use it as many times on the same page as needed. You could have a header inside every section on your page, for example.

 Here's what the specification says about header: https://html.spec.whatwg. org/multipage/sections.html#the-header-element.

## The <footer> element

Like the header, the footer element doesn't take part in the outline algorithm (more on that below) so doesn't section content. Instead, it should be used to contain information about the section it sits within. It might contain links to other documents or copyright information, for example. Like the header, it can be used multiple times within a page if needed. For example, it could be used for the footer of a blog but also a footer within a blog post article on that same blog. However, the specification notes that contact information for the author of a blog post should instead be wrapped by an address element.

The specification for the `footer` element can be found here: `https://html.spec.whatwg.org/multipage/sections.html#the-footer-element`.

Now we have looked at these sectioning elements and the kind of content we should be marking up with each, it is worth looking at the well-intentioned, but largely ignored, outline algorithm.

## The HTML5 outline algorithm

Ordinarily, for an HTML document, headings would begin with an `h1` for the main page title and then progress to using lower hierarchy title tags as needed for sub-headings and the like.

However, HTML5 introduced the ability for each sectioning container to have its own self-contained outline. That means it is not necessary to think about which level of heading tag you're at in terms of the entire document. You could just concentrate on the sectioning container you were currently working in. To illustrate why this might be preferable, within a blog, post titles could be set to use `h1` tags, while the title of the blog itself could also have an `h1` tag. For example, consider the following structure:

```
<h1>Ben's site</h1>
<section>
    <h1>Ben's blog</h1>
    <p>All about what I do</p>
</section>
<article>
    <header>
        <h1>A post about something</h1>
        <p>Trust me this is a great read</p>
        <p>No, not really</p>
        <p>See. Told you.</p>
    </header>
</article>
```

Despite having multiple h1 headings, the outline still appears as follows:

**1.** Ben's site

   **1.** Ben's blog

   **2.** A post about something

As such, theoretically, you shouldn't need to keep track of the heading tag you need to use in terms of the whole document. It should be possible to use whatever appropriate level of heading tag is needed within each piece of sectioned content and the HTML5 outline algorithm will order it accordingly.

You can test the outline of your documents using HTML5 outliners at one of the following URLs:

- `https://gsnedders.html5.org/outliner/`
- `https://hoyois.github.io/html5outliner/`

However, the reality is that search engines and the like make no use of the HTML5 outliner at present. Therefore, from a pragmatic viewpoint, it probably makes more sense to continue thinking about headings in terms of the whole document. That will make your documents easier to read for search engines and also aid assistive technology to infer the correct meaning.

## A note on h1-h6 and the <hgroup> element

Be aware that using h1-h6 tags to mark up groups of headings and their associated sub-headings/taglines is discouraged. I'm talking about this kind of thing:

```
<h1>Scones:</h1>
<h2>The most resplendent of snacks</h2>
```

Instead, try and reserve h1-h6 elements for when sections of content require a distinct heading.

So, how should we author such content? It is recommended to group it in an hgroup element like this:

```
<hgroup>
    <h1>Scones:</h1>
    <p>The most resplendent of snacks</p>
</hgroup>
```

You should use an hgroup element with a h1-h6 tag inside, along with any number of p tags before or after.

 The specification for the hgroup element can be found here: `https://html.spec.whatwg.org/multipage/sections.html#the-hgroup-element`.

Right, we've now covered the lion's share of the HTML sectioning elements. Let's now consider grouping elements, like the one we've just seen. These are the elements that are used to contain, you guessed it, groups of other elements.

# The <div> element

The most ubiquitous grouping element is the div. The div is so widely used because it is opinion-less. It conveys nothing. The only implied meaning of a div is that it groups something. Despite that, you will often see a div wrapping nothing but a string of text.

You should only opt for a div as a last resort. It is the element to use when you can think of nothing better.

We have more elements in HTML than ever before so, as we continue, hopefully we can get acquainted with plenty of other elements that can be more suitable for the jobs you currently use a div for.

# The <p> element

The p element is used to mark up a paragraph. However, don't think that means it can only be used on text 3-4 lines long. On the contrary, use it to mark up any text that cannot be better marked up with one of the other elements. For non-specific text, the p element is definitely a better choice than a div.

# The <blockquote> element

A blockquote is used to mark up text that is quoted from somewhere else. You don't have to wrap the text inside with any other element, but you can. For example, knowing what we now do about the p tag, we can use that inside a blockquote, too, if we wish. Here is a simple example using blockquote. First, an introductory section of text in a p tag, and then a blockquote:

```
<p>I did like Ben's book, but he kept going on about Scones. For
example:</p>
<blockquote>
    All this writing about scones in our sample page and there's no image
    of the beauties! I'm going to add in an image of a scone near the top
    of the page; a sort of 'hero' image to entice users to read the page.
</blockquote>
```

There are some good examples of how and when to use blockquotes over on the HTML specification too: https://html.spec.whatwg.org/multipage/grouping-content.html#the-blockquote-element.

# The <figure> and <figcaption> elements

The HTML specification relates that the `figure` element:

*...can thus be used to annotate illustrations, diagrams, photos, code listings, etc.*

So, we use it as an element to call out visuals of any sort and the accompanying `figcaption` provides the means to add some text supporting the visuals. Now, it is worth pointing out here that while we should always provide text in the `alt` attribute of an `img` tag to support assistive technology or to mitigate problems if an image fails to load, it isn't a requirement to provide a `figcaption` with a `figure`. The `figcaption` is added if you want to add a visual description alongside the visuals. Here's how we could use it to revise a portion of markup from the first chapter:

```
<figure class="MoneyShot">
    <img
        class="MoneyShotImg"
        src="img/scones.jpg"
        alt="Incredible scones baked to perfection and ready to eat"
    />
    <figcaption class="ImageCaption">
        This image isn't of scones I have made, instead it's a stock photo
        from Wikipedia
    </figcaption>
</figure>
```

You can see that the `figure` element is used to wrap this little self-contained block. Inside, the `figcaption` is used to provide a caption for the parent `figure` element. It's perfect when images or code need a little caption alongside (that wouldn't be suitable in the main text of the content).

The specification for the `figure` element can be found here: `https://html.spec.whatwg.org/multipage/grouping-content.html#the-figure-element`.

The specification for the `figcaption` is here: `https://html.spec.whatwg.org/multipage/grouping-content.html#the-figcaption-element`.

# <details> and <summary> elements

How many times have you wanted to create a simple open and close "widget" on your page? A piece of summary text that, when clicked, opens a panel with additional information.

Modern HTML facilitates this pattern with the details and summary elements. Consider this markup (you can open example_02-03.html from this chapter's code to play with it for yourself):

```
<details>
    <summary>I ate 15 scones in one day</summary>
    <p>
        Of course I didn't. It would probably kill me if I did. What a way
        to go. Mmmmmm, scones!
    </p>
</details>
```

Opening this in Chrome, with no added styling, shows only the summary text by default:

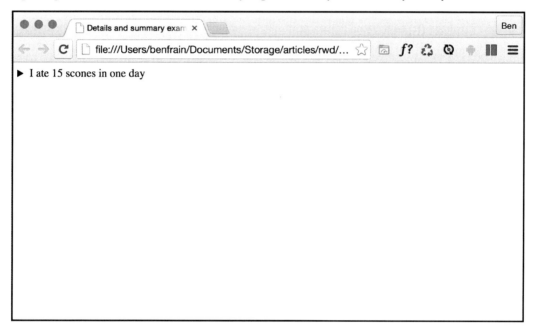

*Figure 2.1: details and summary attempt to solve a common problem but their implementation is limited*

Clicking anywhere on the summary text opens the panel. Clicking it again toggles it shut. If you want the panel open by default, you can add the open attribute to the details element:

```
<details open>
    <summary>I ate 15 scones in one day</summary>
    <p>
```

```
        Of course I didn't. It would probably kill me if I did. What a way
        to go. Mmmmmm, scones!
    </p>
</details>
```

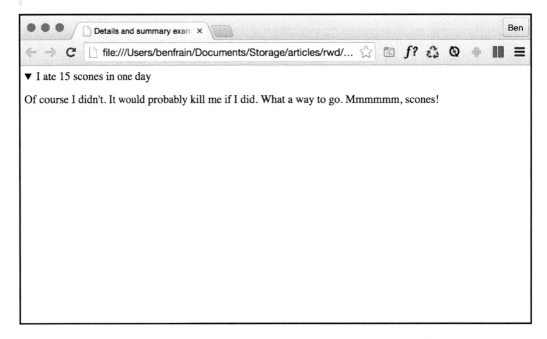

*Figure 2.2: By adding the open attribute, the content is shown by default*

Browsers typically add some default styling to indicate the panel can be opened. Changing the style is frankly a horror show as there is no consensus on how to do this. Different browsers have their own implementations of how we can deal with any visual marker for the details. In Safari, you need to use a proprietary pseudo class (note the -webkit- prefix). So, to remove it entirely:

```
summary::-webkit-details-marker {
    display: none;
}
```

You can, of course, use that same selector to style the marker differently.

To perform the equivalent action in Chrome and Firefox, you can do this:

```
summary::marker {
```

```
        content: none;
    }
```

If that wasn't annoying enough, currently, there is no way of animating the open and close. Without JavaScript, there's also no way of toggling other details panels closed when another details/summary combination is open. I'm not sure either of these desires will (or should) ever be addressed. However, I've therefore found the usefulness of these elements pretty limited by themselves. Rather than an all-in-one open/close drawer solution, you should think of them as a way to more semantically facilitate what you would have done previously with a display: none; toggle on a standard div with the help of JavaScript.

## The <address> element

The address element is to be used explicitly for marking up contact information for its nearest article or body ancestor. To confuse matters, keep in mind that it isn't to be used for postal addresses and the like (unless they are indeed the contact addresses for the content in question). Instead, postal addresses and other arbitrary contact information should be wrapped in good ol' p tags. I'm not a fan of the address element. In my experience, it would be far more useful to mark up a physical address with this element. However, hopefully it makes more sense to you.

For more on what the specification says about the address element, go to the following page: https://html.spec.whatwg.org/multipage/sections.html#the-address-element.

We have now covered the majority of the sectioning elements of HTML, so we will move on to the text-level elements. These are the elements used to mark up individual words, letters, and symbols to provide explicit meaning as to the intent.

## HTML text-level semantics

Before HTML5, text-level semantic elements were referred to in the specifications as inline elements. Therefore, if you are familiar with that description, be aware that we are talking about the same thing here.

The section of the HTML specification that details text-level semantics can be found here: https://html.spec.whatwg.org/multipage/text-level-semantics.html#text-level-semantics.

Let's take a look at the most common and useful text-level elements.

# The <span> element

A span element is the text-level equivalent of a div. It is unopinionated and is the perfect element to reach for when you merely want to wrap text in an element for styling purposes.

# The <b> element

Historically, visuals were defined in the markup and the b element meant "make this bold" (https://www.w3.org/TR/html4/present/graphics.html#edef-B). However, the specification now describes the b element like this:

> *The b element represents a span of text to which attention is being drawn for utilitarian purposes without conveying any extra importance and with no implication of an alternate voice or mood, such as key words in a document abstract, product names in a review, actionable words in interactive text-driven software, or an article lede.*

Although no specific meaning is now attached to it, as it's text-level, it's not intended to be used to surround large groups of markup; use a div for that.

You should also be aware that because it was historically used to bold text, you'll typically have to reset the font weight in CSS if you want content within a b tag to not appear bold.

For example:

```
b {
    font-weight: normal;
}
```

# The <strong> element

If you do want to emphasize something for strength, urgency, or importance, strong is the element for you. Here is how the specification defines these use cases:

> *Importance: The strong element can be used in a heading, caption, or paragraph to distinguish the part that really matters from other parts that might be more detailed, more jovial, or merely boilerplate. Seriousness: The strong element can be used to mark up a warning or caution notice. Urgency: The strong element can be used to denote content that the user needs to see sooner than other parts of the document.*

You can read the full specification for strong here: `https://html.spec.whatwg.`
`org/multipage/text-level-semantics.html#the-strong-element`.

## The <em> element

I'll admit, in the past, I've often used em merely as a styling hook; to provide italic text when I wanted it. I need to mend my ways as the HTML specification tells us:

*The* em *element represents stress emphasis of its contents.*

Therefore, unless you actually want the enclosed contents to be emphasized, consider using a b tag or, where relevant, an i or span tag instead.

## The <i> element

The HTML5 specification describes the i as:

*A span of text in an alternate voice or mood, or otherwise offset from the normal prose in a manner indicating a different quality of text.*

Suffice to say, it's not to be used to merely italicize something. For example, we could use it to mark up the odd name in this line of text:

```
<p>
    However, discussion on the frameset element is now frustraneous as
    it's now gone the way of the <i>Raphus cucullatus</i>.
</p>
```

Or, perhaps if you were marking up a button in a food ordering web application, you might do this:

```
<button type="button">French Fries <i>No Salt Added</i></button>
```

There are plenty of other text-level semantic tags in HTML; for a full rundown, take a look at the relevant section of the specification at the following URL: `https://www.w3.org/TR/html5/`
`text-level-semantics.html#text-level-semantics`.

# Obsolete HTML features

If you have been writing HTML for a few years, you might be surprised to learn there are parts of HTML that are now considered "obsolete." It's important to be aware that there are two camps of obsolete features in HTML; **conforming** and **non-conforming**. Conforming features will still work, but will generate warnings in validators. Realistically, avoid them if you can, but they aren't going to make the sky fall down if you do use them. Non-conforming features may still render in certain browsers but they may not. It's certainly not guaranteed.

In terms of obsolete and non-conforming features, there is quite a raft. I'll confess that many I have never used. Some I've never even seen! It's possible you may experience a similar reaction. However, if you're curious, you can find the full list of obsolete and non-conforming features at `https://html.spec.whatwg.org/multipage/obsolete.html`. Notable obsolete and non-conforming features that you may occasionally encounter are `strike`, `center`, `font`, `acronym`, `frame`, and `frameset`.

# Putting HTML elements to use

It's time to practice using some of the elements we have just looked at. Let's revisit the example from *Chapter 1*. If we compare the markup below to the original markup in *Chapter 1* (remember, you can download all the examples from the `https://rwd.education` website), you can see where the new elements we've looked at have been employed below:

```
<article>
    <header class="Header">
        <a href="/" class="LogoWrapper"
            ><img src="img/SOC-Logo.png" alt="Scone O'Clock logo"
        /></a>
        <h1 class="Strap">Scones: the most resplendent of snacks</h1>
    </header>
    <section class="IntroWrapper">
        <p class="IntroText">
            Occasionally maligned and misunderstood; the scone is a
            quintessentially British classic.
        </p>
```

```
            <figure class="MoneyShot">
                <img
                    class="MoneyShotImg"
                    src="img/scones.jpg"
                    alt="Incredible scones"
                />
                <figcaption class="ImageCaption">
                    Incredible scones, picture from Wikipedia
                </figcaption>
            </figure>
        </section>
        <p>Recipe and serving suggestions follow.</p>
        <section class="Ingredients">
            <h3 class="SubHeader">Ingredients</h3>
        </section>
        <section class="HowToMake"><h3 class="SubHeader">Method</h3></section>
        <footer>
            Made for the book,
            <a href="https://rwd.education">
                'Responsive Web Design with HTML5 and CSS3'
            </a>
            by
            <address><a href="https://benfrain.com">Ben Frain</a></address>
        </footer>
    </article>
</article>
```

I've removed a good portion of the inner content so we can concentrate on the structure. Hopefully you will agree that it's easy to discern different sections of markup from one another. However, at this point, I'd also like to offer some pragmatic advice; it isn't the end of the world if you don't always pick the correct element for every single given situation.

For example, whether or not I used a section or div in the above example is of little real consequence.

If we use an em when we should actually be using an i, I certainly don't feel it's a crime against humanity; the folks at the W3C won't hunt you down and feather and tar you for making the wrong choice. Just apply a little common sense. That said, if you can use elements like the header and footer when relevant, there are inherent accessibility benefits in doing so. I certainly think it's better than using nothing but divs in your markup!

# WCAG accessibility conformance and WAI-ARIA for more accessible web applications

Even since writing the first edition of this book in 2011/2012, the W3C has made strides in making it easier for authors to make the necessary adjustments to code to make web pages more accessible.

## Web Content Accessibility Guidelines (WCAG)

The **WCAG (Web Content Accessibility Guidelines)** exist to provide:

*a single shared standard for web content accessibility that meets the needs of individuals, organizations, and governments internationally*

When it comes to more pedestrian web pages, as opposed to single-page web applications and the like, it makes sense to concentrate on the WCAG guidelines. They offer a number of mostly common-sense guidelines for how to ensure your web content is accessible. Each recommendation is rated by a conformance level: A, AA, or AAA, and each of these levels has a distinct set of acceptance criteria. For more on these conformance levels, look here: `https://www.w3.org/TR/UNDERSTANDING-WCAG20/conformance.html#uc-levels-head`.

You'll probably find that you are already adhering to many of the guidelines, like providing alternative text for images, for example. However, you can get a brief rundown of the guidelines here: `https://www.w3.org/WAI/standards-guidelines/wcag/glance/` and then build your own custom quick reference list of checks here: `https://www.w3.org/WAI/WCAG21/quickref/`.

I'd encourage everyone to spend an hour or two to look down the list. Many of the guidelines are simple to implement and offer real benefits to users.

## WAI-ARIA

The aim of **WAI-ARIA (Web Accessibility Initiative – Accessible Rich Internet Applications)** is principally to solve the problem of making dynamic content on a web page accessible. It provides a means of describing roles, states, and properties for custom widgets, such as dynamic sections in web applications, so that they are recognizable and usable by assistive technology users.

For example, if an onscreen widget displays a constantly updating stock price, how would a blind user accessing the page know that? WAI-ARIA attempts to solve this problem.

How to implement ARIA fully in something like a web application is outside the scope of this book. However, if that's the kind of project you are building, head over to `https://www.w3.org/WAI/standards-guidelines/aria/` for more information.

Instead, for a great overview of getting to grips with ARIA, consider reading the W3C *Using Aria* guide: `https://www.w3.org/TR/using-aria/`.

The easiest thing you can do to aid assistive technologies is to use the correct elements where possible. A `header` element is going to be far more useful than `<div class="Header">`. Similarly, if you have a button on your page, use the `button` element, rather than a `span` or other element styled to look like a button.

## Taking ARIA further

If you want to explore a solid set of accessible design patterns, the W3C has a published set you can peruse here: `https://www.w3.org/WAI/ARIA/apg/example-index/`.

Test your designs for free with **NonVisual Desktop Access (NVDA)**. If you develop on the Windows platform and you'd like to test your ARIA enhanced designs on a screen reader, you can do so for free with NVDA. You can get it at the following URL: `https://www.nvaccess.org`. Google now also ships the free Accessibility Developer Tools for the Chrome browser (available cross-platform); well worth checking out. There's also a growing number of tools that help quickly test your own designs against things like color blindness; for example, deque make their Axe DevTools browser extension available: `https://www.deque.com/axe/devtools/`.

We will also cover a few new color techniques that aid with creating accessible color palettes in *Chapter 7, CSS Color.*

But for now, hopefully, this brief introduction to WAI-ARIA and WCAG has given you a little background information on supporting assistive technology. Perhaps adding assistive technology support to your next HTML project will be easier than you think. As a final resource for all things Accessibility, there are handy links and advice galore on the A11Y project home page at `https://a11yproject.com/`.

# Embedding media in HTML5

For many, HTML5 first entered their vocabulary when Apple refused to add support for Flash technology in their iOS devices. Flash had gained market dominance (some would argue market stranglehold) as the plugin of choice to serve up video through a web browser. However, rather than using Adobe's proprietary technology, Apple decided to rely on HTML5 instead to handle rich media rendering. While HTML5 was making good headway in this area anyway, Apple's public support of HTML5 gave it a major leg up and helped its media tools gain greater traction in the wider community.

We've discussed already that people tend to just use the term *HTML* rather than *HTML5* these days, but that label was important historically in relation to media. Before HTML5, adding video and audio into markup was a bit of a pain. These days, it's easy.

## Adding video and audio in HTML

Here's a "simple as can be" example of how to link to a video file on your page:

```
<video src="myVideo.mp4"></video>
```

HTML allows a single video tag (or audio tag for audio) to do all the heavy lifting. It's also possible to insert text between the opening and closing tag to inform users when there is a problem. There are also additional attributes you'd ordinarily want to add, such as the height and width. Let's add these in:

```
<video src="myVideo.mp4" width="640" height="480">
    If you're reading this either the video didn't load or your browser is
    waaaayyyyyy old!
</video>
```

Now, if we add the preceding code snippet into our page and look at it in some browsers, it will appear, but there will be no controls for playback. To ensure we show the default playback controls, we need to add the controls attribute. For the sake of illustration, we could also add the autoplay attribute.

 These days, you will also usually need to add the muted attribute if you want your video to autoplay. Everyone detested videos automatically blaring out audio into a crowded office (if you want to listen to a little Rick Astley at lunch, who am I to judge) so much that most browsers won't autoplay without the muted attribute present.

Here's an example with the `controls` and `autoplay` attributes added:

```
<video src="myVideo.mp4" width="640" height="480" controls autoplay>
    If you're reading this either the video didn't load or your browser is
    waaaayyyyyy old!
</video>
```

The result of the preceding code snippet is shown in the following screenshot:

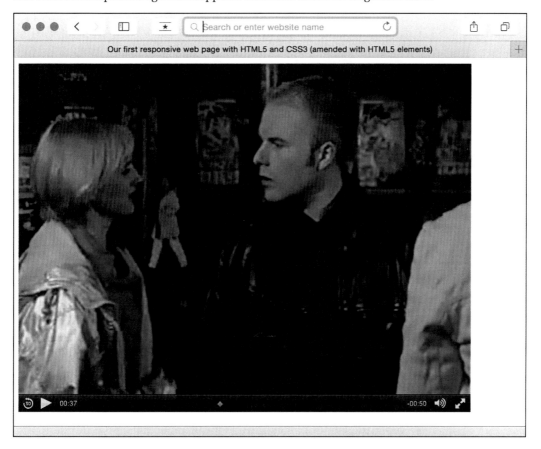

*Figure 2.3: With minimal code, we have inserted a video into our page*

Further attributes include `preload` to control the preloading of media, `loop` to repeat the video, and `poster` to define a poster frame for the video-the image that shows while a video is loading.

To use an attribute, simply add it to the tag. Here's an example that includes all these attributes:

```
<video
    src="myVideo.mp4"
    width="640"
    height="480"
    controls
    autoplay
    muted
    preload="auto"
    loop
    poster="myVideoPoster.png"
>
    If you're reading this either the video didn't load or your browser is
    waaaayyyyyy old!
</video>
```

## Providing alternate media sources

The source tag enables us to provide alternate sources for the media. For example, alongside providing an MP4 version of the video, if we wanted to provide support for a new format, we could easily do so. Further still, if the user didn't have any suitable playback technology in the browser, we could provide download links to the files themselves. Here's an example:

```
<video
    width="640"
    height="480"
    controls
    preload="auto"
    loop
    poster="myVideoPoster.png"
>
    <source src="video/myVideo.sp8" type="video/super8" />
    <source src="video/myVideo.mp4" type="video/mp4" />
    <p>
        <b>Download Video:</b>
        MP4 Format:
        <a href="myVideo.mp4">"MP4"</a>
    </p>
</video>
```

In that case, we first specified a source of a made-up video format called super8. The browser goes top to bottom deciding what to play, so if it doesn't support super8, it moves on to the next source; mp4 in this case. And on and on it goes, moving down to the download link if it can't reconcile any of the sources listed. The type attribute tells the browser the MIME type of the resource. If you fail to specify this, the browser will fetch the content and try and play it anyway. But if you know the MIME type, you should add it in the type attribute. The prior code example and the sample video file (which, incidentally, is me appearing in the UK soap *Coronation Street* back when I had hair and hopes of starring alongside DeNiro) in MP4 format are in the example_02-02.html section of the chapter code.

## Audio and video tags work almost identically

The audio tag works on the same principles as the video tag, with the same attributes (excluding width, height, and poster). The main difference between the two is the fact that audio has no playback area for visible content.

## Responsive HTML5 video and iframes

The only problem with our lovely HTML video implementation is that it's not responsive. That's right; an example in a book on responsive web design with HTML5 and CSS that doesn't "respond." Thankfully, for HTML embedded video, the fix is easy. Simply remove any height and width attributes in the markup (for example, remove width="640" height="480") and add the following in the CSS:

```
video {
    max-width: 100%;
    height: auto;
}
```

However, while that works fine for files that we might be hosting locally, it doesn't solve the problem of videos embedded within an iframe (take a bow YouTube, Vimeo, et al.). The following code will add a film trailer for *Midnight Run* from YouTube:

```
<iframe
    width="960"
    height="720"
    src="https://www.youtube.com/watch?v=B1_N28DA3gY"
    frameborder="0"
    allowfullscreen
></iframe>
```

However, if you add that to a page as is, even if adding that earlier CSS rule, if the viewport is less than 960 px wide, things will start to get clipped.

Historically, the easiest way to solve this problem is with a little CSS trick pioneered by Gallic CSS maestro Thierry Koblentz, here, `https://alistapart.com/article/creating-intrinsic-ratios-for-video`, essentially creating a box of the correct aspect ratio for the video it contains. I won't spoil the magician's own explanation; go take a read.

If you're feeling lazy, you don't even need to work out the aspect ratio and plug it in yourself; there's an online service that can do it for you. Just head to `https://embedresponsively.com/` and paste your `iframe` URL in. It will spit you out a simple chunk of code you can paste into your page. For example, our *Midnight Run* trailer results in this (note the `padding-bottom` value to define the aspect ratio):

```
<style>
    .embed-container {
        position: relative;
        padding-bottom: 56.25%;
        height: 0;
        overflow: hidden;
        max-width: 100%;
    }
    .embed-container iframe,
    .embed-container object,
    .embed-container embed {
        position: absolute;
        top: 0;
        left: 0;
        width: 100%;
        height: 100%;
    }
</style>
<div class="embed-container">
    <iframe
        src="https://www.youtube.com/embed/B1_N28DA3gY"
        frameborder="0"
```

```
            allowfullscreen
        ></iframe>
    </div>
```

That's all there is to it. Simply add to your page and you're done: we now have a fully responsive YouTube video (note: kids, don't pay any attention to Mr. DeNiro; smoking is bad)!

## The modern way to embed iframes and keep aspect ratio

If you only need to support more modern browsers (check at `https://caniuse.com/mdn-css_ properties_aspect-ratio`), you can set the aspect ratio of something like an `iframe` with the `aspect-ratio` CSS property. For an `iframe` we want to keep in a 16:9 ratio, such as a YouTube video, we could add a suitable class and do this:

```
.iframe-16-9 {
    aspect-ratio: 16/9;
    max-width: 100%;
}
```

You can see this in action for yourself in `example_02-04.html` of the chapter code. Of course, the `aspect-ratio` property is not limited to `iframes` – you can use it on any box in CSS that you want to maintain certain proportions with.

# The loading attribute

If you find yourself adding a lot of images or `iframe` elements to your page, consider the `loading` attribute. Setting this attribute to `lazy` means the browser will only go and fetch the item if the user scrolls it into view. This is really useful for any media you know will certainly not be visible when the page first displays, meaning the cost of loading that item is saved until it is actually needed. It's literally as simple as adding it like this:

```
<img src="home-image.png" alt="A rendering of the home page"
loading="lazy" />
```

Or, if you were adding something like a YouTube video embed, you could make the same economy like this:

```
<iframe
    loading="lazy"
    width="560"
    height="315"
```

```
        src="https://www.youtube.com/embed/NkfMBI1tVwY"
        title="YouTube video player"
        frameborder="0"
        allow="accelerometer; autoplay; clipboard-write; encrypted-media;
        gyroscope; picture-in-picture"
        allowfullscreen
    ></iframe>
```

In case you were wondering, the opposite of `lazy` in this context is `eager`, which is the default if you don't add the attribute.

## The <dialog> element

You know what a dialog is, even if you know it by a different name. It's the pop-up you get on a site asking you to subscribe to a newsletter, or log in to a service. Coding this kind of thing has always been problematic. Worse still, if you didn't think they were problematic it is likely because you didn't realize there were accessibility problems with your implementation. It's likely users using only a keyboard could struggle to get focus into the dialog or be unable to leave it.

Thankfully, we now have a specific element to handle these use cases. In the code for this chapter, you will want to consider `example_02-05.html`.

Inside that HTML file is also the relevant CSS and JavaScript to produce a simple but fully working `dialog`.

When the modal `dialog` is opened, it automatically gets centered, focused, and the backdrop of the dialog — which is automatically inserted — covers everything below, preventing any of the underlying content from being interacted with. You can dismiss the `dialog` with the button inside it, or a keyboard press of the *Escape* key; the keyboard support is functionality you get for free!

The `dialog` is a wonderful addition to the web platform.

Here is the relevant HTML from our example:

```
        <button id="launchDialog">Where is the dialog?</button>
        <p id="formResult"></p>
        <dialog id="dialogEle">
            <form method="dialog">
                <h1>How about this? A native Dialog.</h1>
```

```
            <p>So, only thing left to do is dismiss me.</p>
            <button value="Dismissed!">Dismiss Dialog</button>
        </form>
    </dialog>
```

Worth noting here that I have included the content of the dialog in a form. That isn't necessary, but doing so allows you to use the special method="dialog" attribute, which "returns" the value of the button doing the submitting of the form; more in-built functionality that can prove useful!

Also worth noting is that when you click the button to open a dialog, it automatically gets an open attribute, which you can see in the dev tools. This can be used as a styling hook. I've added that in the styles when animating the modal backdrop when it first appears, although it isn't actually necessary in this instance.

Let's take a look at the styles:

```
dialog {
    border-radius: 10px;
}
dialog::backdrop {
    animation: fade 0.5s ease forwards;
}
button {
    height: 40px;
    padding: 5px 10px;
}
button:focus {
    outline: 2px solid #f90;
}
@keyframes fade {
    0% {
        background-color: transparent;
    }
    100% {
        background-color: rgb(0 57 24 / 0.6);
    }
}
```

None of the styles are necessary for the dialog to function, but I do always like to add a stronger :focus style than the default for better accessibility. However, I thought it would also be interesting to bring the ::backdrop pseudo-element to your attention, as that is how you can style the area behind the modal dialog.

If any of the syntaxes or styles in there are unfamiliar to you, don't worry. We cover all of those in detail later in the book. All that is necessary here is to understand that you can style the dialog and backdrop however you see fit.

This book is deliberately light on JavaScript, but we do need to consider some now to understand how the dialog functions:

```
const dialogEle = document.getElementById("dialogEle");
const launchBtn = document.getElementById("launchDialog");
const formResult = document.getElementById("formResult");
launchBtn.addEventListener("click", () => dialogEle.showModal());
dialogEle.addEventListener("close", () => {
    formResult.textContent = dialogEle.returnValue;
});
```

Besides creating const references to the dialog itself, the button that opens it, and a p tag to display the value of the button that can be clicked inside the dialog, we have two event listeners. The first opens the dialog when the launchBtn button is clicked with the showModal() method, and the second listens for the close event. The close is unique to dialog and gets triggered when submitting a form inside a dialog that has a method of dialog, or if the user exits the form with, say, a press of *Escape* on their keyboard.

The default type of a button is submit, so in our example above, where we want to submit the form inside the dialog, there is no need to declare it. However, imagine you are building a form, as we will in detail in *Chapter 13, Forms*, and you have a button in your form for some other purpose; you don't want the form submitting when the user clicks that, rather than the correct submit button. As such, I recommend being in the habit of always adding type="button" whenever you use the button element.

In our example, we are using the returnValue of the dialog to set the text of our p tag. That returnValue is set to the value attribute of the button that submits the form in the dialog. Not essential, but potentially useful depending on your use case.

It's also possible to show a dialog in a non-modal manner. To do that, instead of using the showModal() method, use the show() method. In this situation, no backdrop is inserted and the dialog is inserted using absolute positioning by default.

You now know how to create, control, and style a fully working dialog.

   You can read the specification for the dialog element here: https://html.spec. whatwg.org/multipage/interactive-elements.html#the-dialog-element.

## Summary

We've covered a lot in this chapter. Everything from the basics of creating a page that validates as HTML5 through to embedding rich media (video and audio) into our markup and ensuring it behaves responsively. Although not specific to responsive designs, we've also covered how we can write semantically rich and meaningful code and considered how we might ensure pages are meaningful and usable for users who are relying on assistive technology.

You should now have a decent understanding of the wide and varied vocabulary of HTML elements at your disposal.

# An exercise

In this chapter, we covered a raft of HTML elements. We didn't cover them all, but we certainly covered all the elements you are likely to need day-to-day. I think you're ready to try a little exercise to see how much you have understood. Below is a screenshot of the website for this book:

*Figure 2.4: The design for the website made for this book*

Take a look at the design, and try and create an HTML page for it. Consider the head section and what you need in there. Think about the language the content is in and any meta tags you might need. Then, think about the visuals themselves. What might be the best elements to use to create the navigation section? Or each of those little sections below the book image?

You can see the choices I made by visiting the live site at `https://rwd.education`, but do yourself a favor and don't peek until you've tried it for yourself!

# 3

# Media Queries and Container Queries

This chapter will look in detail at CSS media queries, hopefully providing all that's needed to fully understand their capability, syntax, and future development.

At the end of this chapter, we will also look at container queries. As this chapter is written in mid-2022, there are only experimental versions available of container queries in some browsers, which I wouldn't typically cover. However, we shall enjoy an exception here. Container queries are likely to be a very significant addition to the web platform. As such, we will take a whistle-stop tour of the current implementations and consider some of the considerable possibilities they promise. But, to begin with, let's understand everything we need to know about media queries.

We ended the last chapter with the initial markup for the `rwd.education` website. It wasn't necessarily the final markup, but it was solid enough for us to start working with. For the sake of this chapter, I have taken that markup and added some corresponding basic "mobile" styles.

If you open the index.html file inside this chapter's Start folder in a web browser, you will see that the design looks acceptable at slim viewports such as mobile phones:

*Figure 3.1: The design looks fine at smaller viewports*

However, it quickly starts to look a little stretched when you widen the browser window:

*Figure 3.2: We definitely need to change the styles for wider viewports*

The initial styles are written using a fluid/proportional approach. This means widths are generally written as percentages rather than fixed pixel sizes; the upshot being that the content at least grows and shrinks to fill the browser window regardless of how large or small it gets.

However, this still leaves us with the problem that when you go wide enough, you need to do something a little more drastic, visually, than just making things wider still!

We can fix this problem with media queries.

Media queries allow us to target specific CSS styles depending on the capabilities of a device. For example, with just a few lines of CSS, we can change the way content is displayed based on things such as viewport width, screen aspect ratio, orientation (landscape or portrait), and so on.

In this chapter, we will:

- Understand the meta viewport tag to make media queries work on mobile devices
- Learn why media queries are essential for a responsive web design

- Understand the media query syntax
- Learn how to use media queries in links, in @import statements, and within CSS files
- Understand what device features we can test for
- Consider whether to author alike media queries in one block or wherever it suits
- Consider the latest capabilities added in Media Queries Level 5 that we can use today. Media features like `pointer`, `hover`, `prefers-color-scheme`, and `prefers-reduced-motion`, as well as better ways of dealing with viewport ranges
- Look at what future media queries may provide

Back in *Chapter 1, The Essentials of Responsive Web Design,* we inserted a `meta` tag into the head of our web page to make it work on mobile devices. At that point, I made the promise that *Chapter 3* would explain exactly what that tag was, what it does, and why we still have it. It's time to make good on that promise.

## The meta viewport tag

When Apple released the iPhone in 2007, they introduced a proprietary `meta` tag called the viewport `meta` tag. Its purpose was to provide a way for web pages to communicate to mobile browsers how they would like the web browser to render the page.

Without this `meta` tag, iPhones would render web pages as a 980 px wide window that the user would then have to zoom in or out of.

With this `meta` tag, it's possible to render a web page at its actual size and then adapt the layout to provide the kind of web pages we now all expect to see when we browse the internet on our phones.

For the foreseeable future, any web page you want to be responsive, and render well across small screen devices, will still need to make use of this `meta` tag as Android and a growing number of other platforms also support it.

As you are now aware, the viewport `meta` tag is added within the head tags of the HTML. It can be set to a specific width (which we could specify in pixels, for example) or as a scale, for example, 2.0 (twice the actual size). Here's an example of the viewport `meta` tag set to show the browser at twice (200 percent) the actual size:

```
<meta name="viewport" content="initial-scale=2.0,width=device-width" />
```

Let's break the above `meta` tag down and understand what's going on. The `name="viewport"` attribute tells the browser this tag is dealing with the viewport. The `content="initial-scale=2.0` section is then saying "scale the content to twice the size" (where 0.5 would be half the size, 3.0 would be three times the size, and so on) whilst the `width=device-width` part tells the browser that the width of the page should be equal to `device-width`. The `meta` tag can also be used to control the amount a user can zoom in and out of the page. This example allows users to go as large as three times the device width and as small as half the device width:

```
<meta
    name="viewport"
    content="width=device-width, maximum-scale=3, minimum-scale=0.5"
/>
```

You could also disable users from zooming at all:

```
<meta name="viewport" content="initial-scale=1.0, user-scalable=no" />
```

The `user-scalable=no` being the relevant part.

However, with zooming being an important accessibility requirement for users with reduced visual acuity, it's rare that it would be appropriate to prevent it. In addition, many browsers disable the ability to prevent zooming for that very reason.

Right, we'll change the scale to 1.0, which means that the mobile browser will render the page at 100 percent of its viewport. Setting it to the device's width means that our page should render at 100 percent of the width of all supported mobile browsers. For the majority of responsive web design cases, this `meta` tag would be appropriate:

```
<meta name="viewport" content="width=device-width,initial-scale=1.0" />
```

That should be all you need to know about viewport `meta` tags from a responsive design perspective. In short, ensure you have one added or things are unlikely to look and behave as you might expect! To be certain everything is in order, ensure you test at some point on an actual device.

With the `meta` tag covered, we can now get to the real focus of the chapter: media queries themselves.

# Why media queries are needed for a responsive web design

If you head over to the W3C specification of the CSS3 Media Queries module (`https://www.w3.org/TR/mediaqueries-3/`), you'll see that this is their official introduction to what media queries are all about:

> *A media query consists of a media type and zero or more expressions that check for the conditions of particular media features. Among the media features that can be used in media queries are 'width', 'height', and 'color'. By using media queries, presentations can be tailored to a specific range of output devices without changing the content itself.*

While a fluid layout, created with percentages rather than fixed widths, can carry a design a substantial distance (we cover fluid layouts in full in the next chapter), given the gamut of screen sizes we have to cover, there are times when we need to revise the layout more substantially. Media queries make this possible—think of them as basic conditional logic for CSS.

## Basic conditional logic in CSS

True programming languages all have some facility in which one of two or more possible situations are catered for. This usually takes the form of conditional logic, also known as **control flow**, typified by an **if/else** statement.

If programming vernacular makes your eyes itch, fear not; it's a very simple concept. You probably dictate conditional logic every time you ask a friend to order for you when visiting a cafe: "If they've got triple chocolate muffins I'll have one of those, if not, I'll have a slice of carrot cake." It's a simple conditional statement with two possible (and equally desirable) results based on two equally possible eventualities.

At the time of writing, CSS offers few possibilities when it comes to true conditional logic and programmatic features. Loops and iteration, for example, are still within the sole domain of CSS pre-processors (did I mention a fine book on the subject of the Sass pre-processor, called *Sass and Compass for Designers?*). However, media queries are one mechanism that does allow us to author basic conditional logic; styles applied depending on whether certain media-based conditions are met.

## Media query syntax

So what does a CSS media query look like and, more importantly, how does it work?

Below is a complete but simple web page, with no content but some basic styles and media queries:

```html
<!DOCTYPE html>
<html class="no-js" lang="en">
    <head>
        <meta charset="utf-8" />
        <title>Media Query Test</title>
        <meta name="viewport" content="width=device-width,
        initial-scale=1.0" />
        <style>
            body {
                background-color: grey;
            }
            @media screen and (min-width: 320px) {
                body {
                    background-color: green;
                }
            }
            @media screen and (min-width: 550px) {
                body {
                    background-color: yellow;
                }
            }
            @media screen and (min-width: 768px) {
                body {
                    background-color: orange;
                }
            }
            @media screen and (min-width: 960px) {
                body {
                    background-color: red;
                }
            }
        </style>
    </head>
    <body></body>
</html>
```

Copy and save that into a new file, or, if you have the downloaded code for the book, you can find it as example_03-01.

Now, open the file in a browser and resize the window. The background color of the page will vary depending upon the current viewport size.

A default color is defined first, outside of a media query. Then, when any of the media queries are "true," the styles inside the media query overwrite the default.

The basic syntax of a media query is simple when you get used to it. You use the @media **at-rule** to communicate a media query and then write the media test in parentheses. The test must pass in order for the styles within the curly braces to be applied.

You can write media queries in links in HTML, to load particular style sheets if the media query passes. You can write media queries on CSS @import at-rules to determine which style sheets should be imported. You can also write media queries directly into a CSS file to determine which rules should be applied on the basis of which media queries resolve to true.

Let's look at each in turn.

## Media queries in link tags

Here's what a media query looks like on a link you'd find in the <head> section of markup:

```
<link
    rel="stylesheet"
    media="screen and (orientation: portrait)"
    href="portrait-screen.css"
/>
```

This media query is asking, "Are you a screen and is your orientation portrait?".

## Media query on an @import at-rule

Here's the same rule on an @import statement:

```
@import url("portrait-screen.css") screen and (orientation: portrait);
```

You can see all the same component parts there: the file to be loaded and the test that has to be passed. Different syntax, same outcome.

Using the @import at-rule in CSS makes the browser request the relevant file from the network and this can add to the number of HTTP requests. This can sometimes adversely affect site load speed.

## Media queries in a CSS file

Finally, here's the same media query written inside a CSS file, or within a style tag inside the HTML:

```
@media screen and (orientation: portrait) {
    /* styles here */
}
```

## Inverting media query logic

It's possible to reverse the logic of any media query expression by adding not to the beginning of the media query. For example, the following code would negate the result in our prior example, loading the file for anything that wasn't a screen with a portrait orientation:

```
<link
    rel="stylesheet"
    media="not screen and (orientation: portrait)"
    href="portrait-screen.css"
/>
```

Although using the not keyword is occasionally useful, I find it is far simpler to just think about applying styles when you do want them. This way you can stick to writing the most terse and simplest forms of media queries.

## Combining media queries

It's also possible to string multiple expressions together. For example, let's extend one of our prior examples and also limit the file to devices that have a viewport greater than 800 pixels:

```
<link
    rel="stylesheet"
    media="screen and (orientation: portrait) and (min-width: 800px)"
    href="800wide-portrait-screen.css"
/>
```

# A number of different media queries

Further still, we could have a list of media queries. If any of the listed queries are true, the file will be loaded. If none are true, it won't. Here is an example:

```
<link
    rel="stylesheet"
    media="screen and (orientation: portrait) and (min-width: 800px),
    projection"
    href="800wide-portrait-screen.css"
/>
```

There are two points to note here. Firstly, a comma separates each media query, effectively acting like an or command. Secondly, you'll notice that after `projection`, there is no trailing and or feature/value combination in parentheses. That's because, in the absence of these values, the media query is applied to all media types. In our example, the styles will apply to all projectors.

 You should be aware that you can use any CSS length unit to specify media queries. **Pixels** (px) are the most commonly used, but **ems** (em) and **rems** (rem) are equally valid and applicable.

# Everyday media queries

At this point, it's probably prudent of me to tell you that in most situations, you don't actually need to specify `screen`. Here's the key point in the specification:

*A shorthand syntax is offered for media queries that apply to all media types; the keyword 'all' can be left out (along with the trailing 'and'). I.e. if the media type is not explicitly given it is 'all'.*

Therefore, unless you want to target styles to particular media types, just leave the `screen` and part out. That's the way we will be writing media queries in the example files from this point on. For example:

```
@media (min-width: 750px) {
    /* styles */
}
```

# What can media queries test for?

When building responsive designs, the media queries that get used most usually relate to a device's viewport width (width). In my own experience, I have found little need, with the occasional exception of resolution and viewport height, to employ the other capabilities. However, just in case the need arises, here is a list of all capabilities that Media Queries Level 3 can test for. We will look at some other queries from later versions of the specification later in the chapter. For now, hopefully, some will pique your interest:

- `width`: The viewport width.
- `height`: The viewport height.
- `device-width*`: The rendering surface's width (for our purposes, this is typically the screen width of a device).
- `device-height*`: The rendering surface's height (for our purposes, this is typically the screen height of a device).
- `orientation`: This capability checks whether a device is portrait or landscape in orientation.
- `aspect-ratio`: The ratio of width to height based on the viewport width and height. A 16:9 widescreen display can be written as `aspect-ratio: 16/9`.
- `device-aspect-ratio*`: This capability is similar to `aspect-ratio` but is based on the width and height of the device's rendering surface, rather than the viewport.
- `color`: The number of bits per color component. For example, `min-color: 16` will check that the device has 16-bit color.
- `color-index`: The number of entries in the color lookup table (the table is how a device changes one set of colors to another) of the device. Values must be numbers and cannot be negative.
- `monochrome`: This capability tests how many bits per pixel are in a monochrome frame buffer. The value would be a number (integer), for example, `monochrome: 2`, and cannot be negative.
- `resolution`: This capability can be used to test screen or print resolution; for example, `min-resolution: 300dpi`. It can also accept measurements in dots per centimeter; for example, `min-resolution: 118dpcm`.

- scan: This can be either progressive or interlace, features largely particular to TVs. For example, a 720p HD TV (the "p" part of 720p indicates "progressive") could be targeted with scan: progressive, while a 1080i HD TV (the "i" part of 1080i indicates "interlaced") could be targeted with scan: interlace.

- grid: This capability indicates whether or not the device is grid orbitmap-based.

All the above features, with the exception of scan and grid, can be prefixed with min or max to create ranges. For example, consider the following code snippet:

```
@import url("tiny.css") screen and (min-width: 200px) and (max-width:
360px);
```

Here, a minimum (min) and maximum (max) have been applied to width to set a range. The tiny.css file will only be imported for screen devices with a minimum viewport width of 200 pixels and a maximum viewport width of 360 pixels.

**\*Features deprecated in CSS Media Queries Level 5**

It's worth being aware that the draft specification for Media Queries Level 5, which in turn consumed the Media Queries Level 4 draft, deprecates the use of a few features (https://www.w3.org/TR/mediaqueries-5/#mf-deprecated), most notably device-height, device-width, and device-aspect-ratio. Support for those queries will remain in browsers but it's recommended you refrain from writing any new style sheets that use them.

# Using media queries to alter a design

If you've read, and at least partially understood, what we have been through so far in this chapter, you should be ready to start using media queries in earnest.

I'd suggest opening the index.html file and the associated index.css file from the Start folder of this chapter's code. Then try and add some media queries to alter some areas of the page at certain viewport widths. Let's make a couple of changes together and then you can practice some of your own.

Let's look at the header section of what we have currently (viewport around 1200 px wide):

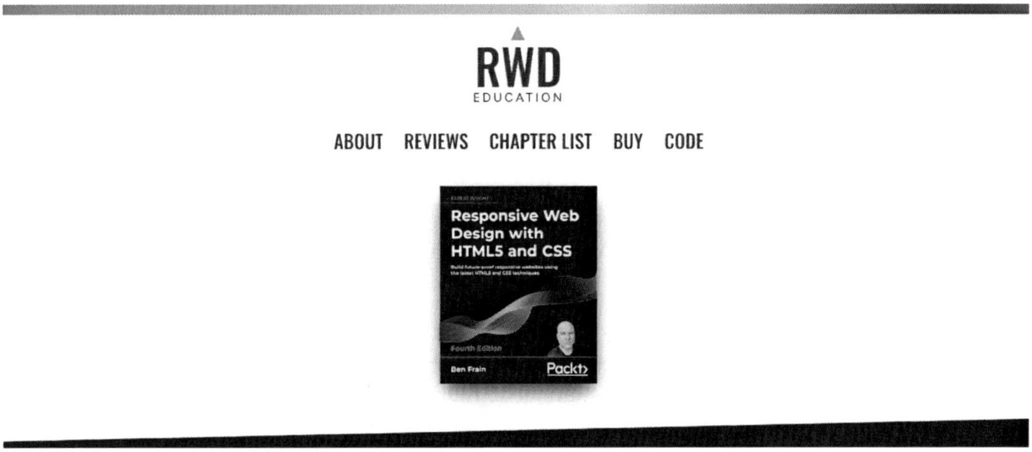

*Figure 3.3: On wider viewports, what we have in the browser doesn't match the design*

And here is the layout we are trying to achieve:

*Figure 3.4: The design calls for a different layout at wider viewports*

We need to keep the design as it is for smaller viewports but amend it for larger ones. Let's start by adding a media query that makes the navigation links and the logo appear at opposite sides at 1200 px and above:

```
@media (min-width: 800px) {
    .rwd-MastHead {
        flex-direction: row;
        justify-content: space-between;
        max-width: 1000px;
        margin: 30px auto;
    }
}
```

If any of those styles don't make sense now, don't worry. We will be covering Flexbox layout in *Chapter 4, Fluid Layout and Flexbox*. What is important to understand is the media query itself. What we are saying is "apply this rule, but only at a minimum width of 800 px."

And here is the effect of that rule in the browser:

*Figure 3.5: Our first media query gets our logo on the left and navigation over to the right*

Now, the keen-eyed among you may realize that despite this new rule, which gets our logo and navigation links spread out, we have some styles applied that we no longer need at this size. The following grab shows the no-longer needed margin above and inline padding within the main navigation links:

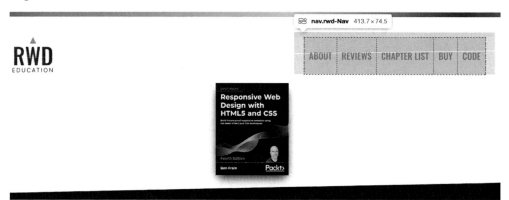

*Figure 3.6: There are styles being applied that we want to reset at this viewport*

Let's write another media query to fix that. We'll make this change at a slightly smaller screen width, as that extra space is unneeded even at 1000 px wide:

```
@media (min-width: 1000px) {
    .rwd-Nav {
        margin: 0;
```

```
        padding: 0;
    }
  }
```

In this instance, we are saying "at 1000 px and beyond, make the margin and padding zero for the `.rwd-Nav` element." Notice that each time, in our media query, we only amend the specific properties we need to change. By writing our "base" styles as we have, outside of any media query, our actual media queries only need to encapsulate the differences needed.

It might seem a little reductive, but the above process is essentially all there is to working with media queries. Write the basic styles without media queries and then work wider and wider, adding media queries and changes wherever needed to affect the design as required.

If you have the time, I implore you to try writing some media queries for yourself. Whether it's the test page here or something of your own you want to work with. Pick something you want to change, pick a viewport width, and add a media query to make the change happen. Once you have written a few, making the changes you want to see, you will realize how straightforward but powerful they are.

**Testing responsive designs on emulators and simulators**

 Although there is no substitute for testing your development work on real devices, there are emulators for Android and a simulator for iOS (for the pedantic, a simulator merely simulates the relevant device whereas an emulator actually attempts to interpret the original device's code). The Android emulator for Windows, Linux, and Mac is available free by installing Android Studio from `https://developer.android.com/studio`. The iOS simulator is only available to macOS users and comes as part of the Xcode package (free from the Mac App Store). Browsers themselves are also including ever-improving tools for emulating mobile devices in their development tools.

# Advanced media query considerations

The following section deals with concerns for when you are highly proficient in writing media queries. Think of these topics as micro-optimizations. If you are just starting with media queries, you certainly shouldn't be worrying about any of these topics yet. Jump on to the *Media Queries Level 5* section instead!

OK, media query uber-geekery, here we go...

## Do media queries affect which files get downloaded or how the page renders?

Ordinarily, for a browser, CSS is considered to be a **render blocking** asset; the browser needs to fetch and parse a linked CSS file before the rendering of the page can complete. This stands to reason, as the browser needs to know what styles to apply for laying out and painting the page. However, modern browsers are smart enough to discern which style sheets (linked with media queries in the head) need to be analyzed immediately and which can be deferred until after the initial page rendering. The upshot of this is that for these browsers, CSS files that are linked with media queries that don't apply to the current environmental situation can be *deferred* until after the initial page load, providing some performance advantage. There's more on this topic over on Google's developer pages: https://web.dev/critical-rendering-path-render-blocking-css/.

However, I would like to draw your attention to this part in particular:

*...note that "render blocking" only refers to whether the browser will have to hold the initial rendering of the page on that resource. In either case, the CSS asset is still downloaded by the browser, albeit with a lower priority for non-blocking resources.*

To reiterate, all the linked files will still be downloaded; they just may not necessarily require the browser to hold the rendering of the page.

Therefore, a modern browser loading a responsive web page with four different style sheets linked with different media queries (to apply different styles for different viewport ranges) will download all four CSS files, but probably only parse the applicable one initially before rendering the page. Take a look at example_03-02 in the chapter's example code, which you may find more convenient to view at https://benfrain.com/playground/mq-downloads/. If you view that page with a slim viewport and you are proficient enough with your browser's developer tools, you can look in the network area and check that all files are downloaded, regardless of whether the media queries are actually being applied.

## Should you split media queries into their own files?

Let's suppose you have a style sheet with a bunch of different media queries. Suppose there are a bunch for min-widths of 800 px, and another load for widths above 1200 px. Should you separate them out into their own style sheets? In short, I would say no.

Apart from preference and/or compartmentalization of code, there is rarely a great tangible advantage in separating different media query styles into separate files. After all, using separate files increases the number of HTTP requests needed to render a page, which in turn can make the pages slower in certain other situations. Nothing is ever easy on the Web! It is, therefore, really a question of evaluating the entire performance of your site and testing each scenario on different devices.

As a default approach, unless the project has considerable time available for performance optimizations, this is one of the last places I would look to make performance gains.

More practically, only once I am certain all images are compressed, all scripts are squished as small as possible with concatenation and minification, all assets are being served gzipped, all static content is being cached via CDNs and all surplus CSS rules have been removed, would I start looking to split up media queries into separate files for potential performance gains.

In all but exceptional circumstances, I recommend adding media queries within an existing style sheet alongside the "normal" rules. If you are happy to do the same, that leads to one further consideration: should media queries be declared underneath the associated selector? Or split off into a separate block of code at the end for all alike media queries? Glad you asked.

## Consolidate media queries or scatter them where it suits?

I'm a fan of writing media queries underneath the original "normal" rule. For example, let's say I want to change the width of a couple of different elements, at different places in the style sheet, depending on the viewport width. I would typically do this:

```
.thing {
    width: 50%;
}
@media (min-width: 30rem) {
    .thing {
        width: 75%;
    }
}
/* More styles for different elements */
.thing2 {
    width: 65%;
}
```

```
@media (min-width: 30rem) {
    .thing2 {
        width: 75%;
    }
}
```

Can you see in this example that we have two separate media queries that are testing for the same thing: @media (min-width: 30rem)? Surely duplicating media at-rules like this is overly verbose and wasteful? Shouldn't I be advocating grouping all the like media queries into a single block like this:

```
.thing {
    width: 50%;
}
.thing2 {
    width: 65%;
}
/* Styles affecting other elements */
@media (min-width: 30rem) {
    .thing {
        width: 75%;
    }
    .thing2 {
        width: 75%;
    }
}
/* A few more styles go after */
```

That is certainly one way to do it. However, from a maintenance point of view, I find this more difficult. There is no "right" way to do this, but my preference is to define a rule for an individual selector once and have any variations of that rule (such as changes within media queries) defined immediately after. That way I don't have to search for separate blocks of code to find the declaration that is relevant to a particular selector.

With CSS preprocessors, associating all alike rules can be even more convenient as the media query "variant" of a rule can be nested directly within the initial ruleset. But that's a technique for a different book. Curious? Take a look here: `https://ecss.benfrain.com/chapter8.html#h-H2_1`.

We also have native nesting due to arrive in CSS; more on that in *Chapter 14, Cutting-Edge CSS Features*.

## What about file size?

It would seem fair to argue against the former technique on the grounds of verbosity. Surely file size alone should be enough reason not to write media queries in this manner? After all, no one wants a big, bloated CSS file to serve their users. However, the simple fact is that gzip compression, which should be compressing all possible assets on your server, reduces the difference to a completely inconsequential amount. I've done various tests on this in the past, so if it's something you would like to read more about, head over to: `http://benfrain.com/inline-or-combined-media-queries-in-sass-fight/`. The bottom line is: I don't believe you should concern yourself with file size if you would rather write media queries directly after the "standard" styles.

As a final note on this, if you want to author your media queries directly after the original rule but have all alike media queries definitions merged into one, there are a number of build tools that facilitate this (at the time of writing, PostCSS and Gulp both have relevant plugins).

That should give you everything you need to start wielding media queries like a pro. However, before we move on, there are a number of media query features in Media Queries Level 5 we can actually start using today. Let's take a sneak peek!

# Media Queries Level 5

Specifications at the W3C go through a ratification process, from **Working Draft** (**WD**) to **Candidate Recommendation** (**CR**) to **Proposed Recommendation** (**PR**) before finally arriving, many years later, at W3C **Recommendation** (**REC**). So modules at a greater maturity level than others are generally safer to use. For example, CSS Spatial Navigation Level 1 is in progress as I write this (`http://www.w3.org/TR/css-nav-1/`), at Working Draft status with no support in browsers. Meanwhile, the topic of this chapter until this point has been Media Queries Level 3, which is implemented in every modern browser.

If you have a spare day, you can knock yourself out reading all about the official explanation of the standards ratification process at http://www.w3.org/2005/10/Process-20051014/tr.

At the time of writing, whilst CSS Media Queries Level 5 enjoys a draft specification: https://www.w3.org/TR/mediaqueries-5, not all the features it documents enjoy browser implementations. So, in this section, we will concentrate on Media Queries Level 5 features that we can make use of: features already implemented in browsers.

## Interaction media features

Interaction media queries are concerned with pointing devices and hover capability. Let's see what each of these can do for us.

## The pointer media feature

Here is the W3C introduction to the pointer media feature:

*The pointer media feature is used to query about the presence and accuracy of a pointing device such as a mouse. If a device has multiple input mechanisms, the pointer media feature must reflect the characteristics of the "primary" input mechanism, as determined by the user agent.*

There are three possible states for the pointer features: none, coarse, and fine.

A coarse pointer device might be a finger on a touchscreen device. However, it could equally be a cursor from a games console that doesn't have the fine-grained control of something like a mouse:

```
@media (pointer: coarse) {
    /* styles for when coarse pointer is present */
}
```

A fine pointer device might be a mouse but could also be a stylus pen or any future fine-grained pointer mechanism:

```
@media (pointer: fine) {
    /* styles for when fine pointer is present */
}
```

Browsers report whether the value of pointer is fine, coarse, or none, based on the "primary" pointing device.

Therefore, consider that just because a device has the capability of a fine pointer, it doesn't mean that will be the primary pointing device. Think of tablets where the primary pointer is a finger (coarse), but that has an attached stylus (a fine pointing device).

 The safest bet is always to assume users are using touch-based input and size user interface elements accordingly. That way, even if they are using a mouse they will have no difficulty using the interface with ease. If, however, you assume mouse input and don't provide affordance for coarse pointers, it might make for a difficult user experience.

Read the draft of this feature here: https://www.w3.org/TR/mediaqueries-5/#pointer.

## The hover media feature

As you might imagine, the hover media feature tests the device's ability to hover over elements on the screen. If the user has multiple inputs at their disposal (touch and mouse, for example), characteristics of the primary input are used. Here are the possible values and example code:

For users that have no ability to hover, we can target styles at them with a value of none:

```
@media (hover: none) {
    /* styles for when the user cannot hover */
}
```

Or, as before, we might choose to make the non-hover scenario the default and then only add hover styles for devices that take advantage of them:

```
@media (hover) {
    /* styles for when user can hover */
}
```

Be aware that there are also any-pointer or any-hover media features. They are like the above hover and pointer but test the capabilities of any of the possible input devices.

That way, if you want to apply styles if any input device is capable of hover, regardless of whether that input device is the primary one, you can:

```
@media (any-hover: hover) {
    /* styles if any input device is capable of hover */
}
```

If you wanted to style an element a certain way based upon whether any attached pointer device was coarse, you could use any-pointer like this:

```
@media (any-pointer: coarse) {
    /* styles to be applied if any attached pointer is coarse */
}
```

# User preference media features

There are a number of features in the Media Queries Level 5 draft that cater to the preferences and needs of users. Some of these can be seen as largely superficial, while others have more concrete applications such as enhancing accessibility. Let's look at some next.

## The prefers-color-scheme media feature

In the last couple of years, popular operating systems for both desktop and mobile computers have given users the option of a dark mode. To supplement this, operating systems expose this user preference to the browser by way of the prefers-color-scheme media feature.

At present there are three possible preferences: light, dark, and no-preference. To exemplify this feature's use, we might amend the default colors for a page like this:

```
body {
    background-color: #e4e4e4;
    color: #545454;
}
@media (prefers-color-scheme: dark) {
    body {
        background-color: #333;
        color: #ddd;
    }
}
```

In the same vein as I'm recommending you to write your default "mobile" styles in the root of your style sheet, I would recommend writing the default colors in the root too and adding one of these queries to cater for an alternative interface if needed or desired.

You can read the draft specification for the prefers-color-scheme media feature here: https://www.w3.org/TR/mediaqueries-5/#prefers-color-scheme.

# The prefers-reduced-motion feature

If a user has set their device to minimize the amount of motion it provides in its interface and system interactions, this information is exposed to CSS via the prefers-reduced-motion media query.

There are only two settings: no-preference or reduce.

If you find yourself writing more than the occasional animation or transition, it's well worth wrapping such styles up in a no-preference variant like this:

```
@media (prefers-reduced-motion: no-preference) {
    /* animation code here */
}
```

Or if you want to provide a different, subtler animation to your users, you could write your animation code, and then provide another that overwrites the first for users that would like the subtler variant:

```
.ele {
    animation: bezerk 1s;
}
@media (prefers-reduced-motion) {
    .ele {
        animation: subtle 1s;
    }
}
```

Note in the example code that when not explicitly stating a preference, merely using the prefers-reduced-motion query will evaluate to true.

However you prefer to write them, this media query provides a great tool to cater to users sensitive to animations and movement, whether for medical reasons such as vestibular motion disorders or purely from a personal preference point of view.

# Future possibilities

A glance down the Level 5 draft specification reveals a multitude of additional features we haven't discussed here. There is the ability to detect whether scripting is supported (think JavaScript) and the ability to create custom media queries; don't get too carried away, it's only really a nicer way to write them.

Also the ability to specify ranges in a terser syntax. For example, instead of this:

```
@media (min-width: 30rems) and (max-width: 60rems) {
    /* Styles */
}
```

You could write:

```
@media (30rems <= width <= 60rems) {
    /* Styles */
}
```

I don't know if it's lack of exposure, but I find that new syntax quite difficult to parse. We will see how it fares if it makes it to a browser implementation.

Media queries are a very powerful part of CSS. It's always worth checking what they can do for you right now, and also in the near future.

## Container queries

Media queries operate their queries on the capabilities of the device. Practically, when working with responsive designs, it's the width of the container we are typically interested in.

However, suppose we are creating a visual component that might be used in a wider container, such as a main content area, but equally might be used in a thinner, sidebar aside area. We tend to work around these scenarios without container queries by using descendant selectors to give some context and make style changes based on the document structure:

```
.component {
    display: flex;
}


.sidebar .thing {
    flex-direction: column;
}
```

Then, with this override for when the component is in the sidebar established, we can combine these selectors with media queries as needed. Maybe we need one set of styles when in the .sidebar and the screen is a certain size, and then another set of styles when not in the .sidebar but we are still at that viewport size:

```
@media (min-width: 40em) {
    .component {
        /* styles */
    }
    .sidebar .component {
        /* styles */
    }
}
```

That's OK, but in this scenario, we need to be very clear about the environments our piece of user interface may find itself in. It's also quite a broad stroke. What happens when the structure or physical shape of the rendered document is changed, as it is given to do in responsive designs?

As discussed at the beginning of this section, what we are actually interested in is the width of the container our component finds itself in. If only we could query the container!

For years, web developers have been hoping for something that allowed us to do just that. Finally, that is happening. CSS container queries are just now, as I write this in 2022, making their way to browsers in experimental form.

 You may hear of Web Platform features being "Experimental" or "behind a flag." This means the capabilities can be optionally switched on in browsers, but they are not shipping in browsers by default. It is a chance to use the feature in its unfinished form and provide feedback to browser vendors as it is being developed.

## This may change!

This is bleeding-edge stuff as I write this, and hasn't officially shipped in browsers, so before we proceed I want to give you this "it may change" warning! While it's unlikely the principles of container queries will change significantly before they are available in browsers, it is possible some syntax and nuances may be revised.

As such, we will consider example code only for this section; there are no example pages in the downloadable code. What is important for you to appreciate is the possibilities these new tools offer.

## Using a container query

Unlike media queries, which are always available, for container queries, it is necessary to establish some containment for an element. Effectively, this is like saying to the browser, "Hey, I might want to know how wide this is." Without this, we are not able to query the element.

Therefore, in order for a container to be query-able, we first need to tell the browser how the container should be "contained".

As we have established, typically, with a responsive design, width is the axis we are interested in querying. So to start solving our imagined scenario above, we can communicate that we want the elements to be containers that we can query the width of (or the height in the second selector below), and give them a name like this:

```
.main-content {
    container: main / inline-size;
}
.sidebar {
    container: side / block-size;
}
```

The `container` property is actually a shorthand for setting two other properties: `container-name` and `container-type`. You can set them separately with those properties if you prefer.

With those set, elements nested within can query the container.

 In one version of the draft specification, setting the values in the `container` shorthand was done with space-separated values; in the latest draft, it is done using a forward slash (/) to delineate the two parts. This serves as a reminder that readers should check the syntax that actually ships.

As with media queries, there are different types of queries. For width, the equivalent in container queries is the `inline-size`. This is the length of the container in the inline axis. In the Western, left-to-right writing world, that equates to the container width, just as `block-size` would be equivalent to height.

## Why name the container?

If there were no other ancestor containers, then we wouldn't need to bother with a named container. We could just write a container query like this:

```
@container (inline-size > 500px) { /* styles */ }
```

As you have likely gathered, the syntax is purposely modeled after media queries, and if you have read the rest of this chapter, that syntax should make immediate sense.

However, if there is a possibility of more than one ancestral container, this approach may become problematic.

The container name allows us to write container queries specific to a specific container. So, assuming our imaginary component has two ancestral containers, we can have some styles applied when the `main` container is over 500 px wide like this:

```
@container main (inline-size > 500px) {
    .thing {
        /* styles */
    }
}
```

And those styles will only get applied when the `main` container is more than 500 px wide. And, crucially, *not* if the `side` container is more than 500 px wide.

 By default, container queries resolve to their nearest ancestor container that accepts querying on the specified axis, or smallest viewport size if none available.

As named containers provide the ability to query more than one container, we can effectively say, "If the `main` is 400 px wide apply one set of styles, and if the `side` is over 20 rem high, apply these other styles." This provides us a lot of flexibility.

 There are additional queries being specified for container queries such as `style` and `state`; however, right now there aren't even initial experimental implementations in browsers. To read more on those possibilities, keep an eye on the developing specification at `https://drafts.csswg.org/css-contain-3/`.

## Container relative lengths

We can size the child elements of containers using container relative lengths.

Here are the proposed units:

- cqi, 1% of the inline-size
- cqw, 1% of the width
- cqb, 1% of the block-size
- cqh, 1% of the height
- cqmin, 1% of the smallest of cqi and cqb
- cqmax, 1% of the largest of cqi and cqb

These resolve to the nearest ancestor container that accepts queries on that axis. This is an important concept to fully grasp. Let's assume you specified 40cqh. If the nearest ancestor container is set to inline-size, then it won't be 40% of the height of that container. It will be the nearest ancestor container set for block-size.

Whether or not these details change in the shipping version of container queries, your humble author is unable to know.

## Possibilities

While, at this point, it's not possible to be certain of the syntaxes we will end up with, let's reflect on some of the possibilities that should be possible. What about headings that scale with the size of the container? That would be as simple as:

```
.heading {
    font-size: calc(14px + 2cqi);
}
```

Or changing layout if the container ends up taller than it is wide:

```
@container (orientation: portrait) {
    /* styles */
}
```

Remember we will be able to make all these styling forks independently or in conjunction with things going on with the viewport.

Exciting times are coming as CSS provides further means to define and codify our designs with hitherto impossible flexibility.

## Summary

In this chapter, we've covered everything you are likely to need when using media queries for a responsive design. You now understand how to change a layout based on the characteristics of the environment your web pages find themselves in.

We learned what media queries are, why we need them, and how to include them in our CSS files in all manner of ways. We've also learned how to use the meta viewport tag to make browsers render pages in the manner we'd like.

As I'll no doubt repeat in later chapters, don't get bogged down with or intimidated by the syntax. Just get an understanding of the underlying principles and you can look up the syntax anytime; after all, that's what all developers do! As long as you understand what you can accomplish with media queries, our work here is largely done.

While only experimental as I write this, we have also considered container queries and some of the exciting abilities they provide. Modeled after media queries, they let us style elements based on their containers, allowing us even greater control over our designs.

Back in *Chapter 1*, we noted that the three tenets of responsive web design are media queries, flexible layouts, and flexible media. We're three chapters in and we've only covered media queries! We're going to put that right in the next chapter.

In *Chapter 4*, we are going to take a deep dive into fluid layouts with Flexbox. We will cover how to convert a fixed-width design into a fluid proportional layout and lay out our page elements with Flexbox.

It's going to be another packed chapter, so get yourself comfy and I'll see you there!

# Join our book's Discord space

Stumped by media queries? Join the book's Discord workspace to discuss all your responsive web design concerns directly with the author and interact with other readers:

https://packt.link/RWD4e

# 4

# Fluid Layout and Flexbox

At the end of the last chapter, we reminded ourselves that the three core tenets of responsive web design are fluid layout, media queries, and flexible media. We spent *Chapter 3* learning all about media queries. Now we know how to wield them to change a layout at a particular **breakpoint**. In this chapter, we will focus on another pillar of responsive web design: fluid layout.

Eons ago, in the mists of time (well, the late 1990s), websites were typically built with their widths defined as percentages. These percentage-based widths fluidly adjusted to the screen and were known as fluid layouts.

In the years after, in the mid-to-late 2000s, there was an intervening fixation on fixed-width designs—I blame those pesky print designers and their obsession with pixel-perfect precision! Nowadays, as we build responsive web designs, we need to look back to fluid layouts and remember all the benefits they offer.

Until fairly recently, web developers have used several CSS layout mechanisms to create great fluid layouts. If you've worked on the web for any length of time, you will be familiar with blocks, inline-blocks, tables, and other techniques to achieve any given layout. As I write this in 2022, there seems little benefit in giving those old techniques more than a cursory mention. We now have two powerful CSS layout mechanisms at our disposal: CSS Flexbox and CSS Grid.

This chapter will deal with CSS Flexbox. In *Chapter 5*, *Layout with CSS Grid*, I've got a feeling you can guess what we will be covering.

Flexbox is so useful because it can do more than merely provide a fluid layout mechanism. Do you want to center content easily, change the source order of markup, and generally create amazing layouts with ease? Flexbox has you covered.

In this chapter, we will:

- Learn how to convert fixed pixel layouts into proportional sizes
- Recognize Flexbox as a practical path beyond these limitations
- Understand the Flexible Box Layout Module and the benefits it offers

Let's crack on with our first task: converting fixed designs into fluid relationships. This is a task that you'll need to perform constantly when building responsive web designs.

## Converting a fixed pixel design into a fluid proportional layout

Graphic composites, or **comps**, as they are often called, exported from a program such as Photoshop, Illustrator, Figma, or Sketch all have fixed pixel dimensions. At some point, the designs need to be converted into proportional dimensions when recreating the design as a fluid layout for the browser.

There is a beautifully simple formula for making this conversion that the father of responsive web design, Ethan Marcotte, set down in his 2009 article, *Fluid Grids* (`https://alistapart.com/article/FLUIDGRIDS`):

$$target / context = result$$

Put another way, divide the units of the thing you want by the thing it lives in. Let's put that into practice. Understanding it will enable you to convert any fixed dimension layouts into responsive/fluid equivalents.

Consider a very basic page layout intended for desktop. In an ideal world, we would always be moving to a desktop layout from a smaller screen layout; however, for the sake of illustrating the proportions, we will look at the two situations back to front.

Here's an image of the layout:

*Figure 4.1: A basic "desktop" layout*

The layout is 960 px wide. Both the header and footer are the full widths of the layout. The left-hand area is 200 px wide, and the right-hand area is 100 px wide. That leaves 660 px for the main content area. Our job is to convert this fixed-width design into a fluid layout that retains its proportions as it is resized. For our first task, we need to convert the middle and side sections into proportional dimensions.

We will begin by converting the left-hand side. The left-hand side is 200 units wide. This value is our target value. We will divide that target size by 960 units, our context, and we have a result: .208333333. Now, whenever we get our result with this formula, we need to shift the decimal point two points to the right. This gives us a value that is the target value described as a percentage of its parent. In this case, the left-hand section is 20.8333333% of its parent.

Let's practice the formula again on the middle section. Our target value is 660. Divide that by our context of 960 and we get .6875. Move the decimal two points to the right and we have 68.75%.

Finally, let's look at the right-hand section. Our target is 100. We divide that by the context of 960 and we get .104166667. Move the decimal point and we have a value of 10.4166667%.

That's as difficult as it gets. Say it with me: target, divided by context, equals result.

 You can use values with long decimal values with no issues in CSS. Or, if you would rather see more palatable numbers in your code, rounding them to two decimal points will work just as well for the browser.

To prove the point, let's quickly build that basic layout as blocks in the browser. To make it easier to follow along, I have added a class to the various elements that describes which piece of the **comp** they are referring to. Ordinarily, it's not a good idea to name things based on their location. The location can change, especially with a responsive design. In short, do as I say and not as I do here!

You can view the layout as example_04-01. Here is the HTML:

```
<div class="Wrap">
    <header class="Header"></header>
    <div class="WrapMiddle">
        <aside class="Left"></aside>
        <main class="Middle"></main>
        <aside class="Right"></aside>
    </div>
    <footer class="Footer"></footer>
</div>
```

And here is the CSS:

```
html,
body {
    margin: 0;
    padding: 0;
}
.Wrap {
    max-width: 1400px;
    margin: 0 auto;
}
```

```css
.Header {
    width: 100%;
    height: 130px;
    background-color: #038c5a;
}
.WrapMiddle {
    width: 100%;
    font-size: 0;
}
.Left {
    height: 625px;
    width: 20.83%;
    background-color: #03a66a;
    display: inline-block;
}
.Middle {
    height: 625px;
    width: 68.75%;
    background-color: #bbbf90;
    display: inline-block;
}
.Right {
    height: 625px;
    width: 10.41%;
    background-color: #03a66a;
    display: inline-block;
}
.Footer {
    height: 200px;
    width: 100%;
    background-color: #025059;
}
```

If you open the example code in a browser and resize the page, you will see that the dimensions of the `.Left`, `.Middle`, and `.Right` sections remain proportional to one another. You can also play around with the `max-width` of the `.Wrap` values to make the bounding dimensions for the layout bigger or smaller (in the example, it's set to 1400 px).

Now, let's consider how we would have the same content on a smaller screen that flexes to a point and then changes to the layout we have already seen. You can view the final code of this layout in example_04-02.

The idea is that, for smaller screens, we will have a single "tube" of content. The left-hand area will only be viewable as an "off-canvas" area—typically, an area for a menu or similar, which sits off the viewable screen area and slides in when a menu button is pressed. The main content sits below the header, then the right-hand section below that, and finally the footer area. In our example, we can expose the left-hand menu area by clicking anywhere on the header. Typically, when making this kind of design pattern for real, a menu button would be used to activate the side menu.

As you would expect, when combining this with our newly mastered media query skills, we can adjust the viewport and the design just "responds"—effortlessly moving from one layout to another and stretching between the two. I'm not going to list all the CSS properties here; it's all in example_04-02. However, here's an example—the left-hand section:

```
.Left {
    height: 625px;
    background-color: #03a66a;
    display: inline-block;
    position: absolute;
    left: -200px;
    width: 200px;
    font-size: 0.9rem;
    transition: transform 0.3s;
}
@media (min-width: 40rem) {
    .Left {
        width: 20.83%;
        left: 0;
        position: relative;
    }
}
```

You can see that, up first, without a media query, is the small screen layout. Then, at larger screen sizes, the width becomes proportional, the positioning relative, and the left value is set to zero.

We don't need to rewrite properties such as `height`, `display`, or `background-color` as we aren't changing them.

This is progress. We have combined two of the core responsive web design techniques we have covered: converting fixed dimensions into proportions and using media queries to target CSS rules relevant to the viewport size.

 In a real project, we should be making some provision if JavaScript isn't available and we need to view the content of the menu. We deal with this scenario in detail in *Chapter 11, Transitions, Transformations, and Animations.*

We have now covered the essentials of fluid design. To summarize, where needed, make the dimensions of elements proportional rather than fixed. This way, designs adapt to the size of their container. And you now have the simple `target/context` = `result` formula to make the necessary calculations.

Speaking of fluidity, this seems as good a point as any to talk about Flexbox—a layout system designed with fluid layouts in mind.

# Why do we need Flexbox?

We are now going to explore using CSS Flexible Box Layout, or Flexbox, as it is more commonly known.

In previous editions of this book, this is the point where I would have explained the shortcomings of prior CSS layout mechanisms, but as I write this in 2022, it would be like going over why people use cars instead of horses.

There are two capable and powerful layout systems available to us and perfectly suited to responsive design. For laying things out in one direction at a time, we can reach for Flexbox. For two directions at a time, we reach for Grid, the subject of our next chapter.

# Introducing Flexbox

Flexbox was designed to address the shortcomings of the CSS layout mechanisms that had gone before.

Here's a few choice reasons it is so useful:

- It can easily center contents vertically.
- It can change the visual order of elements.

- It can automatically space and align elements within a box, automatically assigning available space between them.

- Items can be laid out in a row, a row going in the reverse direction, a column down the page, or a column going in reverse order up a page.

- It can make you look 10 years younger (probably not, but in low numbers of empirical tests (me), it has been proven to reduce stress compared with other layout techniques).

## The bumpy path to Flexbox

Flexbox has been through a few major iterations before arriving at the stable version we have today. For example, consider the changes from the 2009 version (`https://www.w3.org/TR/2009/WD-css3-flexbox-20090723/`), the 2011 version (`https://www.w3.org/TR/2011/WD-css3-flexbox-20111129/`), and the 2014 version that we are basing our examples on (`https://www.w3.org/TR/css-flexbox-1/`). The syntax differences are marked.

These differing specifications mean there have been three major implementations across browsers. Today, we need not concern ourselves with the differences. However, if you find yourself having to support some incredibly old browser (I'm talking IE11 old), be aware that you will need to ensure you have a decent autoprefixing solution as part of your build step.

## Choosing your autoprefixing solution

For the sake of your sanity, to accurately and easily add vendor prefixes to CSS, use some form of automatic prefixing solution. Right now, I favor Autoprefixer (`https://github.com/postcss/autoprefixer`). It's fast, easy to set up, and very accurate.

There are versions of Autoprefixer for most setups, including text editors, so you don't necessarily need a command line-based build tool.

There are also more recent CSS minifier tools like Parcel CSS that can perform the same task: `https://github.com/parcel-bundler/parcel-css`.

## Getting Flexy

Flexbox has four key characteristics: direction, alignment, ordering, and flexibility. We'll cover all of these characteristics and how they relate to each other by way of a few examples.

The examples are deliberately simplistic; we are just moving some boxes and their content around so that we can understand the principles of how Flexbox works.

## Perfect vertically centered text

Note that this first Flexbox example is example_04-03:

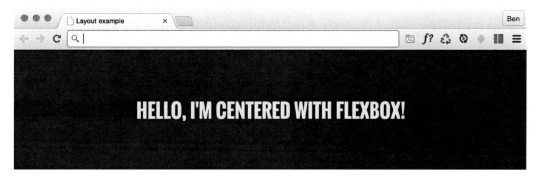

*Figure 4.2: Centering is simple with Flexbox*

Here's the markup:

```
<div class="CenterMe">Hello, I'm centered with Flexbox!</div>
```

Here is the entire CSS rule that's styling that markup:

```
.CenterMe {
    background-color: indigo;
    color: #ebebeb;
    font-family: "Oswald", sans-serif;
    font-size: 2rem;
    text-transform: uppercase;
    height: 200px;
    display: flex;
    align-items: center;
    justify-content: center;
}
```

The majority of the property/value pairs in that rule are merely setting the colors and font sizes. The three properties we are interested in are:

```
.CenterMe {
    /* other declarations */
```

```
    display: flex;
    align-items: center;
    justify-content: center;
}
```

If you have not used Flexbox or any of the properties in the related Box Alignment specification (https://www.w3.org/TR/css-align-3/), these properties probably seem a little alien. Let's consider what each one does:

- `display: flex`: This is the bread and butter of Flexbox. This merely sets the item to be a Flexbox, as opposed to a block or inline-block.
- `align-items`: This aligns the items within a Flexbox in the cross axis, vertically centering the text in our example.
- `justify-content`: This sets the main axis, centering the content. With a Flexbox row, you can think of it as the button in a word processor that sets the text to the left, right, or center (although there are additional `justify-content` values that we will look at shortly).

 Flexbox has an even more convenient way of positioning items and that's with `place-items`. This provides a shorthand for setting align and justify items. As you become familiar with the alignment properties in this chapter, you can try setting them at once with `place-items`. The first value is for the align value, and the second is for the justify value. If you just pass one value, it gets used for both. So to center both, it is just `place-items: center`.

OK, before we get further into the properties of Flexbox, we will consider a few more examples.

 In some of these examples, I'm making use of the Google-hosted font "Oswald," with a fallback to a sans serif font. In *Chapter 6, CSS Selectors, Typography, and More*, we will look at how we can use the @font-face rule to link to custom font files.

## Offset items

How about a simple list of navigation items, but with one offset to one side?

Here's what it looks like:

*Figure 4.3: Flexbox makes it simple to offset one link in a list*

You can play about with this in the example_04-04 code. Here's the markup:

```
<div class="container">
    <a href="#" class="item">Home</a>
    <a href="#" class="item">About Us</a>
    <a href="#" class="item">Products</a>
    <a href="#" class="item">Policy</a>
    <a href="#" class="last-item">Contact Us</a>
</div>
```

And here is the CSS:

```
.container {
    background-color: indigo;
    font-family: "Oswald", sans-serif;
    font-size: 1rem;
    min-height: 2.75rem;
    display: flex;
    align-items: center;
    padding: 0 1rem;
}
.item,
.last-item {
    color: #ebebeb;
    text-decoration: none;
}
.item {
    margin-right: 1rem;
}
.last-item {
    margin-left: auto;
}
```

When you set display: flex; on a wrapping element, the children of that element become flex items, which then get laid out using the flex layout model. The magical property here is margin-left: auto;, which makes that item use all of the available margin on that side.

## Reverse the order of items

Want to reverse the order of the items?

*Figure 4.4: Reversing the visual order with Flexbox*

It's as easy as adding flex-direction: row-reverse; to the wrapping element and changing margin-left: auto; to margin-right: auto; on the offset item:

```
.container {
    background-color: indigo;
    font-family: "Oswald", sans-serif;
    font-size: 1rem;
    min-height: 2.75rem;
    display: flex;
    flex-direction: row-reverse;
    align-items: center;
    padding: 0 1rem;
}
.item,
.last-item {
    color: #ebebeb;
    text-decoration: none;
}
.item {
    margin-right: 1rem;
}
.last-item {
    margin-right: auto;
}
```

You can find that as example_04-05.

 Be aware that when using the reverse-based properties, you are only changing the order in presentation. This won't change the order of the content for people using a screen reader, for example. If the order of the items is essential to the understanding of the content, ensure you make the changes in the DOM to benefit all users.

## How about if we want them laid out vertically instead?

Simple. Change to flex-direction: column; on the wrapping element and remove the auto margin:

*Figure 4.5: Items laid out vertically instead*

Here's the code for it:

```
.container {
    background-color: indigo;
    font-family: "Oswald", sans-serif;
    font-size: 1rem;
    min-height: 2.75rem;
    display: flex;
    flex-direction: column;
    align-items: center;
    padding: 0 1rem;
}
.item,
.last-item {
    color: #ebebeb;
    text-decoration: none;
}
```

## Column reverse

Want them stacked in the opposite direction? Just change to `flex-direction: column-reverse;` and you're done.

 There is a `flex-flow` property that is shorthand for setting `flex-direction` and `flex-wrap` in one go. For example, `flex-flow: row wrap;` would set the direction to a row and set the wrapping on. However, at least initially, I find it easier to specify the two settings separately.

# Inline-flex

Flexbox has an inline variant: `display: inline-flex;`. Thanks to its beautiful centering abilities, you can do some wacky things with very little effort:

*Figure 4.6: The inline equivalent of flex is the aptly named "inline-flex"*

Here's the markup:

```
<p>
    Here is a sentence with an
    <em class="InlineFlex">inline-flex</em>.
</p>
```

And, using the same basic styles as the previous examples for the fonts, font sizes, and colors, here is the CSS needed:

```
.InlineFlex {
    display: inline-flex;
    align-items: center;
    height: 120px;
    padding: 0 4px;
```

```
        background-color: indigo;
        text-decoration: none;
        border-radius: 3px;
        color: #ddd;
    }
```

When items are set as inline-flex anonymously, which happens if their parent element is not set to display: flex, then they retain whitespace (which can often manifest as an unwanted gap between elements), just like inline-block or inline-table do. However, if they are within a flex container, then whitespace is removed. Of course, you don't always have to center items within a Flexbox. There are a number of different options. Let's look at those now.

# Flexbox alignment properties

If you want to play along with this example, start with example_04-06s.

The important thing to understand with Flexbox alignment is the concept of the axis. There are two axes to consider, the **main axis** and the **cross axis**. What each of these represents depends on the direction the Flexbox is set to. For example, if the direction of your Flexbox is set to row, the main axis will be the horizontal axis and the cross axis will be the vertical axis.

Conversely, if your Flexbox direction is set to column, the main axis will be the vertical axis and the cross axis will be the horizontal axis. The specification (https://www.w3.org/TR/css-flexbox-1/#box-model) provides the following illustration to aid authors:

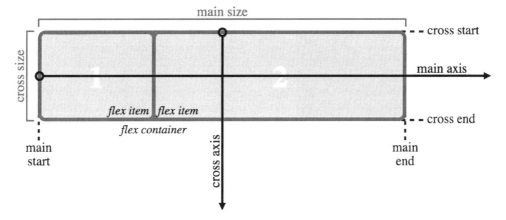

*Figure 4.7: This image from the specification shows that the main axis always relates to the direction the flex container is heading*

Here's the basic markup of our example you'll need to add into the example file:

```
<div class="container">
    <div class="item one">Item One</div>
</div>
```

Let's set a few basic Flexbox-related styles:

```
.container {
    background-color: indigo;
    display: flex;
    height: 200px;
    width: 400px;
}

.item {
    background-color: #34005b;
    display: flex;
    height: 100px;
    width: 200px;
}
```

In the browser, that produces this:

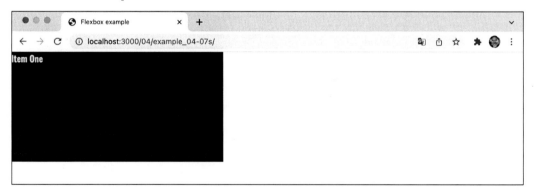

*Figure 4.8: With no alignment set, child elements default to the top left*

Right, let's test drive the effects of some of these properties.

# align-items

The `align-items` property positions items in the cross axis. Let's apply this property to our wrapping element, like so:

```
.container {
    background-color: indigo;
    display: flex;
    height: 200px;
    width: 400px;
    align-items: center;
}
```

As you would imagine, the item within that box gets centered vertically:

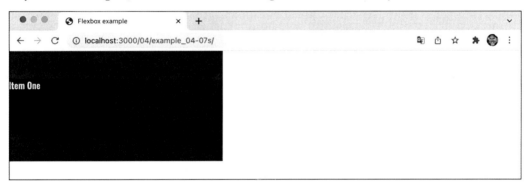

*Figure 4.9: A one-liner provides cross-axis centering*

The same effect would be applied to any number of children within.

# align-self

Sometimes, you may want to pull just one item into a different alignment. Individual flex items can use the `align-self` property to align themselves.

At this point, let's *remove the previous alignment properties* in the CSS and also add another two `div` elements to the markup, both also with a class of `item`. In the middle one of these three items, we will add an additional class of `AlignSelf`. We'll use that class in the CSS to add the `align-self` property. So here's the HTML:

```
<div class="container">
    <div class="item">Item One</div>
```

```
        <div class="item AlignSelf">Item Two</div>
        <div class="item">Item Three</div>
    </div>
```

And here is the CSS for that one item we want to move:

```
    .AlignSelf {
        align-self: flex-end;
    }
```

Here is the effect in the browser:

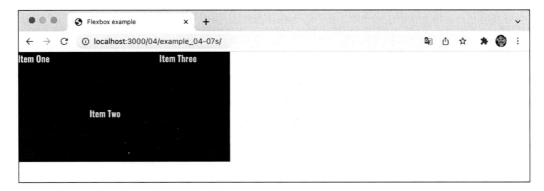

*Figure 4.10: Individual items can be aligned in a different manner*

Wow! Flexbox really makes these kinds of changes trivial. In the example, the value of `align-self` was set to `flex-end`. Let's consider the possible values we could use on the cross axis before looking at alignment in the main axis.

## Possible alignment values

For cross-axis alignment, Flexbox has the following possible values:

- `flex-start`: Setting an element to `flex-start` makes it begin at the "starting" edge of its flex container.
- `flex-end`: Setting to `flex-end` aligns the element at the end of the flex container.
- `center`: This puts it in the middle of the flex container.
- `baseline`: This sets all the flex items in the container so that their baselines align.
- `stretch`: This makes the items stretch to the size of their flex container (in the cross axis).

There are some particulars inherent to using these properties, so if something isn't playing happily, always refer to the specification for any edge case scenarios: https://www.w3.org/TR/css-flexbox-1/#align-items-property.

## justify-content

Alignment in the main axis is controlled with justify-content. Possible values for justify-content are:

- flex-start
- flex-end
- center
- space-between
- space-around
- space-evenly

The first three do exactly what you would now expect. However, let's take a look at what the last three do. Consider this markup:

```
<div class="container">
    <div class="item">Item One</div>
    <div class="item">Item Two</div>
    <div class="item">Item Three</div>
</div>
```

And then consider the following CSS. We are setting the three div elements with a class of item to each be 25% width, wrapped by a flex container, with a class of container, set to be 100% width:

```
.container {
    background-color: indigo;
    display: flex;
    justify-content: space-between;
    height: 200px;
    width: 100%;
}
.item {
    background-color: #34005b;
```

```
    display: flex;
    height: 100px;
    width: 25%;
}
```

As the three items will only take up 75% of the available space, `justify-content` explains what we would like the browser to do with the remaining space. A value of `space-between` puts an equal amount of space between the items, and `space-around` puts it around the items. Perhaps a screenshot, or two, here will help—this is `space-between`:

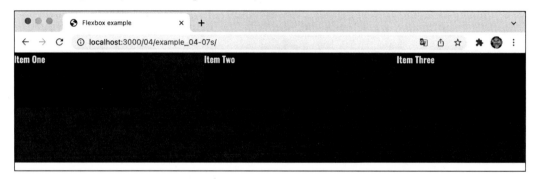

*Figure 4.11: Main axis alignment is carried out with the justify-content property*

And here is what happens if we switch to `space-around`:

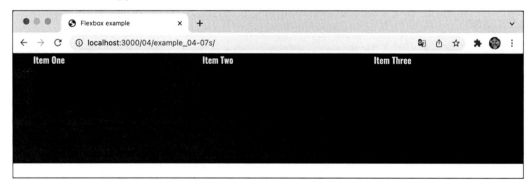

*Figure 4.12: Subtly different, but notice the space around, not just between, items*

Finally, let's look at what `space-evenly` does. This takes the available space and adds an equal amount to every gap:

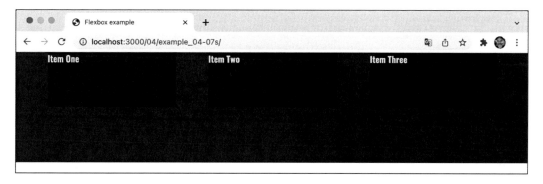

*Figure 4.13: An even space between items with space-evenly*

The various alignment properties of Flexbox are currently being specified in CSS Box Alignment Module Level 3. This should give the same fundamental alignment powers to other display properties, such as `display: block;` and `display: table`. The specification is still being worked on, so you can keep checking the status at `https://www.w3.org/TR/css3-align/`.

## The flex property

We've used the `width` property on those flex items, but it's also possible and preferable to define the width, or "flexiness," if you will, with the `flex` property. To illustrate, consider an example with the same markup as the last, but with an amended CSS for the items:

```
.item {
    background-color: #34005b;
    display: flex;
    height: 100px;
    flex: 1;
    border: 1px solid #ebebeb;
}
```

And here is what we get in the browser:

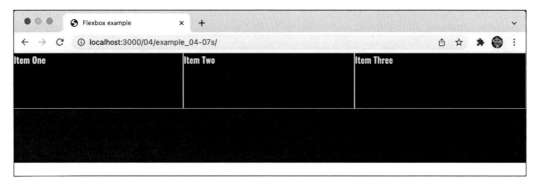

*Figure 4.14: Our first foray into using the flex shorthand*

Those three items have gobbled up all the space. So what's going on?

The flex property is actually a shorthand way of specifying three separate properties: flex-grow, flex-shrink, and flex-basis. The specification covers these individual properties in more detail here: https://www.w3.org/TR/css-flexbox-1/#flex-components. However, the specification recommends that authors use the flex shorthand property, so that's what we will be learning here, capiche?

*Figure 4.15: Understanding the three possible values of the flex property*

For items within a flex container, if a flex property is present, it is used to size the item rather than a width or height value (if also present). Even if the width or height value is specified after the flex property, it will still have no effect.

 However, it is important to note that if the item you are adding the flex property to is not a flex item, the flex property will have no effect.

Now, let's look at what each of these flex properties actually does:

- flex-grow is the first value you can pass to flex. It is the amount, in relation to the other flex items, that the flex item can grow when free space is available.

- `flex-shrink` is the second value you can pass. It is the amount the flex item can shrink, in relation to the other flex items, when there is not enough space available.

- `flex-basis` is the final value you can pass to `flex`. It is the basis size the flex item is sized to. If you don't set an item to shrink, you can use `flex-basis` like a `min-width`.

Although it's possible to just write `flex: 1` and have that interpreted to mean `flex: 1 1 0`, I recommend writing all the values into a `flex` shorthand property yourself. I think it's clearer to understand what you intend to happen that way.

For example, `flex: 1 1 auto` means that the item will grow into one part of the available space. It will also shrink one part when space is lacking, and the basis size for the flexing is the intrinsic width of the content, that is, the size the content would be if `flex` wasn't involved.

Let's try another: `flex: 0 0 50px` means this item will neither grow nor shrink, and its basis is 50 px (so it will be 50 px regardless of any free space).

What about `flex: 2 0 50%`? That's going to take two "lots" of available space, it won't shrink, and its basis size is 50%. What do you think will happen if you have three items all set to that width in a fixed-width container? Well, let's think this through. Our shorthand has the `flex-basis` set to 50%, so each item is going to start out at 50% of the container. And as there are three of them, one is going to overflow. Now, we don't have any `flex-shrink` set, so none of them are going to get any smaller. And although we have `flex-grow` set to 2, there is no room to grow, so we get this:

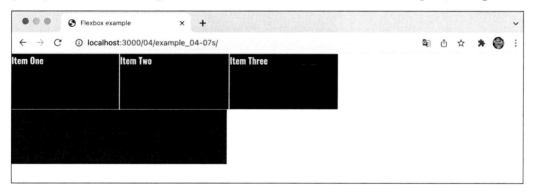

*Figure 4.16: If items don't fit, like anything else they overflow, wrap, or scroll if you set them to do so*

Hopefully, these brief examples have demystified the `flex` property a little, and this incredibly powerful property is starting to make a little sense. If you take a look at `example_04-06e`, the first item is set to `flex: 1.5 0 auto;`. Hopefully, you can imagine what that will look like before opening it in the browser to find out.

I could write chapters and chapters on Flexbox! There are so many examples we could look at.

However, for now, there are just two more things I would like to share with you.

## Simple sticky footer

Suppose you want a footer to sit at the bottom of the viewport when there is not enough content to push it there. Historically, this has been a pain to achieve, but with Flexbox it's simple. Consider this markup, which is example_04-07:

```
<body>
    <main>
        Here is a bunch of text but not enough to push the footer to the
        bottom of the page.
    </main>
    <footer>
        I'd like this to be at the bottom and thanks to Flexbox I can be
        put in my place!
    </footer>
</body>
```

And here's the CSS:

```
html,
body {
    margin: 0;
    padding: 0;
    font-family: "Oswald", sans-serif;
    color: #ebebeb;
}

html {
    height: 100%;
}

body {
    background-color: #ebebeb;
    display: flex;
```

```
        flex-direction: column;
        min-height: 100%;
    }

    main {
        flex: 1 0 auto;
        color: #333;
        padding: 0600rem;
    }

    footer {
        background-color: violet;
        color: #fff;
        padding: 1.5rem;
    }
```

Take a look at that in the browser, and test it by adding more content into main. You'll see that when there is not enough content, the footer is stuck to the bottom of the viewport. When there is enough, it sits below the content.

This works because our flex property is set to grow where space is available. As our body is a flex container of 100% minimum height, the main content can grow into all of that available space. Beautiful!

# Changing the source order

Flexbox has the ability to re-order items. Prior to Flexbox, if you wanted to have something that came after something else in the DOM appear before it instead, you were in for a rough time. However, Flexbox makes such work trivial. Let's have a look at how it works.

Consider this markup, which you can build along with in example_04-08:

```
<div class="container">
    <header class="item">Header</header>
    <aside class="item">Side one</aside>
    <main class="item">Content</main>
    <aside class="item aside-two">Side Two</aside>
    <footer class="item">Footer</footer>
</div>
```

We will add some simple colors to more easily differentiate the sections, and stack them one under another in the same order they appear in the markup:

```css
.container {
    background-color: indigo;
    display: flex;
    flex-direction: column;
}
.item {
    display: flex;
    align-items: center;
    min-height: 6.25rem;
    padding: 1rem;
}
header {
    background-color: #105b63;
}
main {
    background-color: #fffad5;
}
aside {
    background-color: #ffd34e;
}
aside.aside-two {
    background-color: #db9e36;
}
footer {
    background-color: #bd4932;
}
```

That renders in the browser like this:

*Figure 4.17: Here, our boxes are displayed in source order*

Now, suppose we want to switch the order of main to be the first item, visually, without touching the markup. With Flexbox, it's as simple as adding a single property/value pair:

```
main {
    order: -1;
}
```

The order property lets us revise the order of items within a Flexbox simply and sanely. In this example, a value of -1 means that we want it to be before all the others.

If you want to switch items around quite a bit, I'd recommend being a little more declarative and adding an order number for each item. This makes things a little easier to understand when you combine them with media queries.

Let's combine our new source order-changing powers with some media queries to produce not just a different layout at different screen widths but different ordering.

Let's suppose we want our main content at the beginning of a document. Let's amend the content of our earlier example:

```
<div class="container">
    <main class="item">Content</main>
    <aside class="item">Side one</aside>
    <aside class="item aside-two">Side Two</aside>
    <header class="item">Header</header>
    <footer class="item">Footer</footer>
</div>
```

First is the page content, then our two sidebar areas, then the header, and finally the footer. As we'll be using Flexbox, we can structure the HTML in the order that makes sense for the document, regardless of how things need to be laid out visually.

After some basic styling for each flex item, for the smallest screens (outside of any media query), I'll go with the following order:

```
header {
    background-color: #105b63;
    order: 1;
}
main {
    background-color: #fffad5;
    color: #333;
    order: 2;
}
aside {
    background-color: #ffd34e;
    color: #222;
    order: 3;
}
aside.aside-two {
    background-color: #db9e36;
    color: #333;
```

```
        order: 4;
    }
    footer {
        background-color: #bd4932;
        order: 5;
    }
```

That gives us this in the browser:

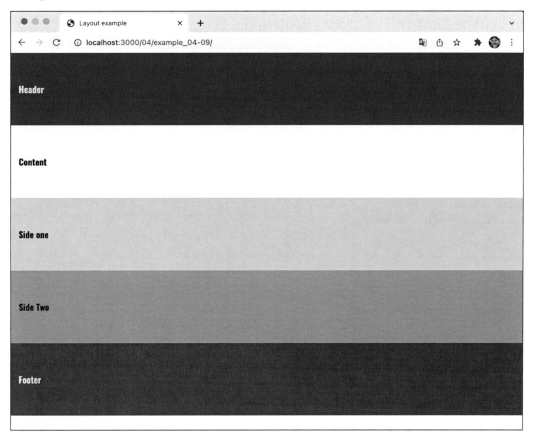

*Figure 4.18: We can move the items in visual order with a single property*

And then, at a breakpoint, I'm switching to this:

```
@media (min-width: 600px) {
    .container {
        flex-flow: row wrap;
```

```
    }
    header {
        flex: 0 0 100%;
    }
    main {
        flex: 1 0 auto;
        order: 3;
    }
    aside {
        flex: 0 0 150px;
        order: 2;
    }
    aside.aside-two {
        flex: 0 0 150px;
        order: 4;
    }
    footer {
        flex: 1 0 100%;
    }
}
```

That gives us this in the browser:

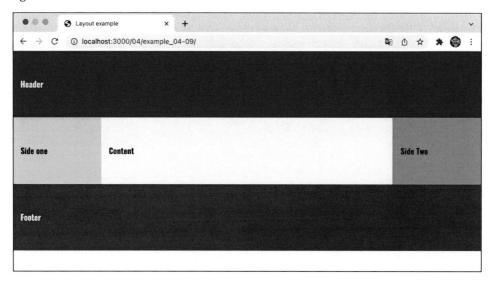

*Figure 4.19: With a media query, we can change the visual order again*

In that example, the shortcut flex-flow: row wrap has been used. flex-flow is actually a shorthand property of sorts that lets you set two properties in one: flex-direction and flex-wrap.

We've used flex-direction already to switch between rows and columns and to reverse elements. However, we haven't looked at flex-wrap yet.

# Wrapping with flex

By default, items in a flex container will shrink to fit and, if they can't, they will overflow the container. For example, consider this markup:

```
<div class="container">
    <div class="item">Item 1</div>
    <div class="item">Item 2</div>
    <div class="item">Item 3</div>
    <div class="item">Item 4</div>
</div>
```

And this CSS:

```
.container {
    display: flex;
    width: 500px;
    background-color: #bbb;
    align-items: center;
    border: 1px solid #111;
}
.item {
    color: #111;
    display: inline-flex;
    align-items: center;
    justify-content: center;
    font-size: 23px;
    flex: 0 0 160px;
    height: 40px;
    border: 1px dashed #545454;
}
```

You may be wondering why the outer container is set with a width and not the flex shorthand property we looked at before. Remember, this is because unless the element is a flex item (inside a Flexbox itself), flex has no effect.

Because there is a width of only 500 px on the flex container, those four elements don't fit:

*Figure 4.20: By default, Flexbox will always keep child elements from wrapping*

However, those items can be set to wrap with flex-wrap: wrap. This wraps the items once they hit the edge of the container.

The likelihood is that there will be times when you want flex items to wrap and other times when you don't. Remember that the default is not to wrap, but you can easily make the change with a single line.

Also, remember that you can set the wrapping by itself with flex-wrap, or as part of the flex-flow direction and wrap shorthand.

Let's solve a real-world problem with flex-wrap. Consider the list of paragraphs in the following image. At this width, they are not easy to read:

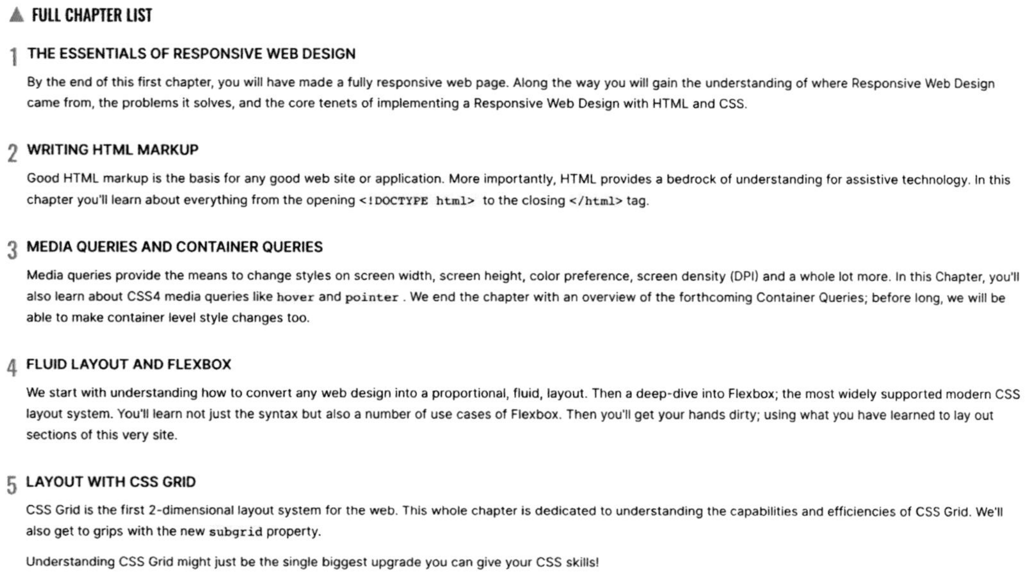

**▲ FULL CHAPTER LIST**

1 **THE ESSENTIALS OF RESPONSIVE WEB DESIGN**

By the end of this first chapter, you will have made a fully responsive web page. Along the way you will gain the understanding of where Responsive Web Design came from, the problems it solves, and the core tenets of implementing a Responsive Web Design with HTML and CSS.

2 **WRITING HTML MARKUP**

Good HTML markup is the basis for any good web site or application. More importantly, HTML provides a bedrock of understanding for assistive technology. In this chapter you'll learn about everything from the opening `<!DOCTYPE html>` to the closing `</html>` tag.

3 **MEDIA QUERIES AND CONTAINER QUERIES**

Media queries provide the means to change styles on screen width, screen height, color preference, screen density (DPI) and a whole lot more. In this Chapter, you'll also learn about CSS4 media queries like `hover` and `pointer`. We end the chapter with an overview of the forthcoming Container Queries; before long, we will be able to make container level style changes too.

4 **FLUID LAYOUT AND FLEXBOX**

We start with understanding how to convert any web design into a proportional, fluid, layout. Then a deep-dive into Flexbox; the most widely supported modern CSS layout system. You'll learn not just the syntax but also a number of use cases of Flexbox. Then you'll get your hands dirty; using what you have learned to lay out sections of this very site.

5 **LAYOUT WITH CSS GRID**

CSS Grid is the first 2-dimensional layout system for the web. This whole chapter is dedicated to understanding the capabilities and efficiencies of CSS Grid. We'll also get to grips with the new `subgrid` property.

Understanding CSS Grid might just be the single biggest upgrade you can give your CSS skills!

*Figure 4.21: This content is overstretched at this viewport width*

Let's amend that layout with a media query and a few choice flex properties. I'm consolidating all of these changes into one media query here for brevity, but remember that you can use as many as you like to organize your code however you see fit. We covered the options extensively in *Chapter 3, Media Queries and Container Queries*:

```
@media (min-width: 1000px) {
    .rwd-Chapters_List {
        display: flex;
        flex-wrap: wrap;
    }
    .rwd-Chapter {
        flex: 0 0 33.33%;
        padding: 0 20px;
    }
    .rwd-Chapter::before {
        left: -20px;
    }
}
```

And that produces this effect in the browser:

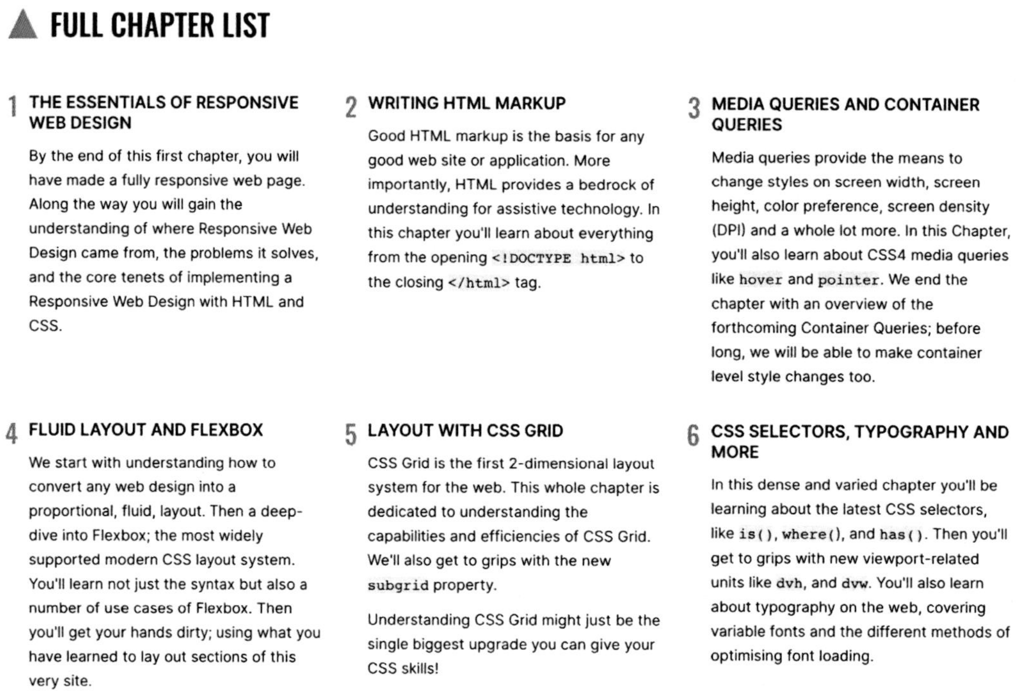

## ▲ FULL CHAPTER LIST

**1 THE ESSENTIALS OF RESPONSIVE WEB DESIGN**

By the end of this first chapter, you will have made a fully responsive web page. Along the way you will gain the understanding of where Responsive Web Design came from, the problems it solves, and the core tenets of implementing a Responsive Web Design with HTML and CSS.

**2 WRITING HTML MARKUP**

Good HTML markup is the basis for any good web site or application. More importantly, HTML provides a bedrock of understanding for assistive technology. In this chapter you'll learn about everything from the opening `<!DOCTYPE html>` to the closing `</html>` tag.

**3 MEDIA QUERIES AND CONTAINER QUERIES**

Media queries provide the means to change styles on screen width, screen height, color preference, screen density (DPI) and a whole lot more. In this Chapter, you'll also learn about CSS4 media queries like `hover` and `pointer`. We end the chapter with an overview of the forthcoming Container Queries; before long, we will be able to make container level style changes too.

**4 FLUID LAYOUT AND FLEXBOX**

We start with understanding how to convert any web design into a proportional, fluid, layout. Then a deep-dive into Flexbox; the most widely supported modern CSS layout system. You'll learn not just the syntax but also a number of use cases of Flexbox. Then you'll get your hands dirty; using what you have learned to lay out sections of this very site.

**5 LAYOUT WITH CSS GRID**

CSS Grid is the first 2-dimensional layout system for the web. This whole chapter is dedicated to understanding the capabilities and efficiencies of CSS Grid. We'll also get to grips with the new `subgrid` property.

Understanding CSS Grid might just be the single biggest upgrade you can give your CSS skills!

**6 CSS SELECTORS, TYPOGRAPHY AND MORE**

In this dense and varied chapter you'll be learning about the latest CSS selectors, like `is()`, `where()`, and `has()`. Then you'll get to grips with new viewport-related units like `dvh`, and `dvw`. You'll also learn about typography on the web, covering variable fonts and the different methods of optimising font loading.

*Figure 4.22: Setting the flex container to wrap means the content can space out equally*

We made the container of the chapters into a flex container. Then, to stop the elements from scrunching up into one another, we set the container to wrap. To limit the chapter section widths to a third of the container, we used the flex shorthand to set 33.33% as the `flex-basis` and prevented the element from growing or shrinking. Padding was used to provide a little space between them. The final small tweak was to bring in the chapter numbers a little.

## Wrapping up Flexbox

There are near endless possibilities when using the Flexbox layout system and, due to its inherent "flex-ability," it's a perfect match for responsive design. If you've never built anything with Flexbox before, all the new properties and values can seem a little odd, and it's sometimes disconcertingly easy to achieve layouts that have previously taken far more work.

# Summary

We've covered a lot of ground in this chapter. We started by understanding how to create fluid layouts that can flex between the media queries we set. We then spent considerable time getting acquainted with Flexbox, learning how to solve common layout problems with relative ease. We learned all about how to easily align content in containers, how to visually re-order things, and how to define the way we want our content to grow and shrink within its context.

As luck would have it, two great layout mechanisms arrived in CSS in relatively quick succession. Hot on the heels of the Flexible Box Layout Module was Grid Layout Module Level 1: `https://www.w3.org/TR/css3-grid-layout/`. Like Flexbox, CSS Grid means learning quite a bit of unique syntax. But don't let that put you off. The next chapter is completely dedicated to Grid: what it can do, how it does it, and how we can bend it to our will.

# 5

# Layout with CSS Grid

Without a doubt, the biggest game changer to CSS layout has been Grid.

We now have a layout system capable of achieving everything we have done before with less code and more predictability, as well as enabling things we simply couldn't do before!

I'd go as far as saying Grid is revolutionary rather than evolutionary. There are entirely new concepts to understand that have no real forebears in past CSS. As such, expect to take some time getting comfortable using it.

But trust me, it is worth it. Let's go!

In this chapter, we will learn the following:

- What CSS Grid is and the problems it solves
- The essential concepts to understand when dealing with Grid Layout
- Grid-specific terminology
- How to set up a Grid
- How to position items in a Grid
- How to create powerful responsive patterns with minimal code
- How to understand and write the grid shorthand syntax
- The latest Grid addition, subgrid

Toward the end of the chapter, you will also be tasked with a small exercise to use some of the techniques we have learned to refactor the layout of a portion of the https://rwd.education website we have been looking at in previous chapters.

Before I ask you to do that, I'd better get on with explaining what Grid is all about.

# What CSS Grid is and the problems it solves

CSS Grid is a two-dimensional layout system. Flexbox, which we covered in the last chapter, concerns itself with items being laid out in a single dimension/direction at a time. A Flexbox container either lays things out in a row, or it lays them out in a column. It cannot facilitate laying out items horizontally and vertically at once; that is what Grid is for.

I should point out at the outset that you don't need to choose between Flexbox or Grid when building projects. They are not mutually exclusive. I commonly use both, even within a single visual component.

To be completely clear, when you adopt Grid, you don't have to forsake any other display methods. For example, a Grid will quite happily allow a Flexbox inside it. Equally, part of your interface coded with Grid can quite happily live inside a Flexbox, standard block, or `inline-block`.

So there are times when using Grid is the most appropriate option, and there are times when Flexbox, or another layout method, is the most appropriate.

The truth is, we've been creating grid-like layouts with CSS for years. We just haven't had a specific `grid` layout mechanism in CSS to do it. We have made use of blocks, floats, tables, and many other ingenious techniques to work around the fact we didn't have a proper Grid Layout system in CSS. Now, thankfully, we do.

Using CSS Grid, we can create grids of virtually infinite permutations and position child elements wherever we want them, regardless of their source order. What's more, Grid even makes provision for when additional items are added and adapts itself to the needs of the content. This might sound hyperbolic, so let's not waste any more text. Let's get to it.

## Basic Grid syntax

In the most simple terms, to use Grid, we need to tell the browser:

- How many rows and columns our grid should have
- How those rows and columns should be sized
- Where we want to place the items of our grid
- What should happen when the size of the grid changes or more items are added to the grid

Relating that to the browser is, therefore, just a matter of understanding the terminology.

# Grid-specific concepts and terminology

The first concept to understand is **explicit** and **implicit** item placement. The Grid Layout you define in your CSS with columns and rows is the explicit grid; it's the layout of the items you have explicitly defined. Meanwhile, the implicit grid is the grid placement of items that happens when additional items you didn't foresee also get added to the grid. The placement of these new items is implied by the layout of your explicit grid. Don't worry if that doesn't make sense yet; it will!

The next concept that commonly confuses people (it certainly did me) is that grid lines are on either side of the grid items. The bit in the middle, between the lines, is referred to as a grid **track**. Where two tracks from different directions intersect is where a **grid area** is formed. This grab from the dev tools of Chrome should help illustrate the point:

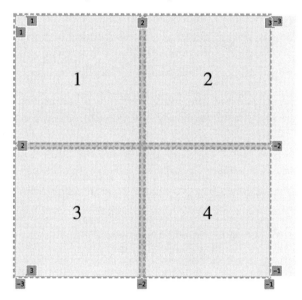

*Figure 5.1: Be aware that grid lines sit on either side of tracks, where the content lives*

A key takeaway is that when you place items within a grid, you can do so by referencing the grid lines (which, therefore, implies a grid area) or the grid areas themselves, if they are named.

There is no limit, theoretically, to the number of tracks a grid can have. However, browsers are at liberty to truncate grids. If you set a value beyond the browser's limit, the grid will be truncated to that limit. Practically, I can't imagine hitting a browser's limit being a likely scenario, but I'm mentioning it here for completeness.

# Setting up a Grid Layout

Here is the introduction to the explicit grid section of the W3C specification (`https://www.w3.org/TR/css-grid-1/#explicit-grids`). It's worth rereading a few times as it is dense with essential information for understanding how the grid works:

*The three properties grid-template-rows, grid-template-columns, and grid-template-areas together define the explicit grid of a grid container. The final grid may end up larger due to grid items placed outside the explicit grid; in this case implicit tracks will be created, these implicit tracks will be sized by the grid-auto-rows and grid-auto-columns properties.*

*The size of the explicit grid is determined by the larger of the number of rows/columns defined by grid-template-areas and the number of rows/columns sized by grid-template-rows/grid-template-columns.*

*Any rows/columns defined by grid-template-areas but not sized by grid-template-rows/grid-template-columns take their size from the grid-auto-rows/grid-auto-columns properties. If these properties don't define any explicit tracks the explicit grid still contains one grid line in each axis.*

*Numeric indexes in the grid-placement properties count from the edges of the explicit grid. Positive indexes count from the start side (starting from 1 for the start-most explicit line), while negative indexes count from the end side (starting from -1 for the end-most explicit line).*

*The grid and grid-template are properties that allow a shorthand to be used to set all three explicit grid properties (grid-template-rows, grid-template-columns, and grid-template-areas) at the same time. The grid shorthand also resets properties controlling the implicit grid, whereas the grid-template property leaves them unchanged.*

Now, I'm conscious that when you haven't worked at all with Grid Layout it can be very intimidating, and that quoted section from the specification might seem completely opaque right now. Hopefully, when you have read this chapter through, and played with Grid Layout yourself, it will make a little more sense.

Again, don't worry if little of that previous text made sense. Let's start our Grid journey in code with a very simple example. First, the world's easiest Grid Layout: four numbered boxes.

It will look like this in the browser and you can find it in the chapter code as example_05-01:

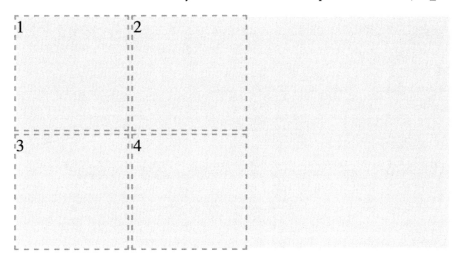

*Figure 5.2: Our first grid; as simple as possible*

Here is the markup:

```
<div class="my-first-grid">
    <div class="grid-item-1">1</div>
    <div class="grid-item-2">2</div>
    <div class="grid-item-3">3</div>
    <div class="grid-item-4">4</div>
</div>
```

The first thing I want you to consider is that with Grid, the markup pattern is a containing element, which is the grid, and the elements of the grid are the direct children. Write the markup for grid child elements in the order that makes the most sense for the content; Grid can place them visually wherever you need them. Here is the related CSS:

```
.my-first-grid {
    display: grid;
    grid-gap: 10px;
    grid-template-rows: 200px 200px;
    grid-template-columns: 200px 200px;
    background-color: #e4e4e4;
}
```

```
.grid-item-1 {
  grid-row: 1;
  grid-column: 1;
}
.grid-item-2 {
  grid-row: 1;
  grid-column: 2;
}
.grid-item-3 {
  grid-row: 2;
  grid-column: 1;
}
.grid-item-4 {
  grid-row: 2;
  grid-column: 2;
}
[class^='grid-item'] {
  outline: 3px dashed #f90;
  font-size: 30px;
  color: #333;
}
```

The parts to concentrate on in that CSS are the grid-specific properties. I've added some outlines and a background to make it easier to see where the grid is and the size and shape of the grid items.

We use display: grid to set our container as a grid and then use grid-template-rows: 200px 200px to set two rows, each 200 px high, and grid-template-columns: 200px 200px to set the grid to have two 200 px-wide columns.

In terms of the child elements of the grid, we use grid-row with a number to tell Grid Layout which row to place the item in and grid-column to tell it which column to place it in.

By default, the child elements of a grid remain as their standard layout type. Although our grid items belong to our grid, in this example, as they are all div elements, they are still computed as display: block. This is important to understand when we start trying to align grid items.

```
.my-first-grid {
  display: grid;
  grid-gap: 10px;
  grid-template-rows: 200px 200px;
  grid-template-columns: 200px 200px;
  background-color: #e4e4e4;
  align-items: center;
  justify-content: center;
}
```

When I first started with Grid Layout and tried something like this, I expected to see the numbers perfectly centered in their respective grid tracks. However, that is not the case:

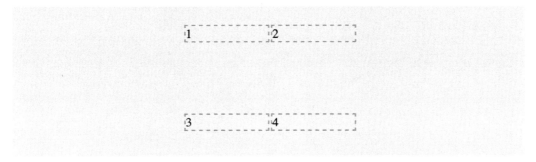

*Figure 5.3: If you don't set a width, a grid will consume the available space*

If we think about what we have done, it does make sense. We made a grid, with two columns and two rows, each 200 px, and asked for the items to be both vertically and horizontally centered. Because we have used `grid` and not `inline-grid`, the grid fills the entire width of the page, despite the fact that our grid items don't need all that space.

Let's tweak this so that the grid is only as wide as its content. Furthermore, let's center the items inside their respective grid items. To do that, we can make the items themselves either Flexbox or Grid. As this is a chapter about Grid, let's try using that:

```
.my-first-grid {
  display: inline-grid;
  grid-gap: 10px;
  grid-template-rows: 200px 200px;
```

```
    grid-template-columns: 200px 200px;
    background-color: #e4e4e4;
  }
  [class^='grid-item'] {
    display: grid;
    align-items: center;
    justify-content: center;
    outline: 3px dashed #f90;
    font-size: 30px;
    color: #333;
  }
```

If that selector with the hat symbol doesn't make sense, don't worry. We cover that in *Chapter 6, CSS Selectors, Typography, and More.*

We switched our container to be an inline-grid, set all the grid items to display: grid, and used the alignment properties justify-content and align-items.

That produces this result:

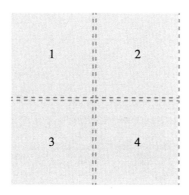

*Figure 5.4: By making the child elements flex or grid, we can center their contents*

You can find the code for this at example_05-02. As an exercise, try moving the position of the grid elements to different rows and columns.

OK, a little progress has been made. Let's move on to the topic of explicit and implicit item placement.

# Explicit and implicit

Earlier in the chapter, we discussed the difference between an explicit and implicit grid, an explicit grid being the structure you define in your CSS when setting up the grid. When more content is placed in that grid than you provisioned for, the implicit grid comes into effect.

Let's look at that again by extending our prior example.

We'll add in another item and see what happens:

```
<div class="my-first-grid">
  <div class="grid-item-1">1</div>
  <div class="grid-item-2">2</div>
  <div class="grid-item-3">3</div>
  <div class="grid-item-4">4</div>
  <div class="grid-item-5">5</div>
</div>
```

With that added, this is what we get in the browser:

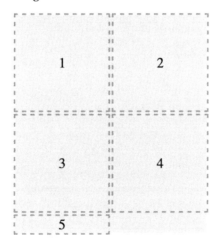

*Figure 5.5: The grid has added our item, but not with the kind of proportions we were hoping for*

That's sort of useful; the grid has created implicit grid lines to create an implicit track for our new item. Now, we didn't tell it what to do with that extra item, so it made the best guess. However, we can control how Grid handles items implicitly with the following properties: grid-auto-rows and grid-auto-columns.

# grid-auto-rows and grid-auto-columns

Let's use `grid-auto-rows` and `grid-auto-columns` to make any extra grid items the same size
as the existing ones:

```
.my-first-grid {
  display: inline-grid;
  grid-gap: 10px;
  grid-template-rows: 200px 200px;
  grid-template-columns: 200px 200px;
  grid-auto-rows: 200px;
  grid-auto-columns: 200px;
  background-color: #e4e4e4;
}
```

Now, without writing any extra CSS, when additional items are placed in our grid, they get the
200 px x 200 px sizing we have defined. Here, we have added another item in the DOM for a
total of six:

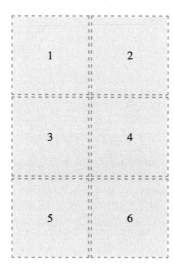

*Figure 5.6: With some auto settings, extra elements can be added at a more preferable size*

You can even make patterns so that the first extra item is one size and the next is another. The
pattern gets repeated:

```
.my-first-grid {
  display: inline-grid;
```

```
    grid-gap: 10px;
    grid-template-rows: 200px 200px;
    grid-template-columns: 200px 200px;
    grid-auto-rows: 100px 150px;
    grid-auto-columns: 100px 150px;
    background-color: #e4e4e4;
}
```

Here's what it looks like:

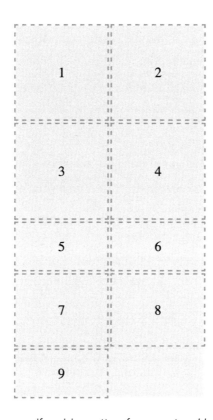

*Figure 5.7: You can specify a sizing pattern for any auto-added rows or columns*

Can you see how item 5 onward uses the pattern we defined in the value of the grid-auto-rows property? First, 5 and 6 are 100 px tall, then 7 and 8 are 150 px, and then back to 100 px for 9.

So far, you can see that the grid items are flowing vertically down the page. You can easily switch this to flow across the page instead! You can play about with this code in example_05-03.

## grid-auto-flow

The grid-auto-flow property allows you to define the direction that any implicitly added items flow inside the grid. Use a value of column when you want the grid to add extra columns to accommodate extra items, and use a value of row when you want the grid to add extra rows.

Let's amend our example by adding grid-auto-flow: column to make the items flow across the page instead of down:

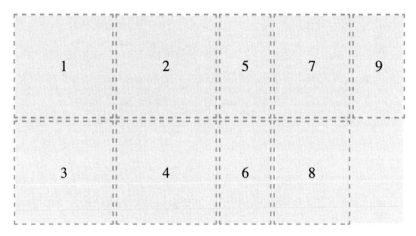

*Figure 5.8: Switching the grid to add extra items horizontally*

There is an additional dense keyword that can be added so that we have grid-auto-flow: column dense or grid-auto-flow: row dense – we'll look at that shortly.

# Placing and sizing Grid Layout items

So far, each item we have added to a grid has taken up a single grid area. We are going to start a new example now (you can find it in the code as example_05-04). This grid will have 20 grid items; these are just random foods and their source order within their container as a number. However, there are quite a few new things to go over in the CSS. Before we go through each new thing step by step, take a look at the code and the screenshot and see how much of it you can make sense of before reading on.

It's also worth mentioning that I've purposely mixed up the use of whitespace in the values. You can write grid-row: 6 / span 2 or grid-row: 6/span 2 – either is just as valid. Just pick which you prefer.

Here's the markup:

```
<div class="container">
   <div class="grid-item1">1. tofu</div>
   <div class="grid-item2">2. egg plant</div>
   <div class="grid-item3">3. onion</div>
   <div class="grid-item4">4. carrots</div>
   <div class="grid-item5">5. swede</div>
   <div class="grid-item6">6. scones</div>
   <div class="grid-item7">7. cucumber</div>
   <div class="grid-item8">8. carrot</div>
   <div class="grid-item9">9. yam</div>
   <div class="grid-item10">10. sweet potato</div>
   <div class="grid-item11">11. peas</div>
   <div class="grid-item12">12. beans</div>
   <div class="grid-item13">13. lentil</div>
   <div class="grid-item14">14. tomato</div>
   <div class="grid-item15">15. butternut squash</div>
   <div class="grid-item16">16. ham</div>
   <div class="grid-item17">17. pizza</div>
   <div class="grid-item18">18. pasta</div>
   <div class="grid-item19">19. cheese</div>
   <div class="grid-item20">20. milk</div>
</div>
```

Here is the CSS:

```
.container {
   font-size: 28px;
   font-family: sans-serif;
   display: grid;
   gap: 30px;
   background-color: #ddd;
   grid-template-columns: repeat(4, 1fr);
   grid-auto-rows: 100px;
   grid-auto-flow: row;
}
[class^='grid-item'] {
   outline: 1px #f90 dashed;
   display: grid;
```

```
    background-color: goldenrod;
    align-items: center;
    justify-content: center;
  }
  .grid-item3 {
    grid-column: 2/-1;
  }
  .grid-item6 {
    grid-row: 3/6;
    grid-column: 3 / 5;
  }
  .grid-item17 {
    grid-row: 6 / span 2;
    grid-column: 2/3;
  }
  .grid-item4 {
    grid-row: 4 / 7;
  }
```

And here is what we get in the browser:

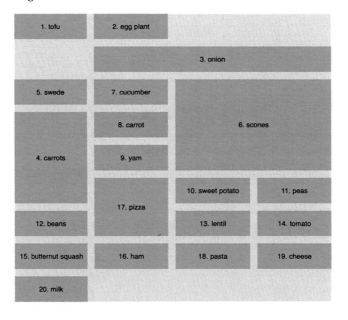

*Figure 5.9: Grid items sized arbitrarily*

We've introduced a few new things here. Let's cover each in turn, starting with how we have achieved a nice uniform gap between grid elements.

## gap

I've used gap in some of the prior code samples, but I've not explained it. Forgive me! The gap property lets you specify a gap between grid tracks. It is actually shorthand for both row-gap and column-gap. Just like when you specify a margin with two values, the first value applies to the top and bottom (row), and the second to the left and right (columns). If you specify a single value, as we have, it applies to both.

It's especially useful because, unlike dealing with padding or margin when laying things out, you don't need to worry about undoing it again on the final item; gap only applies between the items. You should also be aware that all modern browsers allow you to apply gap to Flexbox items too!

## repeat

If you were making a grid with 30 identical columns, it would get a little tiring having to write auto 30 times, for instance, grid-template-columns: auto auto auto auto auto auto...; in fact, I got bored just writing that!

Thankfully, the Grid Layout specification writers have blessed us with repeat(). As you might have guessed, the repeat() function provides a convenient way of stamping out the need for any number of items. In our example, we have used it to create four columns, all 1fr in width:

```
repeat(4, 1fr);
```

The format of the syntax is that, inside the parentheses, the first value is the number of times you want something repeated, and the second value is the width of each item.

Don't worry, I'll explain fr units in a moment; for now, just know that you can create multiple columns/rows with ease. Do you want 15 columns, all 100 px wide? It's as easy as repeat(15, 100px).

## fr units

The fr unit represents "flexible length" and stands for "flex fraction." It's used to communicate how much of any available free space we want something to gobble up, much like the flex-grow unit we covered for Flexbox in *Chapter 4, Fluid Layout and Flexbox*.

The specification doesn't say so, but I conceptualize fr as standing for "free room" when I'm thinking about a layout. In our example, we have made four columns, each taking up one portion of the available free room.

# Placing items in the grid

Before this example, we have been positioning each grid item in a single grid area. However, here, we have certain grid items being assigned spans of columns or rows numerically.

Let's take the grid-item3 example:

```
.grid-item3 {
  grid-column: 2/-1;
}
```

Here, the grid-column property is being set to start at the second grid line and end at the -1 grid line. The -1 looks pretty odd at first, but it is part of a very smart piece of syntax.

The first number is the start point, which is separated from the endpoint with a forward slash, /. Positive numbers count from the start side, the left-hand side in our column example, while negative numbers start from the end side, the right, in this instance. So, -1 basically just means the last grid line. So, this nice terse syntax just reads: "Start at line 2 and go to the end."

There's an example of spanning across rows in there too. Take a look at this one again:

```
.grid-item4 {
  grid-row: 4 / 7;
}
```

This one says, "Start at grid row line 4 and end at grid row line 7." If your preference is not telling the Grid where something ends and more how much space something should span, Grid Layout has just the property for you.

## span

Take a look at the CSS for .grid-item17 now:

```
.grid-item17 {
  grid-row: 6 / span 2;
  grid-column: 2/3;
}
```

Can you see how we have done something a little different with the value for grid-row?

Rather than stipulating a definite start and end point when placing grid items, you can give one or the other and then tell the item to span a number of rows/columns from that point either forward or backward. In our example, we told the item to start at grid line 6 and span 2 rows.

I find going backward a little more confusing, but that might just be me! But to illustrate, we could achieve the same visual effect for our example by changing that line to grid-row: span 2 / 8. In this instance, the definite point we have is the endpoint, so we are telling the grid to make the item start at grid row 8 and span 2 back from there.

## dense

Remember when we looked at grid-auto-flow, I mentioned the dense keyword? Well, this is the perfect opportunity to show you what that does. I'll amend the value of the grid-auto-flow property to this: grid-auto-flow: row dense;. And here is what it does in the browser:

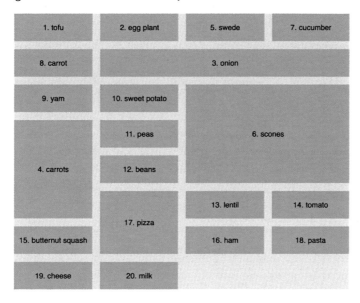

*Figure 5.10: The "dense" keyword rearranges grid items so that gaps are removed*

Can you see how the gaps have been filled? That's what dense does for you. However, while this might seem more aesthetically pleasing, there is a cost. The reason the items are numbered is that I wanted to highlight to you that using dense tells the Grid Layout algorithm to move things, visually, from their source order to any available space. Notice how in this instance the items are not necessarily in source order? That's the cost of the visual nicety.

So far, we have been laying things out using the numbers of the grid lines. However, if you would rather name the grid lines, that is something you can do too.

# Named grid lines

Grid Layout allows authors to work with grids in a number of ways. For example, if you'd rather work with words than numbers, it's possible to name grid lines. Consider a 3-column by 3-row grid.

You can find this example in the book's code as `example_05-05`:

*Figure 5.11: We will use named grid lines to rearrange our elements*

Here's our markup:

```
<div class="my-first-grid">
  <div class="grid-item-1">1</div>
  <div class="grid-item-2">2</div>
  <div class="grid-item-3">3</div>
  <div class="grid-item-4">4</div>
  <div class="grid-item-5">5</div>
  <div class="grid-item-6">6</div>
  <div class="grid-item-7">7</div>
  <div class="grid-item-8">8</div>
  <div class="grid-item-9">9</div>
</div>
```

We set the grid up with this rule. Note the words in square brackets:

```
.my-first-grid {
  display: inline-grid;
  grid-gap: 10px;
  grid-template-columns: [left-start] 200px [left-end center-start] 200px
  [center-end right-start] 200px [right-end];
  grid-template-rows: 200px 200px 200px;
  background-color: #e4e4e4;
}
```

What we are doing inside the square brackets is giving a name to the grid line. In this instance, the first column grid line we have named left-start, and the one after the first column we have named left-end. Notice that, in the center grid line, we have assigned two names: left-end and center-start. We can do this by space-separating the names. In this situation, it makes sense because that grid line is both the end of the left column and the beginning of the center one.

Let's amend our grid-template-row and add some named grid lines there too:

```
grid-template-rows: [top-start] 200px [top-end middle-start] 200px
[middle-end bottom-start] 200px [bottom-end];
```

Here's an example of how we can use these names to position grid items instead of numerical values. This is just the first three of the items we will see in the following diagram:

```
.grid-item-1 {
  grid-column: center-start / center-end;
  grid-row: middle-start / middle-end;
}
.grid-item-2 {
  grid-column: right-start / right-end;
  grid-row: bottom-start / bottom-end;
}
.grid-item-3 {
  grid-column: left-start / left-end;
  grid-row: top-start / middle-start;
}
```

In the example code, I have set each grid item to a random position using this technique. You can see how the three above are placed in this diagram:

*Figure 5.12: You can move things around just as easily with named grid lines*

In specification terms, the name we assign to a grid line is known as a **custom ident**. Because they are just words, avoid using terminology that might interfere with grid keywords. For example, don't start naming grid lines "dense," "auto-fit," or "span"!

Grid Layout has an extra nicety you can make use of when you use named grid lines. If you append your names with -start and -end, as we have in our example, then grid automagically (yes, I know, that's not a real word) makes you a named grid area. Wait, what? Yep, that means that once you have named your grid lines, you can place items in your grid with a one-line grid-area. To prove that point, here are just the first three grid-item rules from earlier rewritten this way:

```
.grid-item-1 {
  grid-area: middle / center;
}
.grid-item-2 {
  grid-area: bottom / right;
}
```

```
  .grid-item-3 {
    grid-area: top / left;
  }
```

I've gotten a little bit ahead of myself now, as I have introduced grid-area without any expla-nation. Let's cover that now.

## grid-template-areas

Yet another way you can work with Grid Layout is to create grid template areas to establish the areas of your grid. Let's rework our prior example and we will remove the named grid lines entirely, starting again with this basic CSS for the grid.

This is example_05-06 in the code:

```
  .my-first-grid {
    display: inline-grid;
    grid-gap: 10px;
    grid-template-columns: 200px 200px 200px;
    grid-template-rows: 200px 200px 200px;
    background-color: #e4e4e4;
  }
  [class^='grid-item'] {
    display: grid;
    align-items: center;
    justify-content: center;
    outline: 3px dashed #f90;
    font-size: 30px;
    color: #333;
  }
```

Now, we will define our grid template areas like this, which we will add to the .my-first-grid rule:

```
  grid-template-areas:
    'one two three'
    'four five six'
    'seven eight nine';
```

With grid-template-areas, we can define rows and columns very simply. A row is defined with quotes (double or single), with the names of each column space-separated inside. Each row in the grid is just another pair of quotes with custom idents inside.

You can use numbers for the start of each grid area, but you then need to **escape** them when you reference them.

 **Escaping** a character, in computer terms, is a means of invoking an alternative interpretation of the character. It is a way of being more explicit about the meaning you would like a certain character to have that could potentially be interpreted in multiple ways.

For example, if one of our areas was named "9," it would have to be referenced like this: grid-area: "\39;". I find that too burdensome, so I suggest using a string for each area or, at least, starting each custom ident with an alpha character.

And that means we can position our items with grid-area like this:

```
.grid-item-1 {
  grid-area: five;
}
.grid-item-2 {
  grid-area: nine;
}
.grid-item-3 {
  grid-area: one;
}
```

Admittedly, this is a simplistic example, but hopefully, you can imagine a more useful scenario: perhaps a blog layout with a header, left-hand sidebar area, main content area, and footer. You might define the necessary grid-template-areas like this:

```
grid-template-areas:
    'header header header header header header'
    'side side main main main main'
    'side side footer footer footer footer';
```

As the specification (the link for the relevant section follows) states that any whitespace character fails to produce a token, which for our purposes simply means delineating one area from another, you could opt to separate columns with tab characters if you would rather, to aid in visually lining up the columns: `https://www.w3.org/TR/css-grid-1/#valdef-grid-template-areas-string`.

When you write the grid template areas, the indentation is not important, nor are the carriage returns; you could lay each row out in a long space-separated list if you liked. As long as the names for each area are inside quotes, with a whitespace character between each, and there is a space between each set of quotes, all is well.

Let's move on to some even more advanced Grid Layout techniques now.

## auto-fit and auto-fill

`auto-fit` and `auto-fill` are "repeat-to-fill" keywords used to describe repetition to Grid.

Thanks to the similarity of their names, I can't help but feel that the `auto-fit` and `auto-fill` keywords are almost guaranteed to confuse – just like `cover` and `contain` do for background image-sizing (we cover them in *Chapter 8, Stunning Aesthetics with CSS*).

The upshot of this is that I frequently have to check which one is which. Thankfully, for both our benefits, we're going to clarify what each of these does now, and why you might want to use them.

Let me start with the why, as that covers both keywords. What if I told you that with the help of `auto-fill` or `auto-fit`, we can create a fully responsive grid that adds/removes columns based upon the available size of the viewport, with no media queries needed?

Compelling, right?

Consider a 9-column grid, where each column is at least 300 px wide. In a slightly back-to-front way, I want to start this by showing you the solution:

```
grid-template-columns: repeat(auto-fit, minmax(300px, 1fr));
```

And here is what that gives you in the browser in a smaller viewport:

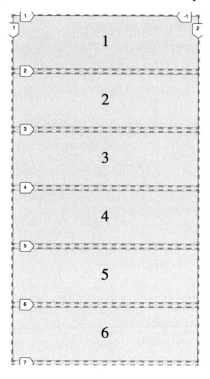

*Figure 5.13: One line with Grid gives you a mobile layout…*

And the same thing on a wider screen:

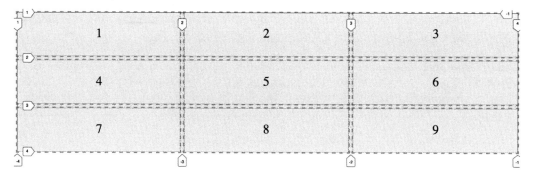

*Figure 5.14: …and also a layout for wider viewports!*

Pretty handy, right?

Let's break down all the magic in that one-liner.

We are using `grid-template-columns`, as we have done before, to set up the columns of our grid. We are using the `repeat()` function to set up a repeating pattern of columns; however, instead of passing in a number of columns, we tell the grid to `auto-fit`. We may have used `auto-fill` there too, but we'll get to the differences between them in a moment. For now, we have told the browser to repeatedly create `auto-fit` columns, and we define the width of those columns using the `minmax` function.

## The minmax() function

Now, if you are new to Grid, it's likely you haven't used `minmax()` before. It's a CSS function that allows you to set up a range for the browser. You specify a minimum size and a maximum size, and it computes something in between based on the available space. In our example, we are passing `minmax()` a minimum size of 300 px and a maximum size of 1 `fr` (remember, it might help to think of `fr` as "free room").

 When dealing with `minmax()`, if you specify a maximum size that is smaller than the minimum, the maximum will be ignored and the minimum will be the computed value.

With that set, the grid "auto-fits" columns that are at least 300 px wide and no more than the size of its content plus a `1fr` share of any remaining space.

In practical terms, this provides a responsive layout that lets our grid resize itself based on the available viewport width.

To more easily show you the difference between `auto-fit` and `auto-fill`, let's revise our one-liner to a minimum of 100 px:

```
grid-template-columns: repeat(auto-fit, minmax(100px, 1fr));
```

That gives us this layout on a wide viewport:

| 1 | 2 | 3 | 4 | 5 | 6 | 7 | 8 | 9 |
|---|---|---|---|---|---|---|---|---|

*Figure 5.15: Using auto-fit will fit our content into the available space*

Note how the columns span the entire width of the page. Now we will change to `auto-fill`:

```
grid-template-columns: repeat(auto-fill, minmax(100px, 1fr));
```

Here is what that produces:

Figure 5.16: Using auto-fill, any spare space is filled up with invisible columns

Notice the space at the end? What happened there?

The key to understanding the difference comes down to whether spare columns are collapsed or not.

When the browser creates the grid in both `auto-fit` and `auto-fill`, it initially lays them out the same. However, when using `auto-fit`, any extra columns left, having laid out the content, are collapsed, leaving that space free to be distributed evenly between the items in the row. In our example (play about with it in the code as `example_05-07`), because each item also has a maximum size of `1fr` unit, each takes up an equal portion of that free space. This results in columns that span the entire width of the space.

However, with `auto-fill`, once the items (in our example, 100 px wide) are laid out, if there is any extra space, the extra empty columns are not collapsed. They remain in situ, filled up, and subsequently the space is not free for the grid items to gobble up. The result is that we get space at the end.

There will be instances where one is more appropriate than the other; just be aware that you can achieve either.

# Shorthand syntax

There are a couple of shorthand syntaxes you can use with Grid: one relatively straightforward, one less so. The first one that you'll probably find most utility for is `grid-template`.

While shorthand syntaxes can be great, my advice would be to write your grids one property at a time, at least to begin with. When you get confident enough that writing each property and value out individually becomes a chore, take the time to learn the shorthand variant.

With that advice dispensed, let's look at these two shorthand methods.

## grid-template shorthand

This allows you to set `grid-template-rows`, `grid-template-columns`, and `grid-template-areas` in one line.

So, for example, for a grid with two 200 px rows and three 300 px columns, we could write:

```
grid-template: 200px 200px / 300px 300px 300px;
```

Or, if you'd rather do it with the repeat function, you could write:

```
grid-template: repeat(2, 200px) / repeat(3, 300px);
```

The part before the forward slash (/) deals with the rows and the bit after the columns. You can add grid-template-areas in there too if you like:

```
grid-template:
  [rows-top] 'a a a' 200px
  'b b b' 200px [rows-bottom]
  / 300px 300px 300px;
```

That computes to this in the browser:

```
grid-template-rows: [rows-top] 200px 200px [rows-bottom];
grid-template-columns: 300px 300px 300px;
grid-template-areas: 'a a a' 'b b b';
```

Personally, I find that once you start mixing in named template areas alongside numerical values, it starts to get too confusing to understand easily. Regardless, some people love the shorthand syntax (maybe you will be one of them), and you should be aware it's possible.

However, we're going to take it up another notch now and deal with the grid shorthand.

## grid shorthand

The other shorthand syntax, grid, lets you define a grid all in one line.

Using this one property, you can set the properties controlling the explicit portion of a grid: grid-template-rows, grid-template-columns, and grid-template-areas, as well as the properties controlling the implicit part of a grid: grid-auto-rows, grid-auto-columns, and grid-auto-flow.

An essential concept to hold onto when writing the grid shorthand is that a grid can only grow implicitly with either rows or columns, not both.

At first, that might seem odd, but if you think about it, how would a grid that could add both rows and columns implicitly lay items out? How would it decide whether to add rows or columns?

So, with that in mind, we can endeavor to wrap our heads around the grid shorthand.

The grid shorthand is not for the faint-hearted, so don't be discouraged if it spits you back out a few times before you get to grips with it. I consider myself pretty familiar with CSS (I know, you'd hope so, right?), but it took me hours rather than minutes to feel confident with what the grid shorthand syntax was doing.

I hope you know your Backus-Naur form, because here is how the property is described in the specification:

```
<'grid-template-rows'> / [ auto-flow && dense? ] <'grid-auto-columns'>? [
auto-flow && dense? ] <'grid-auto-rows'>? / <'grid-template-columns'>
```

Simple, right?

I kid, of course. At this point, when trying to understand a specification, I tend to search out this piece on understanding CSS specifications: https://www.smashingmagazine.com/2016/05/understanding-the-css-property-value-syntax/.

After rereading that, I'll now do my best to distill that piece of the specification into something more human-friendly.

What that means is, the grid shorthand can accept any one of three different sets of syntax as its value.

## grid shorthand value — option one

This is the same value that you would use if you were using grid-template. For example, here is a grid with two 100 px rows and three 200 px columns:

```
grid: 100px 100px / 200px 200px 200px;
```

Just like with our grid-template examples from earlier, you can also use grid-template-areas if you like.

## grid shorthand value — option two

This involves specifying a set of lengths for explicit grid rows, then, separated by a forward slash, a definition for how you want to handle implicit columns. This can be auto-flow to set grid-auto-rows, with the option of setting grid-auto-flow by adding dense too. Or, alternatively, you could add a length value for the width of the columns if you want to set grid-template-columns instead.

Phew, that's a lot to compute. Take a look at some examples.

So, for a grid with two explicit 100 px rows and any number of explicit columns that are 75 px wide:

```
grid: 100px 100px / repeat(auto-fill, 75px);
```

With this grid, should you have too many items, they will spill over into the implicit rows with a default size of auto.

In the browser, that shorthand will compute to the following:

```
grid-template-rows: 100px 100px;
grid-template-columns: repeat(auto-fill, 75px);
grid-template-areas: none;
grid-auto-flow: row;
grid-auto-rows: auto;
grid-auto-columns: auto;
```

Let's try another. Say we want to lay out a grid that has only one row, 100 px high, but any number of columns, potentially running off the side of the container:

```
grid: 100px / auto-flow;
```

That rule computes to the following:

```
grid-template-rows: 100px;
grid-template-columns: none;
grid-template-areas: none;
grid-auto-flow: column;
grid-auto-rows: auto;
grid-auto-columns: auto;
```

It's also worth knowing that, when you use the grid shorthand, you are resetting all of the values it deals with back to their initial state. You can see that if you look at the computed values of styles in the developer tools of your browser.

## grid shorthand value – option three

The final syntax you can pass to grid is effectively the opposite of option two. This time, you set grid-auto-flow to handle implicit rows (with an optional dense) with an optional grid-auto-rows value for the size of the rows. Then, after the forward slash, we handle grid-template-columns.

With this kind of value, we are getting our grid to lay out in rows when needed, rather than in columns, as in the previous option. Here are some examples.

How about a grid that creates as many 100 px rows as needed and 5 columns that occupy 1fr each?

```
grid: auto-flow 100px / repeat(5, 1fr);
```

That computes to this:

```
grid-auto-columns: auto;
grid-auto-flow: row;
grid-auto-rows: 100px;
grid-template-areas: none;
grid-template-columns: 1fr 1fr 1fr 1fr 1fr;
grid-template-rows: none;
```

Or, what about a grid that creates a single column with as many 100 px rows as needed for the content?

```
grid: auto-flow 100px / auto;
```

That computes to this:

```
grid-auto-columns: auto;
grid-auto-flow: row;
grid-auto-rows: 100px;
grid-template-areas: none;
grid-template-columns: auto;
grid-template-rows: none;
```

You can see that the grid shorthand is very powerful but, arguably, not particularly intuitive. For some people, the shorthand is preferable. For some, it is maddening. There is no right or wrong – just what is right or wrong for you.

It won't be long into working with Grid before you hit a seemingly ridiculous shortcoming. If you are dealing with nested elements and wondering why on earth you are not able to make them align with your grid, welcome to the long list of other developers who have thought that very thing. So, what can we do about it?

# Allowing nested elements to take part in the Grid

It is important to be aware that when you define a grid, it is only the direct descendant elements of that grid element that can participate in the layout. The children of those direct descendants cannot.

There are more flexible solutions to this shortcoming on the horizon in the form of `subgrid`. However, right now, `subgrid` only has an implementation in Firefox and Safari, so we will only take a cursory look at that in a moment.

One way we can work around this particular problem right now is with `display: contents`.

What the `display: contents` declaration does is effectively make the layout aspect of the element it is set on – and crucially, not the accessibility side – disappear, allowing the children of that element to behave visually, as if the parent element didn't exist.

Let's consider this markup, and try this out for yourself as we go, by playing with `example_05-08`:

```
<div class="container">
    <div class="child">Child-1</div>
    <div class="child">Child-2</div>
    <div class="parent">
        <div class="grandchild">Grandchild 3</div>
        <div class="grandchild">Grandchild 4</div>
    </div>
</div>
```

And then this CSS:

```
.container {
    display: grid;
    grid: repeat(2, 200px) / repeat(2, 200px);
}

[class*='child'] {
    border: 2px dashed orange;
}
```

And by default, that gives us something like this in the browser:

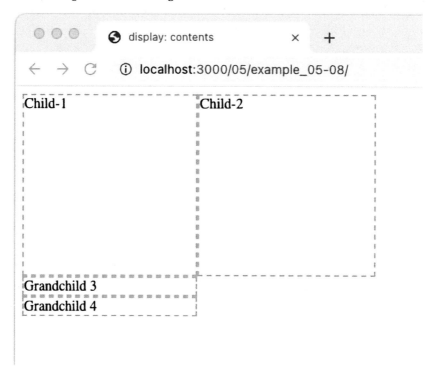

*Figure 5.17: By default, descendants of grid items cannot take part in the grid*

You can see that the two grandchildren elements are not taking part in the grid. We can solve that like this:

```
.parent {
    display: contents;
}
```

By setting the parent element to have `display: contents`, we are allowing the element to display its contents and therefore allowing those elements to participate in the grid layout.

*Figure 5.18: Setting display: contents on an element stops it from producing its own box, allowing child elements to take part in the layout*

You are then able to position those elements in the grid as if the parent element didn't exist.

## The subgrid value

Part of the Level 2 CSS Grid Layout specification deals with the subgrid value. There is every chance that, as you read these words, subgrid will already be available to use. However, support for it will not be ubiquitous for some time.

As ever, you can check support levels at https://caniuse.com/css-subgrid, and read the specification here: https://www.w3.org/TR/css-grid-2/#subgrids.

In essence, subgrid provides a mechanism for non-direct child elements of a grid ancestor to inherit their grid tracks. Using subgrid is as simple as setting subgrid as the value of either grid-template-columns or grid-template-rows, or both.

Let us start with the subgrid value by solving the same problem we solved with display: contents in the last section.

When using the subgrid value, instead we would set the CSS for the .parent like this (you can view the full code in example_05-09):

```
.parent {
    display: grid;
    grid-template-columns: subgrid;
    grid-column: span 2;
}
```

And just like that, this particular problem is solved.

However, for solving that particular problem, we have actually used more code than the prior solution with display: contents, but bear with me. We can understand how it works with this simple example before we look at something more involved.

First, we are making the .parent element a grid, and then crucially telling it that we want the template for the columns to be a subgrid, so that it will inherit the columns from the ancestor grid it is part of.

Next, we need to tell the browser how big this element is going to be in the ancestor grid it is part of. Here we have set it to span 2 columns, making it the full width of the ancestor grid, as, remember, the ancestor grid is made up of two columns.

With that in place, the .grandchild elements happily position themselves in the next available column. We don't need to do anything extra with them.

Let's look at one further, slightly more involved example. Consider this screenshot:

*Figure 5.19: Without subgrid, the labels at the bottom are out of alignment*

Here, we have a horizontally scrolling component containing images of different planets of our Solar System. Crucially, notice how, due to the information text that accompanies each planet, the caption for the image doesn't sit at the same level? While that is a problem we could fix with other means and approaches, subgrid is a perfect fit.

Here it is with our subgrid code in place. Notice how the captions below each planet line up perfectly? Let's look at how this is done.

*Figure 5.20: subgrid allows us to inherit the row and column tracks of a parent grid*

Firstly, consider the markup. We have a containing element with the class of .Scroll_Wrapper to create the scrolling section, and then a number of figure elements, each with a class of .Item, and containing a planet image and associated information.

For brevity, I'll just show you the HTML for the opening of the containing element, and one of the planets (the full code is at example_05-10):

```
<div class="Scroll_Wrapper">
    <figure class="Item">
        <img src="Sun.jpg" alt="Our Sun in space" />
        <figcaption class="Caption">The Sun</figcaption>
        <p>
```

```
        The Sun is a yellow dwarf star, a hot ball of glowing gases
        at the heart of our solar system. Its gravity holds everything
        from the biggest planets to tiny debris in its orbit.
    </p>
</figure>
```

To set up the outer grid on the container, we have this:

```
.Scroll_Wrapper {
    display: grid;
    width: 100%;
    overflow-y: hidden;
    overflow-x: auto;
    gap: 0 20px;
    grid-template-rows: auto auto;
    grid-auto-columns: auto;
    grid-auto-flow: column;
}
```

Those are all grid-related properties you have seen already in this chapter. Now, as we are interested in positioning the contents of each planet, our .Item element, against that grid, we need to introduce subgrid.

We need our element to be a grid itself and, crucially, we need the rows to inherit from the nearest ancestor grid:

```
.Item {
    grid-row: 1/-1;
    display: grid;
    grid-template-rows: subgrid;
    grid-template-columns: 100px 200px;
    gap: 0 20px;
    margin: 0;
}
```

As the .Item is itself part of an outer grid, we need to tell it how it should be positioned in that grid, so setting grid-row: 1/-1 tells it to start at the first row and end at the last.

We then set the rows for this item's own grid with grid-template-rows, but use subgrid to get the row layout from the parent (the .Scroll_Wrapper).

With that in place, we can set the row and column positions of child elements inside the grid as we would normally. But the "magic" part is: because our rows are connected to the outer grid via the `subgrid` value, it means they are sized with the largest child in mind, which in turn means that all the internal elements of each `.Item` can line up.

When you hit these kind of child element problems with Grid, if you simply need to remove a containing element, as if it wasn't there, opt for `display:contents`. If, however, you need to keep the containing element – perhaps it has a background color or image – then `subgrid` is the best choice.

This is but one simple use case of a layout conundrum that can be easily solved with `subgrid`. The exercise that follows will present another to put your mind to.

## Applying what you have learned so far

As an exercise, consider this section of the `https://rwd.education` website:

**400+ INFO PACKED PAGES**

CSS Layers, Color Functions, Media Queries, SVG, animations, transforms, accessibility, Flexbox, Grid, Scroll Snap and much, much more.

**SAMPLE CODE**

Each chapter has associated code examples to follow along with. You also get the source code for this site which utilises many of the techniques you'll master throughout.

**4<sup>th</sup>**

**LATEST EDITION**

The 4th Edition of Packt's best-selling Responsive Web Design title since 2012. Updated in 2022 to include all the new and essential CSS and HTML features.

**IS IT FOR YOU?**

Are you a full-stack developer who needs to boost their front-end skills? Perhaps you work on the front-end and you need a definitive overview of all modern HTML and CSS has to offer?

Maybe you have done a little website building but you need a deep understanding of how responsive web designs work and how to achieve them? This is a book for you!

**WHAT WILL YOU LEARN?**

Understand the most fundamental parts of building a modern web site or application that will work across all devices. You'll learn the best approaches for having a fast and accessible website that works just as well on the latest iPhone or Android as a desktop computer.

The book covers everything from choosing the right tag to mark up content, to understanding the benefits of modern image formats like AVIF and WebP — and everything essential in-between. It also covers all the latest features of CSS: Custom Properties, variable fonts, CSS Grid and much, much more.

**BUY FROM PACKT**   **BUY FROM AMAZON**

*Figure 5.21: Can you use your grid knowledge to lay out this section?*

If you look in the Start folder for this chapter's code, you will see that, currently, those sections are just one under the other. Try to amend the code for that section using Grid Layout. Perhaps think about how you could easily have it showing one or two of those sections when screen space is limited, and the layout that is shown in the preceding screenshot when space allows.

And what about if the headings for those sections wrap? Do you want to make use of the subgrid value to ensure they stay visually aligned?

## Summary

If you are fairly new to building on the web, you almost have an advantage when it comes to learning CSS Grid: a "beginner's mind," if you like. For people that have been laying things out with other techniques over the years, the difficulty, in some ways, is undoing what you already know about layout with CSS.

Having read this chapter, you should have some understanding of what is possible with Grid Layout and how you might employ it.

Plus, with subgrid more recently joining the existing capabilities of CSS Grid, we now have an incredibly powerful, complete, and expressive method of laying out elements on our page with CSS.

I should also ask that, if you were in any way successful with the exercises, you congratulate yourself; there's a lot to consider when you first start using Grid. If you accomplished something with your first effort, you did admirably.

At this point, I'll also reiterate that Grid is tricky at first. It comes with a lot of possibilities but also quite a few new pieces of terminology and concepts. Expect to take a few runs at it the first time you use it.

Personally, I found the easiest approach was to start remaking a few things I already had built in Flexbox with Grid. Start simple, and write the style of syntax that makes the most sense for you. I still rarely write the shorthand versions, as despite the attractiveness of a terse one-liner, I find them hard to interpret and understand at a glance. For me, clarity trumps brevity.

Regardless of the approach you take, I promise that, once you get competent, CSS Grid will pay you back handsomely for your investment.

These last two chapters, on Flexbox and Grid, have covered single topics in some detail. The next chapter is going to be more broad: a veritable grab-bag of CSS goodies. Turn that page, and let's move on to *Chapter 6, CSS Selectors, Typography, and More.*

# Section II

## Core Skills for Effective Front-End Web Development

If you've read from the beginning to this point, you should have a solid understanding of the fundamentals needed for responsive web design. In fact, you're likely a step ahead, in that you will be building your designs using the most recent layout mechanisms, Flexbox and Grid.

If we just needed to cover responsive web design, at this point, my work here would be pretty much done. But there is so much more we can look at.

This next section of the book aims to take you into more advanced and specialty areas. It's not every day you will need to reach for a `clamp` function, or know when and why you would employ a `where()` selector. But in this section, we are going into greater depth, understanding what, primarily, CSS can offer you to solve the everyday challenges that are going to come your way as a developer.

Again, don't think you need to remember all the detail of this stuff. Take it in, get a grasp of what's possible, and know that you can dip back in in future, when you remember that "I think there's a way to do that with CSS."

There's every chance that there probably is!

# 6

# CSS Selectors, Typography, and More

In the last few years, CSS has enjoyed a raft of new features. Some enable us to animate and transform elements. Others allow us to create multiple background images, gradients, and mask and filter effects, and others allow us to bring SVG elements to life.

We will get to all those capabilities in the next few chapters. Firstly, I think it will be useful to look at more recent improvements to some of the fundamentals of CSS.

No one can know every nuance, capability, and syntax in the CSS language. I've been working with CSS for two decades and on a weekly basis, I still discover something new (or just as likely rediscover something I'd forgotten). As such, I don't feel that trying to know every possible CSS property and value permutation is actually a worthy pursuit. Instead, I think it's more sensible to develop a good grasp of what's possible and what capabilities exist that solve the most common problems.

As such, we are going to concentrate in this chapter on some of the techniques, units, and se-lectors I have found most useful when building responsive web designs. I'm hoping you'll then have the requisite knowledge to solve most problems that come your way when developing a responsive web design.

As there are quite a few topics to cover, they have been grouped as follows:

Selectors, units, and capabilities:

- `::before` and `::after` pseudo-elements

- Attribute selectors and substring matching
- Structural pseudo-classes, including `:last-child`, `:nth-child`, `:empty`, and `:not`
- Combinator selectors, including child, next sibling, and subsequent sibling
- Functional pseudo-class selectors (`:is` and `:where`)

Viewport-related units and feature queries:

- Viewport-related length units, `vh`, `vw`, `vmax`, and `vmin`, and their dynamic variants
- Writing feature queries using `@supports` to fork CSS

Web typography:

- `@font-face` rule
- Font formats, including `.woff` and `.woff2`
- Font loading control with the `font-display` property
- Variable fonts and font features

As you can see, we have a lot to get through. Let's begin.

# Selectors, units, and capabilities

Although they may not seem like the most exciting of subjects, selectors, units, and capabilities are the "meat and potatoes" of CSS. Master these and your power to solve problems with CSS will increase substantially. So, skip this section at your peril!

## Anatomy of a CSS rule

Before exploring some of the recent additions to CSS, to prevent confusion, let's establish the terminology we use to describe a CSS rule. Consider the following example:

```
.selector {
    /* comment */
    property: value; /* declaration */
}
```

This rule is made up of the selector (`.selector`) and then, inside the curly braces, the declaration. The declaration is further defined by the property and the value. Happy we're on the same page? Great, let's press on.

# Pseudo-elements and pseudo-classes

There is potential for some confusion when we go on shortly to talk about "pseudo" classes. The reason being is that, in CSS, there are both pseudo-classes and pseudo-elements. Let's therefore take a moment to establish the difference.

The word "pseudo" in this context means something that is *like* something, but not really it. So, a pseudo-element is something that is like an element but not really one, and a pseudo-class is something that selects something that isn't really something, but rather the *state* of something. So, :hover is a pseudo-state, as it selects something when in a certain state. It's possible I'm starting to sound like the Riddler now from Batman! Let's clarify with some code. Here is how you create a pseudo-element in CSS:

```css
.thing::before {
    content: "Spooky";
}
```

That inserts a ::before pseudo-element into the .thing element with the content "Spooky". A ::before behaves like a first child of the element it is defined on, and an ::after behaves like a last child.

The following image might help. It shows a single element represented in the Firefox developer tools, containing text with both a ::before and an ::after pseudo-element added in CSS:

```html
<!DOCTYPE html>
▼ <html class="" lang="en"> event
  ▶ <head> ⋯ </head>
  ▼ <body>
    ▼ <div class="thing">
        ::before
        Here is text in the element
        ::after
      </div>
    </body>
  </html>
```

*Figure 6.1: The Firefox developer tools will show you where pseudo-elements are in the DOM*

The key thing to remember with pseudo-elements is that if you don't provide a value for content, nothing will show on the page. Notice the double colon before before? Officially, that is how you should code pseudo-elements as it helps differentiate them from pseudo-classes, which only use one. However, a single colon worked with the first implementations of ::before and ::after and so you can still write them that way too.

You can't do the same with pseudo-classes; they always have a single colon. For example, `:hover`, `:active`, and `:focus` are all pseudo-classes and are written with a single colon.

Hopefully, the difference between pseudo-classes and elements is now clear.

With that distinction made, let's move on and look at some of the powerful selectors available to us today in CSS.

# CSS selectors — beyond the normal!

CSS now provides incredible power for selecting elements within a page. If you are only used to selecting elements based on their class, ID, or element type, these techniques may open your eyes to new possibilities. I'd better qualify that bold claim.

## CSS attribute selectors

You've probably used CSS attribute selectors to create rules. For example, consider the following markup:

```
<img src="https://placeimg.com/640/480/any" alt="an inquisitive cat" />
```

And this CSS:

```
img[alt] {
    border: 3px dashed #e15f5f;
}
```

This would select the `img` element in the preceding code, and any others on the page provided that they have an `alt` attribute.

In fact, to make something a little more useful, we could combine this with the `:not` negation selector (we will look at that in detail later in this chapter) to add a red border around any images that have no `alt` attribute or an `alt` attribute with no value:

```
img:not([alt]),
img[alt=""] {
    border: 3px solid red;
}
```

That would be useful from an accessibility point of view, as it would visually highlight any images that didn't have alternate text included for assistive technology.

As another example, let's say we wanted to select all elements with a data-sausage attribute:

```
[data-sausage] {
    /* styles */
}
```

The key thing here is to use square brackets to specify the attribute you want to select.

 The data attribute was introduced in HTML5 to provide a place for custom data that can't be stored sensibly by any other existing mechanism. The specification description for these can be found here: https://www.w3.org/TR/2010/WD-html5-20101019/elements. html#embedding-custom-non-visible-data-with-the-data-attributes.

You can also narrow things down by specifying what the attribute value is. For example, consider the following rule:

```
img[alt="Sausages cooking"] {
    /* Styles */
}
```

This would only target images that have an alt attribute value of "Sausages cooking"; for example:

```
<img src="img/sausages.png" alt="Sausages cooking" />
```

So far, so "big deal, we could do that in CSS2." I hear you. Let's turn things up a notch, shall we?

## CSS substring matching attribute selectors

We also have the ability to select elements based on the substring of their attribute selector. That sounds complicated. It isn't! The three options are whether the attribute:

- Begins with a certain substring
- Contains an instance of a certain substring
- Ends with a certain substring

Let's see what they look like.

## The "beginning with" substring matching attribute selector

Consider the following markup:

```
<li data-type="todo-chore">Empty the bins</li>
<li data-type="todo-exercise">Play football</li>
```

Suppose that markup represents two items in a "to-do" list application we are building. Even though they both have different data-type attribute values, we can select them both with the "beginning with" substring matching attribute selector, like this:

```
[data-type^="todo"] {
    /* Styles */
}
```

The key character in all this is the ^ symbol. That symbol is called the **caret**, although it is often referred to as the **hat** symbol too. In this instance, it signifies "begins with." Because both data-type attributes have values that begin with "todo", our selector selects them.

## The "contains an instance of" substring matching attribute selector

The "contains an instance of" substring matching attribute selector has the following syntax:

```
[attribute*="value"] {
    /* Styles */
}
```

Like all attribute selectors, you can combine them with a type selector (one that references the actual HTML element used) if needed, although I would only do that if I had to—in case you want to change the type of element used. Let's try an example. Consider this markup:

```
<p data-ingredients="scones cream jam">Will I get selected?</p>
```

We can select that element like this:

```
[data-ingredients*="cream"] {
    color: red;
}
```

The key character in all this is the * symbol, which in this context means "contains." The "begins with" selector would not have worked in this markup as the string inside the attribute didn't begin with "cream". It did, however, contain "cream", so the "contains an instance of" substring attribute selector finds it.

# The "ends with" substring matching attribute selector

The "ends with" substring matching attribute selector has the following syntax:

```
[attribute$="value"] {
    /* Styles */
}
```

An example should help. Consider this markup:

```
<p data-ingredients="scones cream jam">Will I get selected?</p>
<p data-ingredients="toast jam butter">Will I get selected?</p>
<p data-ingredients="jam toast butter">Will I get selected?</p>
```

Suppose we only want to select the element with "jam" at the end of the data-ingredients attribute (which would be the first element of those three). We can't use the "contains an instance of" (it will select all three) or "begins with" (it will only select the last one) substring attribute selector. However, we can use the "ends with" substring attribute selector:

```
[data-ingredients$="jam"] {
    color: red;
}
```

The key character in all this is the $ (dollar) symbol, which means "ends with."

Right, we have some pretty handy attribute-related selectors now. But it's also worth knowing that you can chain attribute selectors, just like you can class selectors.

## Chaining attribute selectors

You can have even more possibilities for selecting items by grouping attribute selectors. Suppose we had this markup:

```
<li
    data-todo-type="exercise"
    data-activity-name="running"
    data-location="indoor"
>
```

```
        Running
    </li>
    <li
        data-todo-type="exercise"
        data-activity-name="swimming"
        data-location="indoor"
    >
        Swimming
    </li>
    <li
        data-todo-type="exercise"
        data-activity-name="cycling"
        data-location="outdoor"
    >
        Cycling
    </li>
    <li
        data-todo-type="exercise"
        data-activity-name="swimming"
        data-location="outdoor"
    >
        Swimming
    </li>
```

Let's suppose I only wanted to select "indoor swimming." I can't use just data-location="indoor" as that would get the first element too. I can't use data-activity-name="swimming" as that would get me the second and the fourth, but I can do this:

```
[data-activity-name="swimming"][data-location="indoor"] {
    /* styles */
}
```

This selects elements that have "swimming" as the activity name, as long as they also have "indoor" as the location.

Attribute selectors allow you to select IDs and classes that start with numbers. Before HTML5, it wasn't valid markup to start IDs or class names with a number. HTML5 removes that restriction. When it comes to IDs, there are still some things to remember. There should be no spaces in the ID name, and it must be unique on the page. For more information, visit `https://html.spec.whatwg.org/multipage/dom.html#the-id-attribute`. Now, although you can start ID and class values with numbers in HTML5, CSS still restricts you from using ID and class selectors that start with a number (`https://www.w3.org/TR/CSS21/syndata.html#characters`). Luckily for us, we can easily work around this by using an attribute selector; for example, `[id="10"]`.

Right, I think our attribute selecting skills are now pretty good. Let's move on to how we can deal with selecting elements based on where they are in the document.

# CSS structural pseudo-classes

CSS gives us more power to select elements based on where they sit in the structure of the DOM. Let's consider a common design treatment; we're working on the navigation bar for a larger viewport and we want to have all but the last link over on the left. Historically, we would have needed to solve this problem by adding a class name to the last link so we could select it, like this:

```
<nav class="nav-Wrapper">
    <a href="/home" class="nav-Link">Home</a>
    <a href="/About" class="nav-Link">About</a>
    <a href="/Films" class-"nav-Link">Films</a>
    <a href="/Forum" class="nav-Link">Forum</a>
    <a href="/Contact-Us" class="nav-Link nav-LinkLast">Contact Us</a>
</nav>
```

This in itself can be problematic. For example, sometimes, just getting a content management system to add a class to a final list item can be frustratingly difficult. Thankfully, in those eventualities, we can solve this problem and many more with CSS structural pseudo-classes.

# The :last-child selector

Way back in CSS 2.1, we already had a selector applicable for the first item in a list, the :first-child selector:

```
div:first-child {
    /* Styles */
}
```

However, CSS Level 3 added a selector that can also match the last:

```
div:last-child {
    /* Styles */
}
```

Let's look at how that selector could fix our prior problem if we didn't want to, or couldn't, add another class at the desired point in the markup:

```
.nav-Wrapper {
    display: flex;
}
.nav-Link:last-child {
    margin-left: auto;
}
```

There are also useful selectors for when something is the only item (:only-child) and the only item of a type (:only-of-type).

# The nth-child selectors

The nth-child selectors let us solve even more difficult problems. With the same markup as before, let's consider how nth-child selectors allow us to select any arbitrary link(s) we want within the list.

Firstly, what about selecting every other list item? We could select the odd ones like this:

```
.nav-Link:nth-child(odd) {
    /* Styles */
}
```

Or, if you wanted to select the even ones, you could do this:

```
.nav-Link:nth-child(even) {
    /* Styles */
}
```

# Understanding what nth rules do

For the uninitiated, nth-based selectors can look pretty intimidating. However, once you've mastered the logic and syntax, you'll be amazed at what you can do with them. Let's take a look.

Here are the nth-based selectors at our disposal:

- `nth-child(n)`
- `nth-last-child(n)`
- `nth-of-type(n)`
- `nth-last-of-type(n)`

We've seen that we can use (`odd`) or (`even`) values already in an nth-based expression, but the (`n`) parameter can be used in another couple of ways:

- As an integer; for example, `:nth-child(2)` would select the second item. Passing a number/integer into the nth selector is easy enough to understand; just enter the element number you want to select.
- You can also pass a numeric expression. For example, `:nth-child(3n+1)` would start at the first element, and then select every third element.

The numeric expression version of the selector is the part that can be a little baffling at first. Let's break it down.

## Breaking down the math

Let's consider 10 spans on a page (you can play about with these by looking at `example_06-01`):

```
<span></span>
<span></span>
<span></span>
<span></span>
<span></span>
<span></span>
<span></span>
<span></span>
<span></span>
<span></span>
```

We will style them like this:

```
span {
    height: 2rem;
    width: 2rem;
    background-color: blue;
    display: inline-block;
}
```

As you might imagine, this gives us 10 squares in a line:

*Figure 6.2: We will test our nth-child selection skills on these 10 identical elements*

OK, let's look at how we can select different ones with nth-based selections.

For practicality, when considering the expression within the parentheses, I start from the right. So, for example, if I want to figure out what (2n+3) will select, I start with the right-most number (the "3" here indicates the third item from the left) and know it will select every second element from that point on. So, adding this rule:

```
span:nth-child(2n + 3) {
    background-color: #f90;
    border-radius: 50%;
}
```

Results in this in the browser:

*Figure 6.3: Anything that matches our nth-child selector is turned round and orange*

As you can see, our nth selector targets the third list item and then every subsequent second one after that too. If there were 100 list items, it would continue selecting every second one.

How about selecting everything from the second item onward? Well, although you could write :nth-child(1n+2), you don't actually need the first number 1 as, unless otherwise stated, n is equal to 1. We can, therefore, just write :nth-child(n+2). Likewise, if we wanted to select every third element, rather than write :nth-child(3n+3), we could just write :nth-child(3n) as every third item would begin at the third item anyway, without needing to state it explicitly.

The expression can also use negative numbers; for example, :nth-child(3n-2) starts at minus 2 and then selects every third item.

You can also change the direction. By default, once the first part of the selection is found, the subsequent ones go down the elements in the DOM (and therefore from left to right in our example). However, you can reverse that with a minus; for example:

```
span:nth-child(-2n + 3) {
    background-color: #f90;
    border-radius: 50%;
}
```

This example finds the third item again, but then goes in the opposite direction to select every two elements; up the DOM tree and therefore from right to left in our example:

*Figure 6.4: With a minus symbol, we can select in the opposite direction*

Hopefully, the nth-based expressions are making more sense now. nth-child and nth-last-child differ in that the nth-last-child variant works from the opposite end of the document tree. For example, :nth-last-child(-n+3) starts at 3 from the end and then selects all the items after it. Here's what that rule gives us in the browser:

*Figure 6.5: nth-last-child lets you start from the opposite end of the elements*

Finally, let's consider :nth-of-type and :nth-last-of-type. While the previous examples count any children, regardless of type (always remember the nth-child selector targets all children at the same DOM level, regardless of classes), :nth-of-type and :nth-last-of-type let you be specific about the type of item you want to select. Consider the following markup (example_06-02), which is a mixture of div and span elements, albeit with the same class:

```
<span class="span-class"></span>
<span class="span-class"></span>
<span class="span-class"></span>
<span class="span-class"></span>
```

```
<span class="span-class"></span>

<div class="span-class"></div>
<div class="span-class"></div>
<div class="span-class"></div>
<div class="span-class"></div>
<div class="span-class"></div>
```

If we used the selector:

```
.span-class:nth-of-type(-2n + 3) {
    background-color: #f90;
    border-radius: 50%;
}
```

Even though all the elements have the same `span-class` class, they don't get seen as one group. The selector applies once to the `span` elements, and then to the `div` elements. Here is what gets selected:

*Figure 6.6: nth-of-type selectors work on each type of element they find*

 CSS doesn't count like JavaScript! If you're used to using JavaScript, you'll know that it counts from 0 upward (zero index-based). For example, when selecting an element in JavaScript, an integer value of 1 is actually the second element. CSS, however, starts at 1 so that a value of 1 is the first item it matches.

## nth-based selection in responsive web designs

Just to close out this little section, I want to illustrate a real-life responsive web design problem and how we can use nth-based selection to solve it. Imagine we are building a page showing our sun and the various planets of our solar system. Our content management system simply spits all the items out in a list, but we want to show them in a grid of sorts.

For some viewports, we will only be able to make it two items wide. However, as the viewport increases in width, we can show three items, and at larger sizes still, we can show four.

Here is the problem, though. Regardless of the viewport size, we want to prevent any items on the bottom row from having a border on the bottom. You can view this code at example_06-03. Here is how it looks when it's four items wide:

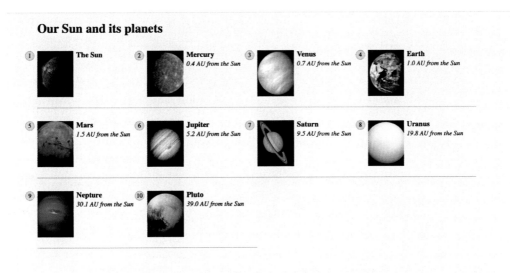

*Figure 6.7: Our task here is to remove the border on the bottom row, regardless of how many items are showing*

See that pesky border below the bottom two items? That's what we need to remove. However, I want a robust solution so that if there was another item on the bottom row (if another planet is suddenly discovered hiding behind Uranus!), the border would also be removed from that too.

Now, because there is a different number of items on each row at different viewports, we will also need to change the nth-based selection at different viewport widths. But we can use media queries for that. For the sake of brevity, I'm not going to show you the selection for each media query. I'll just show you the selection that matches four items per row, as you can see in the preceding screenshot. However, you can open the code sample to see the selections for each different viewport:

```
@media (min-width: 55rem) {
    .Item {
        width: 25%;
    }
    /* Get me every fourth item and, of those, only ones that are in the
    last four items */
    .Item:nth-child(4n + 1):nth-last-child(-n + 4),
```

```
    /* Now get me every one after that same collection too. */
    .Item:nth-child(4n + 1):nth-last-child(-n + 4) ~ .Item {
        border-bottom: 0;
    }
}
```

You'll notice here that we are chaining the nth-based pseudo-class selectors, much like we chained attribute selectors earlier in this chapter. It's important to understand when you chain nth selectors like this that the first selector doesn't "filter" the selection for the next selector; rather, the element has to match each of the selections.

So, for the line like this:

```
.Item:nth-child(4n + 1):nth-last-child(-n + 4),
```

.Item has to be the first item of four and also be one of the last four:

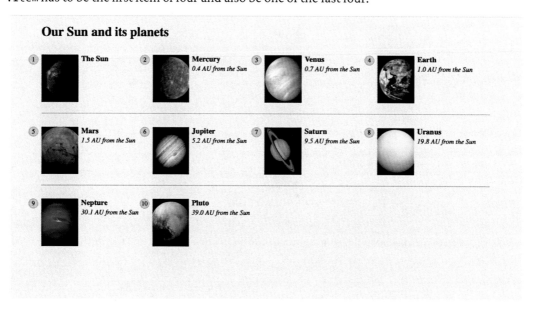

*Figure 6.8: Achievement unlocked—using nth-child selectors like some kind of nth-child wizard!*

Nice! Thanks to nth-based selections, we have a defensive set of rules to remove the bottom border, regardless of the viewport size or the number of items we are showing. You can view the completed code in example_06-04.

Now, one nifty bit of selection we are doing in that prior example is using the "subsequent sibling" selector. We haven't looked at that, so we will cover it next.

# Combinator selectors — child, next sibling, and subsequent sibling

Sometimes you want to do something particular to an element but only if it follows another, or perhaps only if it is the child of another element. We are going to look now at how we can do that.

I'm making the assumption at this point that you understand the basic selector pattern where one class followed by another selects any descendant that matches. For example, .parent .descendant {} would select any element that was a descendant of the .parent element with a class of .descendant, no matter how many levels deep.

## The child combinator

The child combinator only selects direct descendants. Consider this markup:

```
<div class="parent">
    <div class="descendant child">
        <div class="descendant grandchild"></div>
    </div>
</div>
```

We can select only the direct "child" of the parent element, like this:

```
.parent > .descendant {
    /* Styles */
}
```

Notice the right-angle bracket between the two class names in the selector; that's the child combinator symbol.

## The next sibling

Consider another example:

```
<div class="item one">one</div>
<div class="item">two</div>
<div class="item">three</div>
<div class="item">four</div>
<div class="item">five</div>
<div class="item">six</div>
```

Let's suppose we wanted to select an item, but only if it is the next sibling of .one. With that markup, we could select the second element in that list like this:

```
.one + .item {
    border: 3px dashed #f90;
}
```

The + symbol there means "next sibling," so select the next sibling element of .one, our second element.

## The subsequent sibling

With the same markup from the previous example, if we wanted to select all items after the third, we could do this:

```
.item:nth-child(3) ~ .item {
    border: 3px dashed #f90;
}
```

The ~ symbol, called a **tilde**, says "every subsequent sibling."

## The negation (:not) selector

Another handy selector is the negation pseudo-class selector. This is used to select everything that isn't something else. Consider this:

```
<div class="a-div"></div>
<div class="a-div"></div>
<div class="a-div"></div>
<div class="a-div not-me"></div>
<div class="a-div"></div>
```

And then these styles:

```
.a-div {
    display: inline-block;
    height: 2rem;
    width: 2rem;
    background-color: blue;
}
```

```
.a-div:not(.not-me) {
    background-color: orange;
    border-radius: 50%;
}
```

Our final rule will make every element with a class of .a-div orange and round, with the exception of the div that also has the .not-me class. You can find that code in the example_06-05 folder of the code samples (remember, you can grab them all at https://rwd.education):

*Figure 6.9: The negation selector allows you to exclude elements from selection*

So far, we have looked primarily at what's known as structural pseudo-classes (full information on this is available at https://www.w3.org/TR/selectors/#structural-pseudos). However, CSS has many more selectors. If you're working on a web application, it's worth looking at the full list of UI element state pseudo-classes (https://www.w3.org/TR/selectors/#resource-pseudos) as they can, for example, help you target rules based on whether something is selected or not.

## The empty (:empty) selector

I've encountered situations where I have an element that includes some padding on the inside and gets content dynamically inserted. Sometimes, it gets content inserted, while sometimes it doesn't. The trouble is, when it doesn't include content, I still see the padding. Consider the HTML in example_06-06:

```
<div class="thing"></div>
```

And here's the CSS:

```
.thing {
    padding: 1rem;
    background-color: violet;
}
```

Without any content in that element, I still see the background color. Thankfully, we can easily hide it, like this:

```
.thing:empty {
    display: none;
}
```

However, just be careful with the :empty selector. For example, you might think this is empty:

```
<div class="thing"> </div>
```

It isn't! Look at the whitespace in there. Whitespace is not "no" space! And neither is something like a line break.

However, just to confuse matters, be aware that a comment doesn't affect whether an element is considered empty or not. For example, this is still considered empty:

```
<div class="thing"><!--I'm empty, honest I am--></div>
```

# Grouping selectors

Ordinarily, when we want to share a bunch of properties across a number of things, we just comma-separate the selectors into a list:

```
.thing1,
[data-thing],
#thing {
    /* styles */
}
```

That works fine for a few things. All those comma-separated selectors get the same styles applied, but it can start to become unwieldy and repetitive in more complicated scenarios:

```
.blog-post > h1,
.blog-post > h2,
.blog-post > h3,
.blog-post > h4,
.blog-post > ul,
.blog-post > ul li,
.blog-post > p,
.blog-post > a {
    /* shared styles */
}
```

The other downside is that a single mistake in that group renders the whole list invalid:

```
.blog-post > h1,
.blog-post > h2,
```

```
.blog-post > h3,
.blog-post > h4,
.blog-post > ul,
.blog-post > ul < li,
.blog-post > p,
.blog-post > a {
    /* shared styles */
}
```

That accidental "less than" symbol will mean this rule won't apply any styles to any of the selectors. Now, I don't think that is something to concern yourself with too much, but there are newer selectors that can solve these issues.

## The :is() functional pseudo-class

This is also known as the "matches any" selector. Let's use it to refactor that prior example, and then talk about the differences:

```
.blog-post > :is(h1, h2, h3, h4, ul, ul < li, p, a) {
    /* shared styles */
}
```

Not only is this more compact, but it has the added benefit that even though that invalid selector is still present, the entire rule is not invalidated; just that one. Nice, eh?

Now, it is important to be aware that the :is functional gives all selectors within the specificity of the most specific selector. And that can be problematic. Here is the relevant portion of the specification:

> *The specificity of an* :is(), :not(), *or* :has() *pseudo-class is replaced by the specificity of the most specific complex selector in its selector list argument.*

So, suppose you have a grouping like this:

```
:is(.thing, .another-thing, and-another) {
    /* styles */
}
```

Each of those selectors will only have a specificity of 0,1,0, as the most specific selector in the selector list is a class.

However, if I add an ID selector in there:

```
:is(#ouch .thing, .another-thing, and-another) {
    /* styles */
}
```

Each one of those now gets the specificity of the ID: 1,0,0. That can introduce problems in the long term, as it means you have a very high specificity selector in your codebase, and should you ever need to override it at some point, you will need to create a rule with even greater specificity. As such, it is generally advisable to avoid using IDs unless absolutely necessary.

 For more on specificity and the maintenance of larger CSS codebases, you may be interested in another of your author's books, *Enduring CSS!*

However, if you do find yourself in such a pickle, we have just the selector for you.

## The :where() functional pseudo-class

The :where() selector takes a selector list, just as :is() does. However, this selector is snappily known as the "specificity-adjustment pseudo-class." Cripes!

Any selector inside the :where() selector list is given a specificity of zero. Even big bad ID selectors! So, if you do find yourself in a scenario where you need to use an ID selector, you can wrap it in :where() and it will not add to specificity. Let's take a look.

Suppose we had markup like this:

```
<div id="thing" class="hi">hi</div>
```

And we added CSS like this:

```
.hi {
    width: 200px;
    height: 200px;
    background-color: gold;
}

#thing {
    background-color: red;
}
```

You can hopefully guess that the square we have will be red. The ID is an order of magnitude more specific than the class, and it is also written after it in the stylesheet too, so no way that square is going to have a gold background! However, wrap it in a `:where()`:

```css
.hi {
    width: 200px;
    height: 200px;
    background-color: gold;
}

:where(#thing) {
    background-color: red;
}
```

And that ID has zero specificity, meaning our square displays gold. This selector is useful in lots of scenarios but I find it most useful for "reset" styles, or any style you know you'll be overriding later on.

 Remember to check support for your users. As we delve into CSS more and more, don't forget to visit `https://caniuse.com`, if you ever want to know what the current level of browser support is for a particular CSS or HTML5 feature. Alongside showing browser version support (searchable by feature), it also provides the most recent set of global usage statistics from `https://gs.statcounter.com`.

## The :has() relational pseudo-class

A very recent addition to the CSS selectors at our disposal is the `:has()` functional pseudo-class.

In simple terms, it's a way of selecting an element, as long as it has certain child elements or conditions.

Let's suppose you want to do something with a container, but only if it has a video element inside. That would look like this:

```css
.thing:has(video) {
    /* Styles */
}
```

Or you want to add some padding in the block flow direction if an element doesn't have a p element inside of it. That would look like this:

```
.other-thing:not(:has(p)) {
    padding-block: 10px;
}
```

How about an even more convoluted use case; suppose you want to select a h1 if there is an img directly after it. We can do that like this:

```
h1:has(+ img) {
    /* Styles */
}
```

There are so many possibilities with :has()!

If you need to fork your code based on support for :has(), you can do this with feature queries. That would look like this:

```
@supports selector(:has(*)) {
/* Styles */
}
```

Now, don't worry if you've not come across feature queries before; we are going to look at them later on in this very chapter.

### Logical Properties and Values

You may have noticed in one of the previous examples that I used the padding-block shorthand. That's part of the Logical Properties and Values specification and allows us to define spacing and more based on the logical direction of the document. This can be useful when the writing mode being used might not match the physical mappings. For example, in some languages you start reading from the right and not the left. If you use a logical property in that instance, instead of an absolute one, it will work as intended in either case.

Practically, as I don't need to worry about writing modes too often, I find these properties most useful for setting padding or margin on an element in two places at once. For example, if my document is flowing from top to bottom, I can set a margin on either side of an element with margin-inline, which I find preferable to setting it with the margin shorthand, where I would need to set top and bottom and left and right each time.

The specification for these properties can be read at https://www.w3.org/TR/css-logical-1/.

Let's change tack now. We've looked at how we can select items in our responsive world. But how about how we size them? We'll look at viewport percentage lengths next.

# Responsive viewport relative lengths

CSS Values and Units Module Level 3 (https://www.w3.org/TR/css3-values/#viewport-relative-lengths) ushered in **viewport relative units**. These are great for responsive web design, as each unit is a percentage length of the viewport:

- The vw unit, where each vw unit is 1% of the viewport width
- The vh unit, where each vh unit is 1% of the viewport height
- The vmin unit (for viewport minimum; equal to the smaller of either vw or vh)
- The vmax (viewport maximum; equal to the larger of either vw or vh)

Want a modal window that's 90% of the browser height? This is, at least in theory, as easy as:

```
.modal {
    height: 90vh;
}
```

Now, as useful as viewport relative units are, some browsers have had curious implementations. Safari in iOS, for example, changes the viewable screen area as you scroll from the top of a page (it shrinks the address bar), but crucially doesn't make any changes to the reported viewport height. So that thing you sized to be 90% of the viewport may no longer be 90% of the viewport once you scroll.

As such, there is now a bunch of related viewport units coming our way: https://www.w3.org/TR/css-values-4/#viewport-variants:

- lvh/lvw, where the lv is for **largest viewport** percentage units. So in our iOS example, imagine the browser in a state where any shrinking UI is out of the way and the viewport is as large as it can be; this is the size that lvh would be a percentage of.
- svh/svw is for **smallest viewport** units. This represents a percentage of the screen on the basis of any UI being at its largest state.
- dvh/dvw is for **dynamic viewport** units. These represent a percentage of what the browser is currently using, possibly between the largest and smallest. For example, if a browser has two states, a largest and smallest, as is the case with iOS Safari currently, this value would choose one or the other. The problem here is two-fold. Firstly, the browser doesn't necessarily animate between the two values as they change, so it may be choppy. And secondly, if the browser does decide to animate that value as its UI sizes change, it may not always be preferable. Imagine setting your font size using that unit and then seeing all the text resize as you scroll. Probably not the best user experience!

However, you can perhaps find more utility for these units when coupled with fonts. For example, it's now trivially easy to create text that scales in size, depending on the viewport.

For example:

```css
.hero-text {
    font-size: 10vw;
}
```

Now, the text will always be sized as a percentage of the viewport width. However, the limit with something like vw units for text, used in isolation, quickly becomes apparent as you use them. Our example size of 10vw would be a large headline size of 32px at a small viewport size of 320px, but a rather over-the-top size of 130px at a larger viewport of 1300px.

We can solve this kind of issue easily with the CSS clamp function. But that's a whole other topic, and you will need to head over to *Chapter 12, Custom Properties and CSS Functions*, to get the low-down on that.

However, for the newer viewport-related units we just looked at and a whole raft of stuff we haven't yet, it can be really handy to be able to **fork** your code for when those things are supported and when they are not. For that we can reach for feature queries. Let's look at how to use those next.

## Using @supports to fork CSS

When you're building out a responsive web design, attempting to provide a single design that works everywhere, on every device, it's a simple fact that you'll frequently encounter situations when features or techniques are not supported on certain devices. It's also a likely scenario with newer selectors, like :has(), which we looked at earlier in the chapter. In these instances, you'll likely want to create a fork in your CSS. If the browser supports a feature, provide one chunk of code; if it doesn't, it gets different code.

This is the kind of situation that gets handled by if/else or switch statements in JavaScript. In CSS, we use the @supports at-rule.

Now, before we dig into feature queries, it is worth pointing out a straightforward way of providing fallbacks for older browsers. Suppose we want to use some of our new viewport-related length units but ensure we have some kind of fallback for older browsers.

Due to the way in which CSS is parsed we can write the older value first, then the newer style one immediately afterward. For example:

```css
.thing {
    padding: 0 10vw;
    padding: 0 10dvw;
}
```

An older browser that understands vw but not dvw will use the first padding-based declaration and discard the second because it can't understand it. A newer browser that does support dvw units will use the first declaration and then immediately replace it with the second as it comes after it.

Nice and simple. However, that is only really useful for minor fallbacks. There will be times when you need a more sophisticated and robust approach.

## Feature queries

The native solution to forking code in CSS is to use **feature queries**, part of the CSS Conditional Rules Module Level 3 (https://www.w3.org/TR/css-conditional-3/). Support was introduced in iOS and Safari 9, Firefox 22, Edge 12, and Chrome 28.

The great news is, feature queries follow a similar syntax to media queries. So, as you understand media queries, the way we use feature queries should seem instantly familiar. Consider this:

```css
@supports (flashing-sausages: lincolnshire) {
    body {
        sausage-sound: sizzling;
        sausage-color: slightly-burnt;
        background-color: brown;
    }
}
```

Here, the styles will only get applied if the browser supports the flashing-sausages property in combination with the lincolnshire value. I'm quite confident that no browser is ever going to support a flashing-sausages: lincolnshire property/value combination (and if they do, I want full credit), so none of the styles inside the @supports block will be applied.

Let's consider a more practical example. How about we use Grid when browsers support it and fall back to another layout technique when they don't? Consider this example:

```css
@supports (display: grid) {
    .Item {
```

```
            display: inline-grid;
        }
    }
    @supports not (display: grid) {
        .Item {
            display: inline-flex;
        }
    }
```

Here, we are defining one block of code for when the browser supports a feature and another lot for when it doesn't. This pattern is fine if the browser supports @supports (yes, I realize that is confusing), but if it doesn't, it won't apply any of those styles.

If you want to make provision for devices that don't support @supports, you're better off writing your default declarations first and then your @supports-specific one after. That way, the prior rule will be overruled if support for @supports exists, and the @supports block will be ignored if the browser doesn't support it. Our prior example could, therefore, be reworked to:

```
    .Item {
        display: inline-flex;
    }
    @supports (display: grid) {
        .Item {
            display: inline-grid;
        }
    }
```

Sorry, that explanation was tough—hopefully you got through it!

## Combining conditionals

You can also combine conditionals. Let's suppose we only wanted to apply some rules if both Flexbox and pointer: coarse were supported (in case you missed it, we covered the pointer interaction media feature back in *Chapter 3, Media Queries and Container Queries*). Here is what that might look like:

```
    @supports ((display: flex) and (pointer: coarse)) {
        .Item {
            display: inline-flex;
        }
    }
```

Here, we have used the and keyword but we can also use or alongside it in a query, or just instead of it; for example, if we were happy to apply styles if those two prior property/value combinations were supported, or if 3D transforms were supported:

```
@supports ((display: flex) and (pointer: coarse)) or
    (transform: translate3d(0, 0, 0)) {
    .Item {
        display: inline-flex;
    }
}
```

Note the extra set of parentheses that separates the display and pointer conditional from the transform conditional.

Finally, with all the newer selectors we have looked at and future ones coming in time, it is worth knowing you can test for those too. This is what a feature query for :where() would look like:

```
@supports selector(:where(div)) {
    /* styles */
}
```

You place the selector you are interested in testing support for into the selector() function.

All the related not-, or-, and and-related keywords work just the same with selector(). This is incredibly handy, as not only can we then fork our code on a specific feature, but we can do it for the more recent selectors introduced to CSS too.

The only other thing to mention is that you can nest other at-rules inside, such as media queries and keyframes.

And that's everything you are likely to need to understand when it comes to feature queries. As with media queries, put your "default" styles first, and then your enhancement inside a feature query @supports at-rule.

It's time to switch gears one final time in this chapter to cover our last major topic: web typography.

# Web typography

Typography on the web has come on tremendously in the last few years. It was once necessary to limit yourself to system fonts. Then, when custom fonts were made viable, a bevy of different file types was required to satisfy all the competing file implementations.

Mercifully, things have now pretty much settled on `.woff` and the newer `.woff2`. In addition, we have more control over the particulars of our fonts in CSS, and new variable fonts, which we will cover momentarily, are popping up on a monthly basis.

If some of that introduction was lost on you, fear not. Let's try to get through the current state of the art in web typography.

First, however, let's talk about system fonts, as they represent the best-performing web typography choice you can opt for.

## System fonts

Each operating system has its own set of fonts that come pre-installed. However, aside from a few exceptions, there aren't many fonts you can rely upon to be installed on every device a user might view your site with. Subsequently, we've grown accustomed to writing font **stacks**, which enable us to write a font "wish list" for the browser. For example:

```
font-family: -apple-system, BlinkMacSystemFont, Roboto, Ubuntu, "Segoe
UI", "Helvetica Neue", Arial, sans-serif;
```

The browser reads this declaration and goes from left to right until it finds a font it has available, choosing that to render the associated text. In our example system font stack here, macOS users will get San Francisco or Helvetica (`-apple-system` tells Safari to pick San Francisco and `BlinkMacSystemFont` tells Chrome to use Helvetica), Android will get Roboto, the popular Ubuntu Linux distribution will get Ubuntu, Windows users will see Segoe UI, and then we have some last-ditch attempts to get something nice with Helvetica Neue or Arial. If all else fails, we tell the browser to use any sans-serif font it has.

 Some font names contain whitespace, so it is necessary to surround those strings with single or double quotes. You can see in our previous example that both `"Segoe UI"` and `"Helvetica Neue"` are written this way.

For a lot of situations, using system fonts is a compelling choice. There is zero network overhead and you'll never have to worry about fonts not loading or seeing unsightly jumps on the page as one font is replaced with another. Although, as we shall learn shortly, there are means to mitigate that.

The tradeoff is that with system fonts, you can never be entirely sure how your text is being rendered on the user's device. If specific typography is crucial to the project at hand, you'll want to look at web fonts with `@font-face`.

# The @font-face CSS rule

The `@font-face` CSS rule has been around since CSS2 (but was subsequently absent in CSS 2.1). It was even supported partially by Internet Explorer 4 (no, really)! So, what's it doing here, when we're supposed to be talking about the latest CSS?

Well, as it turns out, `@font-face` was reintroduced for the CSS Fonts Module (`https://www.w3.org/TR/css-fonts-3/`). Due to the historic legal quagmire of using fonts on the web, it took years to gain traction as the *de facto* solution for web typography.

Like anything on the web that involves assets, in the beginning, there was no single file format for font delivery. The Embedded OpenType (files with an `.eot` extension) font was Internet Explorer's, and not anyone else's, preferred choice. Others favored the more common TrueType (the `.ttf` file extension), while there was also Scalable Vector Graphics (`.svg`) and then the Web Open Font Format (the `.woff` / `.woff2` extension). Thankfully, as of 2022 you really only need to consider **WOFF** (**Web Open Font Format**), although there are two types: WOFF and WOFF2. Where a user can use WOFF2, that will always be preferable, as it is simply a more efficient way of compressing the font information.

# Implementing web fonts with @font-face

There are a number of online font services for getting beautiful typefaces onto the web. Google Fonts and Adobe Fonts are probably the two most popular. They each have their own variation of the required syntax for getting their fonts onto your websites. However, it's not always possible or preferable to use an online font provider. You may be stuck behind a corporate firewall (or state firewall!) that doesn't allow a certain provider, or you may not want the financial overhead or service availability of a third-party provider. Whatever the reason may be, it is worth knowing how to do it for ourselves.

For this exercise, I'm going to use "Inter" by Rasmus Andersson. It's the font used for the majority of the `https://rwd.education` website. Not only that, it's also what's known as a **variable** font.

Before we look at variable fonts, let's look at the kind of web fonts that you will likely spend the majority of your time dealing with. If you grab the Inter font from `https://rsms.me/inter/`, you will have both the standard and variable fonts at your disposal.

If you can, download a **subset** of your font, specific to the language you intend to use. For example, if you are not going to be using Cyrillic or Greek characters, why include them? The resultant file size will be much smaller as it won't contain glyphs for languages you have no intention of using. You can often choose character sets when you are buying a font, but for an open-source version, there are a growing number of services and utilities, such as Glyphhanger (`https://github.com/zachleat/glyphhanger`), that can subset a font for you.

Having downloaded the Inter font, a look inside the ZIP file reveals folders of the different files available. I'm choosing the `Inter-Regular.woff2` and `Inter-Regular.woff` files for our example.

To make a web font available for use in our CSS, we use the `@font-face` at-rule. This lets us provide a name for the font that we can then reference, and also tells the browser where to go to fetch this file from. Let's look at the syntax:

```
@font-face {
    font-family: "InterRegular";
    src: url("Inter-Regular.woff2") format("woff2"),
        url("Inter-Regular.woff") format("woff");
    font-weight: normal;
    font-style: normal;
    font-display: fallback;
}
```

Inside the `@font-face` braces, we give our font the "`InterRegular`" name. I could have called it "`FlyingBanana`" had I wanted; it wouldn't affect anything other than I would then need to reference this font with that name when I wanted to use it. For example:

```
.hero-Image {
    font-family: "FlyingBanana", sans-serif;
}
```

So, know that you can do this, but it makes sense to use a name similar to the font you are expecting to see!

You can then see two successive url() and format() sections within our src property. Each pair of these is separated with a comma. As we noted previously, .woff2 is always our preference, as it is a better-compressed version of the same font, so we list that first. As long as the browser can understand .woff2 and download the file, it will do so. If, however, the browser can't find that file, or can't understand .woff2, it will download the .woff file listed afterward.

Now, although this block of code is great for fans of copy and paste, it's important to pay attention to the paths the fonts are stored in. For example, if we were to place fonts in a folder inventively called fonts on the same level as a css folder, we would need to amend our paths. So, our @font-face block would become:

```
@font-face {
    font-family: "InterRegular";
    src: url("../fonts/Inter-Regular.woff2") format("woff2"),
        url("../fonts/Inter-Regular.woff") format("woff");
    font-weight: normal;
    font-style: normal;
    font-display: fallback;
}
```

## Optimizing font loading with font-display

If your main font is a web font, it's a good idea to request the file upfront by loading it with a link in the head section of your HTML with the rel attribute value as preload. For example:

```
<link
    rel="preload"
    href="fonts/inter.var.woff2"
    as="font"
    type="font/woff2"
    crossorigin
/>
```

 You can read more about this font optimization technique here: https://web.dev/ optimize-webfont-loading/.

Adding a link with rel="preload" included in this way triggers a request for the web font early in the critical rendering path, without having to wait for the **CSS Object Model** (**CSSOM**) to be created. While this technique is recommended by Google, even if other browsers don't do the same, it is unlikely to do any harm. If you are serving up a .woff and .woff2 file, it's only worth doing this optimization for the .woff2 file; browsers that support .woff2 also support the preload value in the rel attribute.

We can make further optimizations with web fonts by making use of the font-display property.

## font-display

We can also make use of the font-display property of CSS (older browsers that don't understand it will simply ignore it):

```
font-display: fallback;
```

You can also see this property being used in the previous examples. It provides some control over how fonts should get displayed.

The fallback value we have provided sets an extremely short **block** period and a short **swap** period.

To understand what terms like "block" and "swap" mean in this context, we need to consider what the browser does in terms of displaying fonts. I'm talking generically here, but the concepts work for our needs.

Imagine a browser loading our web page in which we have specified a web font for our text. The browser already has the HTML and is parsing the CSS, and learns it needs to download a font in order to display the text it has as intended. Before it draws any text to the screen, it hangs on, waiting for the web font so it can paint the text onto the page as needed. This delay is referred to as a **FOIT**, standing for **Flash of Invisible Text**.

As soon as the font arrives, the browser parses it and paints the text to the screen accordingly.

The hope is that this delay is imperceptible. Where it is not, there are two schools of thought on how best to handle things.

One option is to wait for the font to be downloaded, usually for up to a few seconds but sometimes indefinitely; Safari is the most famous proponent of this option.

The second option is to render the text with a system font initially and then replace the font with the correct font when the browser has it. This redraw of text from system font to the actual intended font is known as a **Flash of Unstyled Text**, or **FOUT** for short.

All the font-display setting does is allow us some control over what we would like to see happen.

The possible values are:

- auto: Whatever the browser determines is most appropriate.
- block: Get a white screen for up to 3 seconds (but the delay is ultimately at the browser's discretion) and then the actual font can replace any system displayed font at any future point.
- swap: There is a very short blocking period (100 ms is the recommended amount) to let the web font load; otherwise, a system font shows and the web font can be swapped in whenever it is available.
- fallback: This option prevents a web font from replacing a system font if a set amount of time has passed (3 seconds is the recommendation). This option blocks for around 100 ms initially and allows a swap for up to 3 seconds, but after that, if the web font subsequently arrives, it doesn't get applied.
- optional: Here, the browser allows a very short duration for the web font to load (100 ms) but no swap period. The result of this is that the browser has the option of canceling the font download if it hasn't arrived, or if it has, using it for subsequent page loads.

 You can read the specification on this property here: https://www.w3.org/TR/css-fonts-4/#font-display-desc.

There are plenty of other font-related properties and values specified in the CSS Font Module Level 4 specification, but font-display is currently the widest implemented and has the most direct relevance to responsive web designs and performance.

So far, we have looked at how to get font files into our project and even considered how best to deal with them from a performance point of view.

However, the most recent development in web fonts, and probably the one that has most developers excited, is **variable** fonts. "What new witchery is this?" I hear you cry. Let's find out.

# Variable fonts

As I write this in 2022, variable fonts have gained decent traction. There is a W3C specification and they are supported in the latest browsers. So, what even is a variable font?

A "normal" font contains the information and glyphs for one variation of a typeface; the regular version of Roboto, for example. By comparison, a variable font, in a single file, would contain everything needed for every variation of Roboto. Bold, Italic, Thin, Black, Medium, and more besides!

This new devilry is not without consequence. A variable version of a font is usually considerably larger in file size terms than a "normal" version. However, it can still make sense when you are making heavy use of a single typeface. It also makes an almost limitless variation of a font possible, effectively making a custom version of a font possible.

Caveats aside, let's look at what we can do with a variable font.

## font-face changes

I'm working with the Inter font we used before, but instead using the variable version. First, let's consider how we tell the browser we are working with a variable font in the first place. It's the @font-face syntax again, but with a few changes:

```
@font-face {
    font-family: "Inter-V";
    src: url("fonts/inter.var.woff2") format("woff2-variations");
    font-weight: 100 900;
    font-style: oblique 0deg 10deg;
    font-display: fallback;
}
```

The first thing to note is the format. We are setting this to woff2-variations to tell the browser this is a font file that makes use of variations.

The next thing to keep in mind is that we are using a range for font-weight. The two-word value syntax we are using here is only understood by browsers that understand variable fonts. It is a way of telling the browser the range of weights this font can use. While font-weight has a range limit of 0-999, other properties may have a different range. Others still simply accept a binary value of 1 or 0.

Another thing to remember is that we have font-style, which is also being provided with a multiple-value syntax. The oblique keyword tells the browser the next values relate to how oblique the font can be, and the two values after that define the range. Be aware that although the range here is positive, you can pass in negative values. We will see that in use momentarily.

Finally, note that we have used the `font-display` property here to tell the browser how we want to handle the loading and display of this font, but that is no different than non-variable fonts.

You can look at this completed example at `example_06-07`.

This is all well and good, Ben, but how do we actually, you know, use it? OK, let's dig in.

# How to make use of a variable font

Variable fonts use what's termed a **variation axis**.

A variation axis is just a way of defining two points at either end of a scale. You can then choose any point along the scale to display your font. The scale doesn't need to be vast; in fact, it can be as simple as "on" or "off" (not much of a scale, I know). Variation axes are subdivided into two groups: registered and custom.

## Registered axis

Registered axes are the most popular ones, which the specification writers have made specific provision for:

- **Weight**: How heavy the text appears; for example, `font-weight: 200`.
- **Width**: How narrow (condensed) or wide the text appears; for example, `font-stretch: 110%`.
- **Italic**: Whether the font is being displayed as italic or not; for example, `font-style: italic`.
- **Slant**: Don't confuse this with italic. This simply alters the angle of the text; it doesn't substitute any glyphs. For example, `font-style: oblique 4deg`.
- **Optical size**: This is the only one of the registered axes that has required a new font property. Using `font-optical-sizing` lets you alter, yes, you guessed it, the optical sizing. But what is that? It's the practice of altering a glyph based upon the size it is displayed at to aid clarity. This means the same glyph displayed at a large size might enjoy thinner stems, for example.

The values you choose to use with these properties should fall within the capabilities of the variable font you are using. For example, there isn't much point in specifying a font weight of 999 if the font you are using can only go up to 600.

There is also a low-level property that lets you bundle up your variable font settings into a single property/value combination:

```
font-variation-settings: "wght" 300, "slnt" -4;
```

Here, we have set the font weight to 300 and the angle of the slant to -4. However, the specification offers the following cautionary advice:

> *When possible, authors should generally use the other properties related to font variations (such as font-optical-sizing), and only use this property for special cases where its use is the only way of accessing a particular infrequently used font variation. For example, it is preferable to use font-weight: 700 rather than font-variation-settings: "wght" 700.*

I'm not sure why this advice is given. The specification doesn't explain the rationale. Hopefully, this detail will be added when the specification is complete. You can find the current version here: `https://www.w3.org/TR/css-fonts-4/`.

 Font variation properties can be animated and transitioned, which can make for some fantastic effects!

Having covered the registered axis group, let's briefly take a look at the custom axis group.

## Custom axis

Variable fonts can include their *own* axis. For example, the FS Pimlico Glow VF font has a "glow" axis. You can amend that like this:

```
font-variation-settings: "GLOW" 500;
```

Notice how this custom axis is written in uppercase; that is, `"GLOW"`? That's how to determine the difference between a registered and custom axis in variable font settings.

If your head isn't already hurting from the seemingly endless possibilities, I also need to tell you about font features, which are sort of similar to the two different axes we just looked at. Don't worry; it will make sense shortly.

## Font features

Variable fonts can also include their own **features**. These features can be literally anything the font designer decides to dream up! Take a look at the choices for Inter:

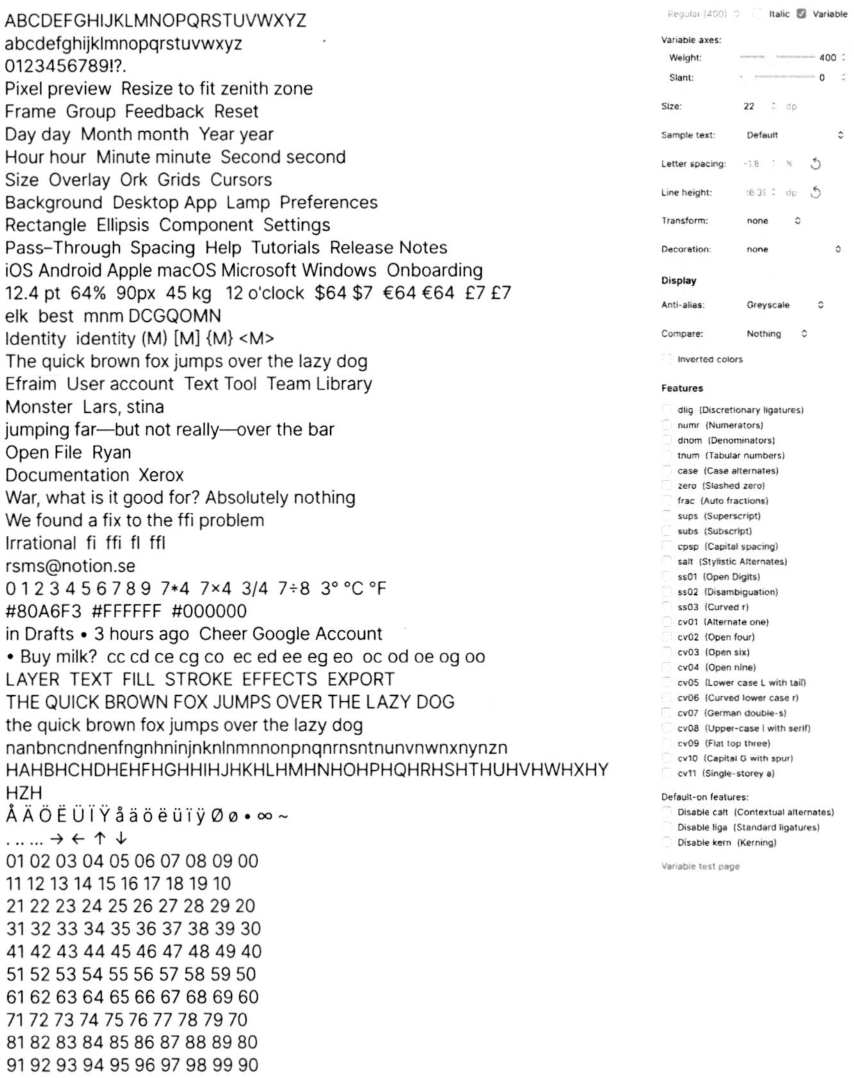
ABCDEFGHIJKLMNOPQRSTUVWXYZ
abcdefghijklmnopqrstuvwxyz
0123456789!?.
Pixel preview Resize to fit zenith zone
Frame Group Feedback Reset
Day day Month month Year year
Hour hour Minute minute Second second
Size Overlay Ork Grids Cursors
Background Desktop App Lamp Preferences
Rectangle Ellipsis Component Settings
Pass-Through Spacing Help Tutorials Release Notes
iOS Android Apple macOS Microsoft Windows Onboarding
12.4 pt 64% 90px 45 kg 12 o'clock $64 $7 €64 €64 £7 £7
elk best mnm DCGQOMN
Identity identity (M) [M] {M} <M>
The quick brown fox jumps over the lazy dog
Efraim User account Text Tool Team Library
Monster Lars, stina
jumping far—but not really—over the bar
Open File Ryan
Documentation Xerox
War, what is it good for? Absolutely nothing
We found a fix to the ffi problem
Irrational fi ffi fl ffl
rsms@notion.se
0 1 2 3 4 5 6 7 8 9 7*4 7×4 3/4 7÷8 3° °C °F
#80A6F3 #FFFFFF #000000
in Drafts • 3 hours ago Cheer Google Account
• Buy milk? cc cd ce cg co ec ed ee eg eo oc od oe og oo
LAYER TEXT FILL STROKE EFFECTS EXPORT
THE QUICK BROWN FOX JUMPS OVER THE LAZY DOG
the quick brown fox jumps over the lazy dog
nanbncndnenfngnhninjnknlnmnnonpnqnrnsntnunvnwnxnynzn
HAHBHCHDHEHFHGHHIHJHKHLHMHNHOHPHQHRHSHTHUHVHWHXHY
HZH
ÅÄÖËÜÏŸåäöëüïÿØø•∞~
. .. ... → ← ↑ ↓
01 02 03 04 05 06 07 08 09 00
11 12 13 14 15 16 17 18 19 10
21 22 23 24 25 26 27 28 29 20
31 32 33 34 35 36 37 38 39 30
41 42 43 44 45 46 47 48 49 40
51 52 53 54 55 56 57 58 59 50
61 62 63 64 65 66 67 68 69 60
71 72 73 74 75 76 77 78 79 70
81 82 83 84 85 86 87 88 89 80
91 92 93 94 95 96 97 98 99 90
Italic Variable
Variable axes:
Weight: 400
Slant: 0
Size: 22
Sample text: Default
Letter spacing:
Line height:
Transform: none
Decoration: none
Display
Anti-alias: Greyscale
Compare: Nothing
Inverted colors
Features
dlig (Discretionary ligatures)
numr (Numerators)
dnom (Denominators)
tnum (Tabular numbers)
case (Case alternates)
zero (Slashed zero)
frac (Auto fractions)
sups (Superscript)
subs (Subscript)
cpsp (Capital spacing)
salt (Stylistic Alternates)
ss01 (Open Digits)
ss02 (Disambiguation)
ss03 (Curved r)
cv01 (Alternate one)
cv02 (Open four)
cv03 (Open six)
cv04 (Open nine)
cv05 (Lower case L with tail)
cv06 (Curved lower case r)
cv07 (German double-s)
cv08 (Upper-case i with serif)
cv09 (Flat top three)
cv10 (Capital G with spur)
cv11 (Single-storey a)
Default-on features:
Disable calt (Contextual alternates)
Disable liga (Standard ligatures)
Disable kern (Kerning)
Variable test page

*Figure 6.10: On the right of the Inter settings page are the enormous possibilities for the font*

All of those "features" are settings that can be turned on with CSS. You can play about with these settings yourself here: `https://rsms.me/inter/lab/?antialias=default`.

When we want to apply these custom features, we make use of the `font-feature-settings` property. This works very similarly to the `font-variation-settings` syntax. For example, to switch on "slashed zeroes," we can do this:

```
font-feature-settings: "zero";
```

This "slashed zeroes" option is a binary choice, so it is not necessary to write "zero" 1. However, if we wanted to toggle this setting off further into our styles, we could write:

```
font-feature-settings: "zero" 0;
```

When you want to apply multiple `font-feature-settings`, you can comma-separate them. So, if we wanted to have "lowercase L with tail" and "uppercase i with serif," we could write this:

```
font-feature-settings: "cv08", "cv05";
```

These are the options switched on in the completed `example_06-07`.

 When looking at the chapter code, don't concern yourself with any additional syntax that doesn't make sense. There are CSS custom properties used, for example, and we will cover those fully in *Chapter 12, Custom Properties and CSS Functions*.

There is plenty more in the way of settings and features specified in CSS Fonts Module Level 4. We have just scratched the surface! To dig in further, take a look at the specification: `https://www.w3.org/TR/css-fonts-4/`.

## Exercise

Have a look at the CSS from our example page:

```
:root {
    --MainFont: "Helvetica Neue", Helvetica, Arial, sans-serif;
}

@font-face {
    font-family: "Inter-V";
    src: url("fonts/inter.var.woff2") format("woff2-variations");
    font-weight: 100 900;
    font-display: fallback;
    font-style: oblique 0deg 10deg;
}
```

```css
body {
    background-color: var(--background);
    color: var(--foreground);
    transition: all 0.35s;
    font-size: 1.2em;
    font-family: "sans-serif";
    font-family: var(--MainFont);
    font-weight: 400;
}

@supports (font-variation-settings: "wdth" 200) {

    body {
        font-family: "Inter-V";
        font-variation-settings: "wght" 300, "slnt" -4;
        font-feature-settings: "cv08", "cv05";
    }
}
```

How much of that can you now understand? We have a system font stack, an @font-face rule loading a variable font (complete with ranges defined for weight and slant), and a sans-serif as the default font-family—which we then immediately overwrite with a font-family defined with a CSS custom property for browsers that understand it. Finally, we use a feature query for variable fonts and define settings for it, also adding in some additional font features we'd like to see.

These are all approaches and techniques that we have covered in this chapter. If you can look at that and have a decent understanding of what is going on, you have done well. There's a lot in there to parse!

# Summary

In this chapter, we've learned how to select almost anything we need on the page with CSS's powerful selection capabilities.

We've also learned how to add custom web typography to a design with the `@font-face` rule, freeing us from the shackles of the humdrum selection of web-safe fonts of yesteryear. We also took a dive into variable fonts and considered many of the possibilities they have to offer.

Alongside all that, we also found time to look at the `@supports` at-rule for providing feature forks in our code.

Despite all these great new features and techniques, we've still only touched the surface of what we can do with CSS.

In the next chapter, we are going to take an extended look at colors in CSS. Recent additions to the specifications mean it's now a bigger topic than ever before. So, let's find out all about that in *Chapter 7, CSS Color*.

# Join our book's Discord space

Variable fonts getting you down? Join the book's Discord workspace to discuss all your responsive web design concerns directly with the author and interact with other readers:

https://packt.link/RWD4e

# 7

# CSS Color

Color is one area of CSS that has enjoyed significant enhancements in the last few years. Previously, if you had an understanding of how to write hex, rgb(), and hsl(), that was all the color knowledge required. Nowadays, you need to understand a whole slew of different formats, alongside color functions to manipulate those formats, to consider yourself "up to speed."

The fine detail of color in CSS is not something you are likely to wrestle with in day-to-day responsive design work. Ordinarily, we take it for granted and paste in the colors from a design file with little thought. However, when you do need to manipulate, or convert, colors, or if you get asked to implement a color in P3, I don't want you looking embarrassed because I didn't explain these concepts to you. So, to repeat advice I have given elsewhere in the book, consider the possibilities presented here but don't worry about remembering the syntax. That's what this chapter is for: to give you some guidance on that fateful day you do need to implement something more involved with color.

Color theory is a dense and notoriously difficult subject. Not just conceptually but mathematically too. As such, we will concentrate almost entirely on the practical side of working with color in CSS. My aim here is to provide conceptual clarity, not necessarily pin-point mathematical accuracy.

With that point made, let's look at what we will be covering in this chapter:

- RGB with hex notation
- RGB transparency with hex notation
- RGB functional notation
- HSL functional notation

- Space-separated functional color notation
- P3 color gamut
- The `@media (color-gamut: )` rule
- The `color()` function
- Lab and LCH
- How to write fallbacks for older browsers
- Relative color syntax
- The `color-mix()` function
- The `color-contrast()` function

To begin our journey through the topic, we will start with a refresher on the basics of working with color in CSS before moving on to the newer color features and formats.

So, let's start with something you will likely already have a solid grasp on: RGB.

# RGB color

**RGB** (**Red**, **Green**, and **Blue**), like many of the formats we will look at, is a coloring system that's been around for decades. It works by defining different values for the red, green, and blue components of a color. For example, a red color might be defined in CSS as a hex (hexadecimal) value, `#fe0208`:

```
.redness {
    color: #fe0208;
}
```

The first two digits are the red value in hexadecimal, the next two are the green, and the last two are the blue.

 For a great post describing how to understand hex values more intuitively, I can recommend this blog post at Smashing Magazine: `https://www.smashingmagazine.com/2012/10/the-code-side-of-color/`.

However, with CSS, that same color can equally be described with an RGB functional notation, where each value can be specified in a range from 0 to 255:

```
.redness {
    color: rgb(254, 2, 8);
}
```

Hex and RGB values are the kinds of values you will be used to seeing in graphics applications.

# HSL color

Besides RGB, CSS also allows us to declare color values as **Hue**, **Saturation**, and **Lightness** (HSL).

HSL isn't the same as HSB! Don't make the mistake of thinking that the **Hue**, **Saturation**, and **Brightness (HSB)** value shown in the color picker of image editing applications such as Photoshop is the same as HSL—it isn't!

What makes HSL comparatively intuitive to use is that it's relatively simple to understand the color that will be represented, based on the values given. For example, unless you're some sort of color-picking ninja, I'd wager you couldn't instantly tell me what color rgb(255, 51, 204) is. Any takers? No, me neither.

However, show me the HSL value of hsl(315, 100%, 60%) and I could take a guess that it is somewhere between a magenta and a red color (it's actually a festive pink color). How do I know this? Simple: "Young Guys Can Be Messy Rascals!" This mnemonic will help you to remember the order of colors in an HSL color wheel, as you'll see shortly. HSL works on a 360° color wheel. It looks like this:

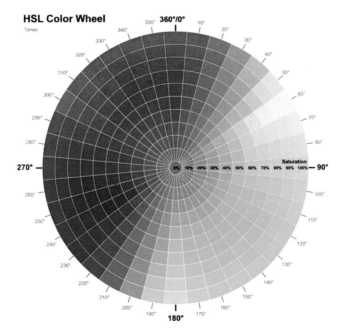

*Figure 7.1: An HSL color wheel created with SVG (*https://codepen.io/websanity/pen/
QWNMRq*)*

The first figure in an HSL color definition represents **hue**. Looking at our wheel, we can see that yellow is at 60°, green is at 120°, cyan is at 180°, blue is at 240°, magenta is at 300°, and finally, red is at 360°. So, as the aforementioned HSL color had a hue of 315, it's easy to know that it will be between magenta (at 300°) and red (at 360°).

The next two values in an HSL definition are for **saturation** and **lightness**, specified as percentages. These merely alter the base hue. For a more saturated or "colorful" appearance, use a higher percentage in the second value. The final value, controlling the lightness, can vary between 0% for black and 100% for white. So, once you've defined a color as an HSL value, it's also easy to create variations of it, merely by altering the saturation and lightness percentages. For example, the same red color we defined in the *RGB color* section can also be defined in HSL values as follows:

```
.redness {
    color: hsl(359, 99%, 50%);
}
```

If we wanted to make a slightly darker color, we could use the same HSL value and merely alter the lightness (the final value) percentage value only:

```
.darker-red {
    color: hsl(359, 99%, 40%);
}
```

In conclusion, if you can remember the mnemonic "Young Guys Can Be Messy Rascals" (or any other mnemonic you care to memorize) for the HSL color wheel, you'll be able to approximately write HSL color values without resorting to a color picker, and also create variations upon it. Show that trick to the savant Ruby, Node.js, and .NET developers at the office party and earn some quick kudos!

## Alpha channels

It won't be long when working with designs on the web before you will be asked if the color of something can be partially transparent to allow some of what's beneath to show through. For that need, with hex, RGB, and HSL, it is possible to define an alpha channel.

## Alpha with hex

With hex, you can define an alpha channel with a four-digit or eight-digit syntax. Here is black with a 50% alpha channel written first as a four-digit hex code:

```
background-color: #0007;
```

And then the same color as an eight-digit hex code:

```
background-color: #00000077;
```

Two things to keep in mind with hex and transparency. Firstly, as the name tells you, it uses a hexadecimal numbering system, where 0-9 are handled with numbers, and 11 to 16 are handled with the "a" to "f" characters. So, if you imagine those characters out in a line:

```
0123456789abcdef
```

You can see that halfway along is the 7 character, which gives us 50% alpha.

The second thing to remember is that the four-digit hex doubles up each value. That's important if you want granularity because you can be more precise with two different digits for each color channel, which means in those scenarios you will want to use the eight-digit variant.

 It used to be necessary to define RGB or HSL colors with an alpha channel using the functional `rgba()` or `hsla()` formats (note the appended a for alpha). However, that's no longer needed unless you need to support a very old browser.

## Alpha with functional notation

Using the functional notation, you can define an alpha channel like this with HSL:

```
.redness-alpha {
    color: hsl(359, 99%, 50%, 0.5);
}
```

Or by using a percentage if you like:

```
.redness-alpha {
    color: hsl(359, 99%, 50%, 50%);
}
```

The RGB syntax follows the same convention as the HSL equivalent:

```
.redness-alpha-rgba {
    color: rgb(254, 2, 8, 0.8);
}
```

The alpha is always represented with either a percentage or a numeric value between 0 and 1.

You may be wondering—why not just use opacity, as CSS allows elements to have opacity set with the `opacity` declaration? When we apply opacity to an element, a value is set between zero and one in decimal increments (for example, opacity set to `0.1` is 10%). However, opacity differs from an alpha channel. Setting an opacity value on an element affects the *entire* element, whereas setting a value by using an alpha channel allows particular *parts* of an element to have an alpha layer. For example, an element could have an alpha value for the background color but a solid color for the text within it.

OK, that brings us to the beginning of the newer CSS color capabilities.

In the last code snippet, we defined an RGB color with an alpha channel using this kind of syntax:

```
.redness-alpha-rgb {
    color:  rgb(254, 2, 8, 0.8);
}
```

However, we can now write things space-separated instead.

## Space-separated functional color notation

Unless you need to support old browsers, you can, and probably should, write colors using the newer **space-separated** syntax. That doesn't get you anything extra for the sRGB-based notations we have already looked at, but as the newer color formats, which we will look at momentarily, also use the space-separated syntax, you may as well just use the same style for all.

So, space-separate the color values, and then if you need an alpha channel, add a forward slash (/) before adding the alpha as either a decimal value or a percentage.

For example:

```
.redness-alpha-rgba {
    color: rgb(254 2 8 / 0.8);
}
```

Or, if you prefer percentages:

```
.redness-alpha-rgba {
    color: rgb(254 2 8 / 80%);
}
```

So, now you know the syntax we will be using for all the new color formats, let's cover some groundwork before taking an in-depth look.

# Color concepts and terminology

With the formats we have looked at so far, it has not been necessary to burden you with too much color background to make practical use of the techniques and syntax we have been using. As we look at the newer formats, syntaxes, and capabilities, we likely need to extend our "palette" (pun intended) of information in order to make better sense of it all.

Therefore, before we get into things proper, it would serve us well to define a couple of terms we will be using throughout the remainder of the chapter.

## Color space

Different color spaces exist to describe varying amounts of color. In the print world, most are familiar with **CMYK** color space, where Cyan, Magenta, Yellow, and Black are mixed to create the colors you wish to see printed. With correctly calibrated equipment, the color you see on screen is the color you will see printed. For us workers in the web world, **sRGB**, the standard color space on the web, is the color space that we are most familiar with (created by HP and Microsoft in 1996 for computer monitors). It is a system that lets us specify colors as varying amounts of Red, Green, and Blue.

From a technical perspective, a color space is a mathematical representation of colors. It is a way of plotting, as numbers, using varying parameters, all the possible colors that a given color space can represent.

As we will see momentarily, CSS now lets us define colors in different color spaces too.

## Gamut

For our purposes, when we talk about **gamut**, we are typically talking about the range of possible colors that a device can display. A modern display can display more colors than the displays of yesteryear. The following image shows the comparative gamuts of a few color spaces.

Notice that the two we are primarily interested in for this chapter, sRGB and P3, are far smaller than others.

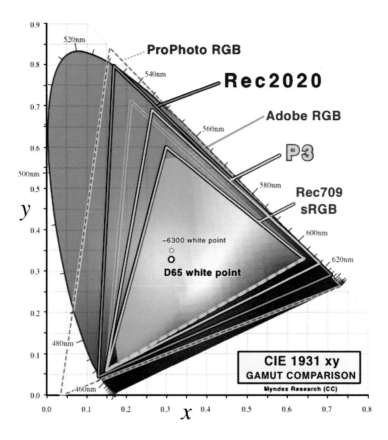

*Figure 7.2: This image from Wikipedia (source: https://en.wikipedia.org/wiki/ DCI-P3) shows how little sRGB represents when compared with P3 and other color spaces*

All you need to appreciate for the understanding of this chapter is that there are many devices these days that are capable of displaying colors that our trusty RGB notations cannot express.

Larger gamuts are becoming more and more of a selling point with hardware. To exemplify, here is the paragraph from Dell's technical specifications describing the colors of the monitor I am looking at:

*See true-to-life color with an incredible color depth of 1.07 billion colors and wide color coverage across industry standards, including 100% sRGB, 100% Rec. 709 and 98% DCI-P3. DCI-P3 (which offers nearly 25% more coverage than sRGB), enables a wider range of colors and is quickly becoming the color standard for creating and viewing content.*

"Wide color coverage" and "wide-gamut" are the kinds of phrases that would indicate you are looking at a screen that can deal with colors (somewhere between 25% and 50% more) you may never have yet seen it display. Probably not with CSS, anyway. Well, we will address that shortly!

If you want to go deeper into this color theory, I recommend the following post on the WebKit blog from 2016 that I keep coming back to time and again: `https://webkit.org/blog/6682/improving-color-on-the-web/`. Don't let the comparatively old date put you off; much of the color work we do these days was figured out in the 1940s and 1950s!

Now we have considered the notion of color space as a mathematical expression of color, and gamut as the range of possible colors a device can display, I think we are finally ready to look at what's new, or imminent, with CSS color.

## The current state of CSS color

As I write this book in 2022, here is the briefest summary this author can manage of the state of CSS color:

- All monitors and browsers can display sRGB colors, and there are various syntaxes to describe them in CSS; hex (for example, `#000`), `rgb(0,0,0)`, `hsl(0 0% 0%)`.
- There are also colors that many modern monitors can display but not all browsers currently support. This category of colors is typically dealt with in CSS with the `color()` function to pass a custom color space (typically `display-P3`) to CSS, or using LCH/Lab.
- Finally, there is a category of colors that humans can see, yet few (if any?) monitors can display. CSS can now also describe such colors with LCH/Lab.
- Right now, in 2022, only the Safari browser supports `lch()`, `lab()`, and `color()`.

## Introductory note

As we work through all these formats, be aware that there is no real "best" color format. They are all useful for certain applications. For example, I tend to use tried and tested hex values the majority of the time; they are the values that designers almost always supply me with and there is no value in converting them to another format. I tend to make use of one of the newer formats when I need to realize a certain style of gradient, for example, or use a color that simply can't be expressed with a hex or rgb(). Hopefully, the notion that there is no "best" format, only a "best format for this job," will become obvious as we work through the chapter.

As we are concentrating on the practicalities of color in CSS, you should be aware there are other color **formats** or syntaxes that may be useful for a specific use case but that we don't cover here. HWB, for example, can also describe sRGB colors and uses a Hue, Whiteness, Blackness syntax. I have never found a need to use HWB, but that doesn't mean you won't! More on HWB here: https://www.w3.org/TR/css-color-4/#the-hwb-notation.

Right, let's get on and show you those colors you have never seen on your screen before.

## Display-P3

P3 is a superset of sRGB and makes up to 50% more colors possible. It's the vivid end of the red, green, and blue colors that benefit the most, particularly the green.

Before I get you too excited, a couple of caveats. Firstly, you will need a browser that supports P3; I'm using Safari 15.4. You'll also need to be using a modern enough screen to see these colors, or this is going to be a letdown on a par with the end of the *Game of Thrones* TV series.

It is also almost redundant to point out that the images in this book will also be unable to convey the colors accurately. You will either have to trust me, or get that browser open and see for yourself.

OK, open example_07-01 and inspect the page with your development tools (in Safari, I'm doing **Develop > Show Web Inspector**). Select the first color "swatch" and open the color picker up for the background-color. What do you notice?

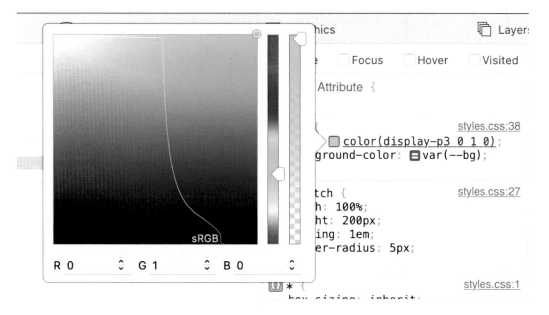

*Figure 7.3: The Safari color picker shows where sRGB ends and P3 takes over*

In Safari, in the color picker tool, I see a representation of the standard sRGB range of colors, but the color we have defined is beyond the sRGB confines we are used to seeing and into the area that only the display-p3 color space can display. I hope your retinas are just a little shocked at the vividness on show!

Because it is a color space we are using, as opposed to a different color model, we use the color() function to pass this predefined color space in, and then set the red, green, and blue values. So, if we want the greenest green that P3 has to offer, we can set it in CSS like this:

```
background-color: color(display-p3 0 1 0);
```

It differs only in that rather than using 0-255 to set each color channel, it uses a decimal between 0 and 1, where 0 is none of that channel and 1 is all of it.

If you don't have access to a browser or hardware that can display this color space, then the following post, also on the WebKit blog, offers some good examples, with comparison pictures of sRGB and P3: https://webkit.org/blog/10042/wide-gamut-color-in-css-with-display-p3/.

Our prior example looks like this in code:

```
color(display-p3 0.135 1 0);
```

Browsers that support P3 should have a color picker capable of playing with it, so you can see as you play with the colors how the values express the different amounts of red, green, and blue. Try another color that plays to the strengths of P3:

```
color(display-p3 0 1 1);
```

That will get you a very vivid cyan color. P3 is great for these kinds of bright colors, and simple to work with, with just a basic understanding of red, green, and blue.

 Browsers that do support wider gamuts like display-p3 can also display images that have a relevant color profile attached. An oft-overlooked fact.

## @media (color-gamut) media query

Although we dealt with media queries in great detail in *Chapter 3*, *Media Queries and Container Queries*, there is one media query better dealt with here. That is the color-gamut media query, which lets us test for the support of certain colors on the host device.

Here is the syntax. In this instance, we are checking for whether a device is capable of supporting the rec2020 gamut, a gamut that includes P3 and more. There is no relevance here other than for illustration:

```
@media (color-gamut: rec2020) {
    .thing {
        color: color(display-p3 0 1 1);
    }
}
```

I don't imagine this is a feature most developers will find themselves needing regularly, if at all, but it is mentioned here just in case.

## LCH with the lch() function

Even the larger gamut of P3 is nowhere near the limits of human visual perception. However, we now have a format in CSS capable of doing that. Lab/LCH are designed to be able to express all of human vision, even if currently our monitors are not capable of it.

LCH is an abbreviation of **Lightness, Chroma, Hue**. It is the same color space as Lab, but using polar coordinates.

 If you aren't familiar with the term **polar coordinates**, it's a way to describe how far something is from a reference point. Imagine looking down on a color wheel that shows all the possible colors of a color space. The center of that wheel is the pole, our reference point. You can describe where one color is in relation to the reference point by giving a direction/angle and a distance along the axis of that angle. That is the essence of how polar coordinates work in CSS color and mathematics.

The syntax is Lightness as a percentage, then two numerical values: one for the Chroma, and the third value for the Hue angle. So, here is an example of a very bright red:

```
background-color: lch(50% 132 43);
```

Like the other functional color notations, you can add a forward slash (/) and then add an alpha channel as a value between 0 and 1 or a percentage.

Arguably one of the more important things to take from LCH/Lab is that the Lightness is designed to look the same across different colors, something that the lightness of HSL does not do. So you should be able to define two different colors with the same lightness in lch() and they should appear to have the same perceptual lightness.

If you compare swatch 3, "hsl() same lightness", and swatch 4, "lch() same lightness", in the example file, hopefully you can appreciate that the lightness of the two colors in the LCH example are more similar than the lightness of the two HSL colors.

*Figure 7.4: Comparison of two colors in HSL (top) and LCH (bottom) that should have the same lightness*

Practically, when working with LCH, lower the lightness value for a darker variant of a color, and increase it for a lighter one.

There are some points to be aware of when using `lch()`. Firstly, you may, as I did, incorrectly assume that as it uses a wheel for the hue then, like HSL, the wheel would be the same one as for HSL. It isn't!

Consider our swatch with the gradient defined with one side as `lch()` and then those values mapped to what you might think would be the equivalent positions in the `hsl()` section (this is swatch 8 in `example_07-01` for the chapter):

```
.lch-hsl {
    background: linear-gradient(
        to right,
        lch(50% 150 45) 50%,
        hsl(45 100% 50%) 0
    );
}
```

Here is what that looks like:

*Figure 7.5: Setting lch and hsl to what you think should be the same color does not produce the same color!*

Hmmmm, nothing is ever easy when it comes to color conversion, I am afraid! Those two look nothing like one another. We would need to remember our earlier HSL mnemonic and move our HSL hue to 0 to make it similar to the position of red in the wheel used by LCH.

 If you are wondering why the gradient defined gives us a hard stop, we cover that in the next chapter, *Stunning Aesthetics with CSS*.

I found the Chroma part of the `lch()` syntax hard to conceptualize initially, as the maximum value of color intensity not only differs between colors and screen gamut, but it is also theoretically limitless. Luckily, an out-of-range value gets normalized in the browser, so if you are after an intense color, just use a high value (say, 150) and the browser will set it accordingly. Whenever I set a value for the Chroma like that, it reminds me of Spinal Tap's "These go to 11!" (kids, ask your parents, or I'll let you search on YouTube for it if you promise to come right back).

For more mathematical clarity on Lab and LCH, head over to `https://www.w3.org/TR/css-color-4/#lab-colors`.

## OKLab and OKLCH

Smart color people recognized shortcomings with Lab and LCH. In late 2020, Bjorn Ottosson introduced us to OKLab, humorlessly titled as such because it is an "OK Lab color space"! You can read all about the background and rationale in this blog post: `https://bottosson.github.io/posts/oklab/`.

Despite its relative newness, it has already made its way into the CSS Color Module Level 4 specification and gets its own polar form `oklch()` and `oklab` functional notations: `https://www.w3.org/TR/css-color-4/#ok-lab`.

In CSS usage, it seems that most people will find it useful for "better" and smoother gradients.

The specification notes that:

> *It was produced by numerical optimisation of a large dataset of visually similar colors, and has improved hue linearity, hue uniformity, and chroma uniformity compared to CIE LCH.*

From my brief experimentation with LCH versus OKLab gradients, I couldn't see an awful lot of difference. Swatches 6 and 7 in the example file show two gradients, the first done with `lch()` and the next with `oklab()`, both using comparable colors from the specification examples. To my eyes, on my screen, I couldn't really see much difference. Your mileage may vary!

## Fallbacks for older browsers

There is a nice, simple way of providing a fallback for older browsers; simply write the standard format first, and then the newer syntax straight after.

So if we wanted that "super green" P3 green but know that we have a nice P3 version for browsers and hardware that don't support P3 (note I'm also using the older syntax with commas for the sake of even older browsers):

```
background-color: rgb(0, 255, 0);
background-color: color(display-p3 0 1 0);
```

Doesn't get much easier than that. Of course, we could also use @supports, which we looked at in detail in the last chapter, *CSS Selectors, Typography, and More*:

```
@supports (color(dispay-p3 0 1 0)) {
    background-color: color(display-p3 0 1 0);
}
```

At first glance, the @supports version may seem more verbose. It is, until you start passing color values around as custom properties instead.

We cover custom properties fully in *Chapter 12, Custom Properties and CSS Functions*, but for now, all you need to understand is in this instance, we are using a custom property as a means of storing a value that we can reuse in multiple places.

We would set up a color to reuse like this:

```
:root {
    --col-accent: rgb(0 255 0);
}
@supports (color: color(display-p3 0 1 0)) {
    :root {
        --col-accent: color(display-p3 0 1 0);
    }
}
```

And then, whenever we wanted to use that color, we only have to write:

```
.thing {
    color: var(--col-accent);
}
```

The user would then get either the rgb() version or the display-p3 version, depending on their system. With it set as a custom property, we can reuse it as many times as we like in that manner and know that each user will get the right syntax for their environment.

## The color-mix() function

This is another very new function for color, so much so that I have had to enable experimental features in one of the only browsers that has an implementation currently – Safari. As ever, check support for features at caniuse.com (https://caniuse.com/?search=color-mix()).

Consider swatch 10 in our example. You should see a color that is like a mix between gold and orange, because that is exactly what it is!

Here, we are using the `color-mix()` function to mix gold and orange:

```
.mix {
    background-color: color-mix(in lch, gold 50%, orange);
}
```

The `color-mix()` function lets you specify a color space to mix in, and then two colors to mix in that color space. It's like kindergarten for web developers!

Here are the essentials to understand. You pass a percentage after the first color (and you can use any of the color notations we have looked at in this chapter) and that is the amount of that color passed into the "mixer." The percentage left is given to the second color.

It's very early days for `color-mix` and, as such, we won't spend much time with it here. However, I hope you agree it's an interesting addition to our color capabilities that is sure to make interesting things possible in the years to come.

You can read the specification for `color-mix()` here: `https://www.w3.org/TR/css-color-5/#color-mix`. It also gives in-depth detail on how the gamuts are mapped when values are passed in that the mixing color space cannot deal with, and lots more.

# The color-contrast() function

As interesting as the `color-mix()` function is, it's not something I can think of immediate use cases for.

However, the `color-contrast()` function is different. The `color-contrast()` function lets you specify a color, then at least another two colors, to effectively compete for the title of "Most Contrasting Color." That's not a real thing by the way, but it does mean a huge difference to day-to-day life as a developer trying to ensure you create suitably contrasting sites for accessibility. Let's take a look at some examples.

This first example of `color-contrast` is the 11th swatch in our example file:

```
.header-text {
    background-color: #333;
    color: color-contrast(#333 vs #666, #545454, #777, #f90);
}
```

In this example, we set the background to a dark gray (#333) to test the contrast against. Then we use the vs keyword to separate the colors that are going to be tested as the color with the highest contrast against that first color. Note that currently, in the experimental version of the syntax, you need a comma after each extra color you want to test against.

OK, take a look at those colors and place your bets. The winner is…

The orange with the hex code of #f90.

Picking the most contrasting color from a list is impressive in itself, but even more useful is being able to specify the *target* contrast. So, if you are trying to achieve AA WCAG accessibility compliance, you can pass a target contrast ratio like this:

```
.header-text {
    background-color: #333;
    color: color-contrast(#333 vs #666, #545454, #777, #f90 to 4.5);
}
```

After the colors, we use the to keyword and then a contrast. We can also pass a contrast like this:

```
.header-text {
    background-color: #333;
    color: color-contrast(#333 vs #666, #545454, #777, #f90 to AA);
}
```

The AA here means a contrast ratio of 4.5:1, which is the ratio required for AA WCAG accessibility with text contrast. Remember we covered accessibility a little more in *Chapter 2, Writing HTML Markup*.

 **Fair warning**: As I write this chapter, there is no implementation that currently supports the to keyword and passing a contrast of AA or AAA; instead, it only supports the number value.

What is especially useful about the to keyword is it gets the first in the list to meet or exceed that contrast. If you look at swatch 12, it is the same as swatch 11, except the contrast is set to 2.5. That's obviously far less than anyone would sensibly want, but it should demonstrate the point:

```
.header-text {
    background-color: #333;
    color: color-contrast(#333 vs #666, #545454, #777, #f90 to 2.5);
}
```

In this case, the color-contrast function returns #777, which is the first color from the list that meets or exceeds the target contrast.

I'm sure you can see the usefulness of this function, especially in situations where you want to use a bunch of pre-defined brand colors while still addressing accessibility concerns. I hope this gets broad browser implementation soon.

# Relative colors with the relative color syntax

One other new feature of the CSS Color Module Level 5 specification that is worth a little exploration is the relative color syntax. This lets you amend a color by kind of deconstructing it. At this point, an example may be more useful. Consider swatch 13 in our example file, which is set with this CSS:

```
.relative {
    --bg: #f90;
    background-color: hsl(from var(--bg) h s calc(l + 10%));
}
```

So, here we have a custom property set to a hex value (#f90). Then, with our hsl() color function notation, we use the from keyword to "pick" where we are generating our relative color from. In this case, it is the hex in the line above, but it could be any color set in any of the notations that CSS allows. Then, we can use the letters of the color type, in this case h, s, and l, to get the component parts of the origin color into our current format and then tweak it. In this instance, I have used the calc() function to brighten the color by 10%. Remember that in HSL, lightness is always a percentage.

Let's look at one more. This is swatch 14:

```
.relative-rgb {
    --bg: hsl(0 100% 50%);
    background-color: rgb(from var(--bg) r 100 b / 80%);
}
```

Here, we take a color defined in our custom property in HSL, then tweak the green value to be 100 and add an 80% alpha layer.

Like the other functions, color-contrast and color-mix, this doesn't have broad support, but is sure to allow plenty of creative expression in the years to come. From a purely practical perspective, it will allow you to manipulate all the colors of a code base in the same way, regardless of whether the authoring format was hex, rgb(), hsl(), or any of the other notations we have considered.

# Summary

In CSS terms, color capability is advancing rapidly. We have looked at the basics of setting colors and alpha layers in CSS using hex and functional notation. We have also considered how to make use of wider gamuts such as P3 and how to provide fallbacks in a couple of ways for older devices.

Later, we looked at the cutting-edge features of color which are just gaining browser support. We have looked at mixing colors with `color-mix()`, creating a color relative to another with the relative color syntax, and, perhaps most usefully, how we can ensure contrasting colors, and gaining better accessibility with the use of the `color-contrast()` function.

As this is such a dense topic, below is a list of resources to read further on the topic. But that doesn't mean we won't look at color more. On the contrary, we will need it in the next chapter, *Chapter 8, Stunning Aesthetics with CSS*, where we will be looking at gradients, shapes, and so much more.

# Resources

- An introduction to OKLab color space: `https://bottosson.github.io/posts/oklab/`
- Great arguments for LCH: `https://lea.verou.me/2020/04/LCH-colors-in-css-what-why-and-how/`
- The latest CSS color specification: `https://www.w3.org/TR/css-color-5/`
- A video from Chris Lilley from the W3C explaining gamut reduction with OKLab: `https://www.youtube.com/watch?v=dOsp6u4bIwI`
- A solid explainer on wide gamut color: `https://webkit.org/blog/10042/wide-gamut-color-in-css-with-display-p3/`
- An excellent and accessible overview of color in CSS: `https://css-tricks.com/new-css-color-features-preview/`

# 8

# Stunning Aesthetics with CSS

In this chapter, we are going to look at a selection of CSS capabilities for enriching your designs. Every year that passes, CSS introduces more features that enable us to do in code what was previously only possible with an image editor.

Replacing images with effects in code is usually a good thing. Not only does it tend to make things more maintainable and flexible, but it also results in less page "weight" for the end user, with images almost always producing a far greater file size than the comparable code.

In this chapter, we will cover:

- How to create text shadows
- How to create box shadows
- How to make linear and radial gradients
- How to make conic gradients
- How to use multiple backgrounds
- Using CSS background gradients to make patterns
- How to implement high-resolution background images with media queries
- How to use CSS filters (and their performance implications)
- Clipping with clipping paths
- Masking elements with image masks
- Mixing the colors of elements with `mix-blend-mode`

These are by no means the only things possible in CSS, but they are a selection of things I have found most useful when building responsive websites and applications for the past decade. Let's dig in.

# Text shadows

Let's make a start by looking at text shadows. Text shadows are a fairly simple way to change the aesthetics of text, and therefore provide a good starting point. Support for text-shadow is also ubiquitous. Let's first consider the basic syntax:

```
.element {
  text-shadow: 1px 1px 1px #ccc;
}
```

The first value is the amount of shadow to the right, the second is the amount down, the third value is the amount of blur (the distance the shadow travels before fading to nothing), and the final value is the color. Shadows to the left and above can be achieved using negative values as the first two values. For example:

```
.text {
  text-shadow: -4px -4px 0px #dad7d7;
}
```

The color value doesn't need to be defined as a hex value. It can just as easily be HSL(A) or RGB(A):

```
text-shadow: 4px 4px 0px hsl(140 3% 26% / 0.4);
```

You can also set the shadow values in any other valid CSS length units such as em, rem, ch, rem, and so on. Personally, I rarely use em or rem units for text-shadow values. As the length values tend to be low, using 1px or 2px generally looks good across all viewports.

Thanks to media queries, we can easily remove text shadows at different viewport sizes too. The key here is the none value:

```
.text {
  text-shadow: 2px 2px 0 #bfbfbf;
}
@media (min-width: 30rem) {
  .text {
    text-shadow: none;
  }
}
```

It's worth knowing that, in CSS, where a value starts with a zero, such as `0.14s`, there is no need to write the leading zero: `.14s` is exactly the same.

If there is no blur to be added to a text shadow, the value can be omitted from the declaration. For example:

```
.text {
  text-shadow: -4px -4px #dad7d7;
}
```

That is perfectly valid. The browser assumes that the first two values are for the offsets if no third value is declared.

## Multiple text shadows

It's possible to add multiple text shadows by comma-separating two or more shadows. For example:

```
.multiple {
  text-shadow: 0px 1px #fff, 4px 4px 0px #dad7d7;
}
```

Also, as CSS is forgiving of whitespace, you can lay out the values like this if it helps with readability:

```
.text {
  text-shadow:
    3px 3px #bbb, /* right and bottom */
    -3px -3px #999; /* left and top */
}
```

 You can read the W3C specification for the `text-shadow` property here: `https://www.w3.org/TR/css-text-decor-3/#text-shadow-property`.

So, that's how you create shadows around text. What about when you want a shadow on a containing element?

# Box shadows

Box shadows allow you to create a box-shaped shadow around the outside or inside of an element. Once you understand text shadows, box shadows are a piece of cake. Principally, they follow the same syntax: horizontal offset, vertical offset, blur, spread (we will get to spread in a moment), and color. Only two of the four length values are required. In the absence of the last two length values, a value of zero is assumed. Let's look at a simple example:

```
.shadow {
  box-shadow: 0 3px 5px #444;
}
```

The default box-shadow is set on the outside of the element. Another optional keyword, inset, allows the box shadow to be applied inside the element.

## Inset shadow

The box-shadow property can also be used to create an inset shadow. The syntax is identical to a normal box shadow, except that the value starts with the keyword inset:

```
.inset {
  box-shadow: inset 0 0 40px #000;
}
```

Everything functions as before, but the inset part of the declaration instructs the browser to set the effect on the inside. If you look at example_08-01, you'll see an example of each type:

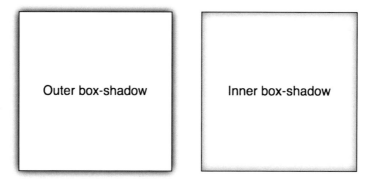

*Figure 8.1: Outer shadows and inner shadows are both easily achievable*

## Multiple shadows

Like text shadows, you can apply multiple box shadows. Separate the box-shadow declarations with a comma. They are applied bottom to top (last to first) as they are listed. Remind yourself of the order by thinking that the declaration nearest to the top in the rule (in the code) appears nearest to the "top" of the order when displayed in the browser. As with text-shadow declarations, you may find it useful to use whitespace to visually stack the different box-shadow declarations:

```
box-shadow:
    inset 0 0 30px hsl(0, 0%, 0%),
    inset 0 0 70px hsla(0, 97%, 53%, 1);
```

 Stacking longer, multiple values one under the other in the code has an added benefit when using version control systems; it makes it easy to spot differences when you compare, or **diff**, two versions of the same file. It can be useful to stack selectors one under the other for that same reason.

## Understanding spread

I'll be honest, for literally years, I didn't truly understand what the spread value of a box-shadow actually did. I don't think the name "spread" is useful. Think of it more as an offset. Let me explain.

Look at the box on the left in example_08-02. This has a standard box shadow applied, with no spread. The one on the right has a negative spread value applied. It's set with the fourth value. Here is the relevant code that deals with each shadow:

```
.no-spread {
  box-shadow: 0 10px 10px;
}
.spread {
  box-shadow: 0 10px 10px -10px;
}
```

Here is the effect of each (element with a spread value on the right):

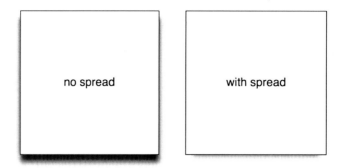

*Figure 8.2: With spread, you can control how much shadow leaks out*

The spread value lets you extend or contract the shadow in all directions by the amount specified. In this example, a negative value is pulling the shadow back in all directions. The result is that we can just see the shadow at the bottom of the right example, instead of seeing the blur "leak" out on all sides.

 You can read the W3C specification for the box-shadow property here: https://www.w3.org/TR/css-backgrounds-3/#the-box-shadow.

Right, so that's shadows. We will go on to deal with more shadows when we look at drop-shadow as part of CSS filters. For now, let's move on to gradients.

## Background gradients

In days gone by, to achieve a background gradient on an element, it was necessary to tile a thin, graphical slice of the gradient. It was a pain to tweak as it meant round trips into a graphics application, and then when a site was live, you would often experience a flash of unloaded gradient while the background image was fetched.

Thankfully, such hassle is now nothing more than a memory; with a CSS background-image gradient, things are far more flexible. CSS now enables us to create linear, radial, and conic background gradients, and repeating versions of each. Let's look at how we can define them.

The specification for CSS Image Values and Replaced Content Module 4 can be found at https://www.w3.org/TR/css-images-4/.

# The linear-gradient notation

The `linear-gradient` notation, in its simplest form, looks like this:

```
.linear-gradient {
  background: linear-gradient(red, blue);
}
```

This will create a linear gradient that starts at red and fades to blue. Unless you tell it otherwise, which we will look at next, it will go from the top to the bottom.

## Specifying gradient direction

If you want to specify a direction for the gradient, there are a couple of ways to do this. The gradient will always begin in the opposite direction to where you are sending it.

For example:

```
.linear-gradient {
  background: linear-gradient(to top right, red, blue);
}
```

In this instance, the gradient heads to the top right. It starts red in the bottom-left corner and fades to blue at the top right.

If you're more mathematically minded, you may believe it would be comparable to write the gradient like this:

```
.linear-gradient {
  background: linear-gradient(45deg, red, blue);
}
```

However, keep in mind that on a rectangular box, a gradient that heads "to top right" (always the top right of the element it's applied to) will end in a slightly different position than 45deg (always 45 degrees from its starting point).

It's worth knowing you can also start gradients before they are visible within a box. For example:

```
.linear-gradient {
  background: linear-gradient(red -50%, blue);
}
```

This would render a gradient as if it had started before it was even visible inside the box. Useful if you want your gradient to begin with "the end" of the fade from one color.

We actually used a color stop in the previous example to define a place where a color should begin and end, so let's look at those more fully.

## Color stops

Perhaps the handiest thing about background gradients is **color stops**. They provide the means to set which color is used at which point in a gradient. With color stops, you can specify something as complex as you are likely to need. Consider this example:

```
.linear-gradient {
  margin: 1rem;
  width: 400px;
  height: 200px;
  background: linear-gradient(
    #f90 0,
    #f90 2%,
    #555 2%,
    #eee 50%,
    #555 98%,
    #f90 98%,
    #f90 100%
  );
}
```

Here's how that linear-gradient renders:

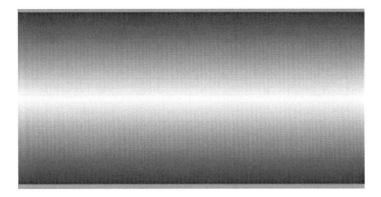

*Figure 8.3: You can add as many stops as you like to a linear gradient*

In this example (example_08-03), a direction has not been specified, so the default top-to-bottom direction applies.

Color stops inside a gradient are written comma-separated and defined by giving first the color, and then the position of the stop. It's generally advisable not to mix units in one notation, but you can. You can have as many color stops as you like and colors can be written as a keyword, hex, RGB, HSL, or any other color format we looked at in the previous chapter.

 You can read the W3C specification for linear background gradients at https://www.w3.org/TR/css-images-3/#linear-gradients.

Having covered linear background gradients, let's now check out radial background gradients.

# Radial background gradients

It's equally simple to create a radial gradient in CSS. These typically begin from a central point and spread out smoothly in an elliptical or circular shape.

Here's the syntax for a radial background gradient (you can play with it in example_08-04):

```css
.radial-gradient {
  margin: 1rem;
  width: 400px;
  height: 200px;
  background: radial-gradient(12rem circle at bottom, yellow, orange,
  red);
}
```

*Figure 8.4: We can set a gradient to start at any point. Here, our "sunrise" gradient starts bottom center*

After specifying the property (background:), we begin the radial-gradient notation. To start with, before the first comma, we define the shape or size of the gradient and the position. We used 12rem circle for the shape and size previously, but consider some other examples:

- circle would be a circle the full size of the container. The size of a radial gradient defaults to farthest-corner if omitted—more on sizing keywords shortly.
- 5em would be a circle 5em in size. It's possible to omit the circle part if giving just a size.
- ellipse would create an ellipse shape that would fit within the element.
- 40px 30px would be an ellipse as if drawn inside a box 40 px wide by 30 px tall.

Next, after the size and/or shape, we define the position. The default position is center, but let's look at some other possibilities and how they can be defined:

- at top right starts the radial gradient from the top right.
- at right 100px top 20px starts the gradient 100 px from the right edge and 20 px from the top edge.

- at center left starts it halfway down the left side of the element.

We end our size, shape, and position parameters with a comma and then define any color stops, which work in exactly the same manner as they do with linear gradients.

To simplify the notation: size, shape, and position before the first comma, then as many color stops as needed after it (with each stop separated by commas).

When it comes to sizing things such as gradients, CSS provides some keywords that are often a better choice than hardcoded values, especially with responsive designs.

## Handy "extent" keywords for responsive sizing

For responsive work, you may find it advantageous to size gradients proportionally rather than using fixed pixel dimensions. That way, you know you are covered (both literally and figuratively) when the size of elements changes. There are some handy sizing keywords that can be applied to gradients.

You would write them like this, in place of any size value:

```
background: radial-gradient(closest-side circle at center, #333, blue);
```

Here is what each of them does:

- closest-side: The shape meets the side of the box nearest to the center (in the case of circles), or meets both the horizontal and vertical sides that are closest to the center (in the case of ellipses).
- closest-corner: The shape meets exactly the closest corner of the box from its center.
- farthest-side: The opposite of closest-side, in that rather than the shape meeting the nearest side, it's sized to meet the one farthest from its center (or both the furthest vertical and horizontal side in the case of an ellipse).
- farthest-corner: The shape expands to the farthest corner of the box from the center.
- cover: Identical to farthest-corner.
- contain: Identical to closest-side.

Practically, the two I find myself using most of the time are cover or contain. They are merely aliases for other keywords, but I find their names are self-explanatory and they are the same keywords you can use for background-size. We look at those keywords again with background-size later in the chapter.

You can read the W3C specification for radial background gradients at `https://www.w3.org/TR/css-images-3/#radial-gradients`.

**The cheat's way to perfect CSS linear and radial gradients**

 If defining gradients by hand seems like hard work, there are some great online gradient generators. My favorite is `https://www.colorzilla.com/gradient-editor/`. It uses a graphics editor-style GUI, allowing you to pick your colors, stops, gradient style (linear and radial gradients are supported), and even the color space (hex, RGB(A), HSL(A)) you'd like the final gradient in. There are also loads of preset gradients to use as starting points. Still not convinced? How about the ability to generate a CSS gradient based on the gradient values in an existing image? Thought that might swing it for you.

# Conic gradients

Where radial gradients pass through any color stops on their way out from a center point, conic gradients pass through any color stops *around* a center point. We set an origin point for the gradient and then specify the color stops as angles around that center point. This accounts for the fact that these types of gradients are also known as **angle** gradients.

Here is an example conic gradient going from white to green and back to white:

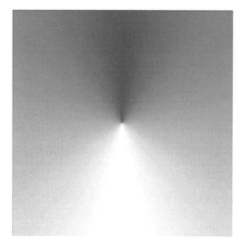

*Figure 8.5: A conic gradient goes around a point, instead of outward from a point*

The code to achieve that looks like this:

```
.conic-gradient {
    width: 200px;
    height: 200px;
    background: conic-gradient(at center, green, white, green);
}
```

If you have looked at the syntax for linear and radial gradients in this chapter already, the conventions will be familiar. You specify the at position for the gradient to start, and then the color stops along the gradient. If you omit the position of the colors, they will be split equally, so that prior example is equivalent to:

```
.conic-gradient {
    width: 200px;
    height: 200px;
    background: conic-gradient(at center, green 0deg, white 180deg,
    green 360deg);
}
```

The one thing that did catch me out when I first started using them is that the angle for the stops isn't just written as degrees around a circle as you might assume; it can also be written as a percentage like other gradients. Imagine that you wanted to change the prior example to be solid green halfway around so it looks like this:

*Figure 8.6: Stops around the center point are typically set in percentages*

Here is the code you would use; just adding a 50% stop on the green or, alternatively, 180deg, would produce an identical result.

```
.conic-gradient {
    width: 200px;
    height: 200px;
    background: conic-gradient(at center, green 50%, white, green);
}
```

One final trick. We can make solid sections with our conic gradients. After the first color stop, if you set another color stop and set it to start at 0deg, it appears as a solid color. Here is an example of a single div using a conic gradient to make four different color sections:

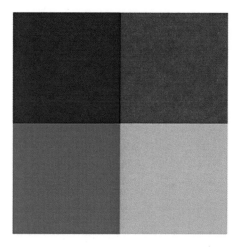

*Figure 8.7: A single element using a conic gradient to create color sections*

This works because the subsequent stops also start at the beginning, but by the time they are visible beneath the color that is listed before, they are already a solid color. Here is the full code for that example:

```
.conic-gradient {
    width: 200px;
    height: 200px;
    background: conic-gradient(at center, red 0 25%, orange 0% 180deg,
    green 0% 75%, blue 0%);
}
```

I've even mixed and matched the units in there to prove you can, but it's usually easier to stick to either percentages or angles in a single gradient—if only for the sake of your own sanity!

Now, if you were a major internet company and wanted to create a nice spinner, all you'd need would be a border-radius of 50% and a CSS animation. I'll leave that as an exercise for you, dear reader.

 You can get hard stops in linear gradients and radial gradients in the same way. Simply use a value of zero as the start of the gradient for subsequent color stops and it will run "behind" the prior one, creating a "hard" transition from one color to the next. I've found this technique very useful when creating bar charts and similar pieces of UI. For example, imagine a bar chart with a 25/75% split. We could achieve that like this:

```
linear-gradient(to right, goldenrod 25%, hotpink 0%)
```

## Repeating gradients

CSS also gives us the ability to create repeating background gradients. Let's take a look at how it's done:

```
.repeating-radial-gradient {
    background: repeating-radial-gradient(black 0px, orange 5px,
    red 10px);
}
```

Here's how that looks (don't look for long, it may cause nausea):

*Figure 8.8: You can use repeating gradients to create all manner of visual effects*

Firstly, prefix the `linear-gradient` or `radial-gradient` with `repeating-`. It then follows the same syntax as a normal gradient. Here, I've used pixel distances between the black, orange, and red colors (`0px`, `5px`, and `10px`, respectively), but you could also choose to use percentages.

 You can read the W3C information on repeating gradients at `https://www.w3.org/TR/css-images-3/#repeating-gradients`.

There's one more way of using background gradients I'd like to share with you.

## Background gradient patterns

Although I've often used subtle linear gradients in designs, I've found less practical use for radial, conic, and repeating gradients. However, clever folks out there have harnessed the power of gradients to create background gradient patterns. Let's look at an example from Lea Verou's collection of CSS background patterns, available at `https://projects.verou.me/css3patterns/`:

```css
.carbon-fibre {
    margin: 1rem;
    width: 400px;
    height: 200px;
    background: radial-gradient(black 15%, transparent 16%) 0 0,
        radial-gradient(black 15%, transparent 16%) 8px 8px,
        radial-gradient(rgba(255, 255, 255, 0.1) 15%, transparent 20%)
        0 1px,
        radial-gradient(rgba(255, 255, 255, 0.1) 15%, transparent 20%)
        8px 9px;
    background-color: #282828;
    background-size: 16px 16px;
}
```

Here's what that gives us in the browser, a carbon fiber background effect:

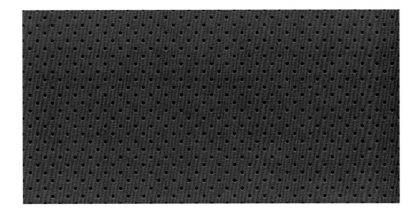

*Figure 8.9: A carbon fiber effect made with pure CSS*

How about that? Just a few lines of CSS and we have an easily editable, responsive, and scalable background pattern.

You might find it useful to add `background-repeat: no-repeat` at the end of the rule to better understand how it works.

As ever, thanks to media queries, different declarations can be used for different responsive scenarios. For example, although a gradient pattern might work well at smaller viewports, it might be better to go with a plain background at larger ones:

```
@media (min-width: 45rem) {
    .carbon-fibre {
        background: #333;
    }
}
```

You can view this example at `example_08-05`.

So far, we have looked at many ways of creating background images using just CSS; however, whether that is linear gradients, radial gradients, or repeating gradients, it is still just one background image. What about when you want to deal with more than one background image at the same time?

# Multiple background images

Although a little out of fashion at the moment, it used to be a fairly common design requirement to build a page with a different background image at the top of the page than at the bottom. Or perhaps to use different background images for the top and bottom of a content section within a page. Back in the day, with CSS 2.1, achieving this effect typically required additional markup (one element for the header background and another for the footer background).

With CSS, you can stack as many background images as you need on an element.

Here's the syntax:

```
.bg {
    background: url('../img/1.png'), url('../img/2.png'),
    url('../img/3.png');
}
```

As with the stacking order of multiple shadows, the image listed first is layered nearest to the top, or closer to the user, in the browser. You can also add a general color for the background in the same declaration if you wish, like this:

```
.bg {
    background: url('../img/1.png'), url('../img/2.png'),
    url('../img/3.png') left bottom, black;
}
```

Specify the color last and this will show up below every image specified in the preceding code snippet.

With the multiple background images, as long as your images have transparency, any partially transparent background image that sits on top of another will show through below. However, background images don't have to sit on top of one another, nor do they all have to be the same size.

# Background size

To set different sizes for each image, use the `background-size` property. When multiple images have been used, the syntax works like this:

```
.bg {
    background-size: 100% 50%, 300px 400px, auto;
}
```

The size values (first width, then height) for each image are declared, separated by commas, in the order they are listed in the background property. As in the preceding example, you can use percentage or pixel values for each image alongside the following:

- `auto`: This sets the element at its native size.
- `cover`: This expands the image, preserving its aspect ratio, to cover the area of the element.
- `contain`: This expands the image to fit its longest side within the element while preserving the aspect ratio.

Having considered size, let's also think about position.

# Background position

If you have different background images, at different sizes, the next thing you'll want is the ability to position them differently. Thankfully, the `background-position` property facilitates that.

Let's put all this background image capability together, alongside some of the responsive units we looked at in previous chapters.

We'll create a simple space scene made with a single element and three background images, set at three different sizes, and positioned in three different ways:

```
.bg-multi {
    height: 100vh;
    width: 100vw;
    background: url('rosetta.png'), url('moon.png'), url('stars.jpg');
    background-size: 75vmax, 50vw, cover;
    background-position: top 50px right 80px, 40px 40px, top center;
    background-repeat: no-repeat;
}
```

You'll see something like this in the browser:

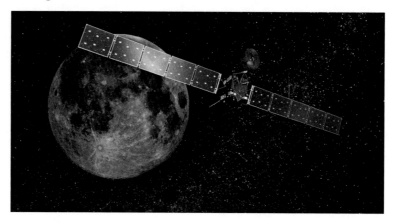

*Figure 8.10: Multiple background images on a single element*

We have the stars image at the bottom, then the moon, and finally an image of the Rosetta space probe on top. View this for yourself in example_08-06. Notice that if you adjust the browser window, the responsive length units work well (vmax, vh, and vw) and retain proportion, while pixel-based ones do not.

Where no background-position is declared, the default position of top left is applied.

## Background shorthand

There is a shorthand method of combining the different background properties together.

However, my experience so far has been that it produces erratic results. Therefore, I recommend the longhand method and that you declare the multiple images first, then the size, and then the position.

 You can read the W3C documentation on multiple background elements here: https://www.w3.org/TR/css-backgrounds-3/.

# High-resolution background images

Thanks to media queries, we have the ability to load in different background images, not just at different viewport sizes, but also at different viewport resolutions.

For example, here is the official way of specifying a background image for a "normal" and a "high" DPI screen. You can find this in example_08-07:

```
.bg {
  background-image: url('bg.jpg');
}
@media (min-resolution: 1.5dppx) {
  .bg {
    background-image: url('bg@1_5x.jpg');
  }
}
```

The media query is written exactly as it is with width, height, or any of the other capability tests. In this example, we are defining the minimum resolution that bg@1_5x.jpg should use as 1.5dppx (device pixels per CSS pixel). We could also use dpi (dots per inch) or dpcm (dots per centimeter) units if preferable. However, despite the poorer support, I find dppx the easiest unit to think about; as 2dppx is twice the resolution, 3dppx would be three times the resolution. Thinking about that in dpi is trickier. "Standard" resolution would be 96dpi, twice that resolution would be 192dpi, and so on.

### A brief note on performance

 Just remember that large images can potentially slow down the feel of your site and lead to a poor experience for users. While a background image won't block the rendering of the page (you'll still see the rest of the site drawn to the page while you wait for the background image), it will add to the total weight of the page, which is important if users are paying for data.

Earlier in this chapter, I told you we would look at more shadows when we got to dealing with CSS filters. That time has come.

# CSS filters

There is a glaring problem with box-shadow. As the name implies, it is limited to the rectangular CSS box shape of the element it is applied to. Here's a screengrab of a triangle shape made with CSS with a box shadow applied:

*Figure 8.11: Box shadows don't always provide the effect you want*

Not exactly what I was hoping for. Thankfully, we can overcome this issue with CSS filters, part of the Filter Effects Module Level 1 (https://www.w3.org/TR/filter-effects/).

Here is that same element with a CSS drop-shadow filter applied instead of a box-shadow (you can view the code in example_08-08):

*Figure 8.12: A drop-shadow filter effect can apply to more than just boxes*

Here is the format for CSS filters:

```
.filter-drop-shadow {
  filter: drop-shadow(8px 8px 6px #333);
}
```

After the `filter` property, we specify the filter we want to use, which is `drop-shadow` in this example, and then pass in the arguments for the filter. `drop-shadow` follows a similar syntax to `box-shadow`, so this one is easy; *x* and *y* offset, blur, then spread radius (both blur and spread are optional), and finally color (also optional, although I recommend specifying a color for consistency).

CSS filters are actually based on SVG filters, which have wider support. We'll look at the SVG-based equivalent in *Chapter 10, SVG*.

## Available CSS filters

There are a few filters to choose from. We will look at each. While images of most of the filters follow, if you are reading a copy of this book with monochrome images, you may struggle to notice the differences. If you're in that situation, remember you can still view the various filters in the browser by opening `example_08-08`. I'm going to list each out now with a suitable value specified. As you might imagine, a greater value means more of the filter applied. Where images are used, the image is shown after the relevant code:

- `filter: url('./img/filters.svg#filterRed')`: Lets you specify an SVG filter to use.
- `filter: blur(3px)`: Uses a single length value (but not as a percentage):

*Figure 8.13: A blur filter applied*

- `filter: brightness(2)`: With brightness, a value of 1 or 100% is normal; less than that, such as 0.5 or 50%, darkens, and more, such as 200% or 2, lightens:

*Figure 8.14: A brightness filter applied*

- `filter: contrast(2)`: A value of 1 or 100% is normal; less than that, for example, 0.5 or 50%, reduces contrast; and more, such as 200% or 2, increases it:

*Figure 8.15: A contrast filter applied*

- `filter: drop-shadow(4px 4px 6px #333)`: We looked at drop-shadow in detail previously.

- `filter: grayscale(.8)`: Use a value from 0 to 1 or 0% to 100% to apply varying amounts of grayscale to the element. A value of 0 would be no grayscale, while a value of 1 would be fully grayscale:

*Figure 8.16: A grayscale filter applied*

- `filter: hue-rotate(25deg)`: Use a value between 0 and 360 degrees to adjust the hue of the colors around the color wheel. You can use a negative value to move the "wheel" backward, and a number greater than 360 just spins it around more! Only really useful if you need to programmatically keep adding to the hue:

*Figure 8.17: A hue-rotate filter applied*

- `filter: invert(75%)`: Use a value from 0 to 1 or 0% to 100% to define the amount the element has its colors inverted:

*Figure 8.18: An invert filter applied*

- `filter: opacity(50%)`: Use a value from 0 to 1 or 0% to 100% to alter the opacity of the element. 1 or 100% is fully opaque, while 0 or 0% would be full transparency. This is similar to the opacity property you will already be familiar with. However, filters, as we shall see, can be combined, and this allows opacity to be combined with other filters in one go:

*Figure 8.19: An opacity filter applied*

- `filter: saturate(15%)`: Use a value from 0 to 1 or 0% to 100% to desaturate an image and anything above 1/100% to add extra saturation:

*Figure 8.20: A saturate filter applied*

- `filter: sepia(.75)`: Use a value from 0 to 1 or 0% to 100% to make the element appear with a more sepia color. 0/0% leaves the element as-is, while anything above that applies greater amounts of sepia, up to a maximum of 1/100%:

*Figure 8.21: A sepia filter applied*

## Combining CSS filters

You can also combine filters easily; simply space-separate them. For example, here is how you would apply `opacity`, `blur`, and `sepia` filters at once:

```
.MultipleFilters {
  filter: opacity(10%) blur(2px) sepia(35%);
}
```

 Apart from `hue-rotate`, when using filters, negative values are not allowed.

I think you'll agree that CSS filters offer some pretty powerful effects. There are also effects that we can transition and transform from situation to situation. We'll look at how to do that in *Chapter 11, Transitions, Transformations, and Animations*.

However, before you go crazy with these new toys, we need to have a grown-up conversation about performance.

## A warning on CSS performance

When it comes to CSS performance, I would like you to remember this one thing:

*"Architecture is outside the braces, performance is inside."*

—— *Ben Frain*

Let me expand on my little maxim: as far as I can prove, worrying about whether a CSS selector (the part outside the curly braces) is fast or slow is pointless. I set out to prove this here: `https://benfrain.com/css-performance-revisited-selectors-bloat-expensive-styles/`.

However, one thing that really can grind a page to a halt, CSS-wise, is *expensive properties* (the parts inside the curly braces). When we use the term "expensive" in relation to certain styles, it simply means it costs the browser a lot of overhead. It's something the browser, or perhaps more accurately, the host hardware, finds overly taxing to do.

It's possible to make a common-sense guess about what will cause the browser extra work. It's basically anything it would have to compute before it can paint things to the screen. For example, compare a standard div with a flat solid background against a semi-opaque image, on top of a background made up of multiple gradients, with rounded corners and a drop-shadow. The latter is more expensive; it will result in far more computational work for the browser and subsequently cause more overhead.

Therefore, when you apply effects like filters, do so judiciously and, if possible, test whether the page speed suffers on the lowest powered devices you are hoping to support. At the least, switch on development tool features, such as continuous page repainting in Chrome, and toggle any effects you think may cause problems. This will provide you with data (in the form of a millisecond reading of how long the current viewport is taking to paint) to make a more educated decision on which effects to apply. The lower the figure, the faster the page will perform—although be aware that browsers/platforms vary, so, as ever, test on real devices where possible. Generally, if you suspect something is slowing things down, just toggling those properties off in the dev tools will show an improvement. These tools just give you hard data to make a more educated decision.

For more on this subject, I recommend the following resource: https://web.dev/rendering-performance/.

*Figure 8.22: Check that fancy effects aren't killing your performance*

OK, grown-up talk finished with now. Let's get back to looking at the fun and powerful stuff we can do with CSS. Next on the list is clipping things.

# CSS clip-path

The `clip-path` property allows you to "clip" an element with a shape. Think of clipping just like drawing a shape on a piece of paper and then cutting around it. This shape can be something simple like an ellipse, something more complicated such as a polygon, or something more complex still, such as a shape defined by an inline SVG path. If you want to view each of these on a page, check out `example-08_09` in this chapter's downloadable code.

# CSS basic shapes

You can use `clip-path` with any of the CSS basic shapes. These are `inset`, `circle`, `ellipse`, and `polygon`, as described here: `https://www.w3.org/TR/css-shapes-1/#supported-basic-shapes`.

Let's take a look at how we would write each of these.

# clip-path with a circle

With `clip-path: circle()`, the first argument you pass is the size, and the second, which is an optional argument, is the position of that shape. So, if you wanted to clip an element down to a circle 20% of the element's height and width:

```
clip-path: circle(20%);
```

If you wanted the same circle `clip-mask` but positioned 60% horizontally and 40% vertically:

```
.clip-circle {
  clip-path: circle(35% at 60% 40%);
}
```

*Figure 8.23: A circular clip-path applied*

Notice the at keyword in there? That's needed to communicate that the lengths after relate to positioning and not size.

It's important to know that pointer events don't occur for areas of an element that have been clipped by a clip mask! To extend our "cutting a shape from a piece of paper" analogy, the bits outside a clip mask are like the discarded pieces of paper that have been cut away. This is useful because you won't be getting clicks on an area where you can't see the subject.

## clip-path with ellipse

With clip-path: ellipse(), the first argument is the *x*-axis radius (horizontal) and the second argument is the *y*-axis radius (vertical). Just like circle(), you specify positioning lengths after the at keyword:

```
.clip-ellipse {
  clip-path: ellipse(100px 50px at 60% 40%);
}
```

*Figure 8.24: An elliptical clip-path applied*

## clip-path with inset

The inset() function for clip-path is a little different. You pass four lengths, and these are how much you want to inset the mask from the edges. Just like when you set margin, the values go clockwise: top, right, bottom, and left. Just like margin, you can also pass just two length values; the first will be top and bottom and the second will be left and right (the three-value syntax works the same too).

There is also an optional round keyword that can be used, followed by another length; this sets how much you would like each corner to be rounded by.

Here is an example with four inset values passed and four different radius values for the corners:

```
.clip-inset {
  clip-path: inset(40px 20px 40px 20px round 0 30px 15px 40px);
}
```

*Figure 8.25: An inset clip-path applied*

## clip-path with polygon

The polygon() function for clip-path allows us to describe a simple shape with a series of comma-separated $x$- and $y$-coordinates. This is what a triangle written with the polygon function looks like:

```
.clip-polygon {
  clip-path: polygon(50% 60px, 100% calc(100% - 40px),
  0% calc(100% - 40px));
}
```

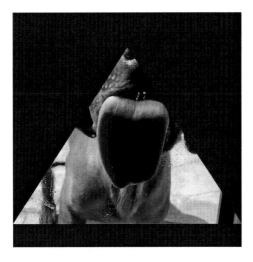

*Figure 8.26: A clip-path applied with a polygon*

Think of this as a way of describing where to start cutting (the first argument), where to go next (any subsequent arguments), and where the last point should be. The polygon then connects the final point to the first to complete the path.

Each argument is made up of an *x*-coordinate described from the top left of the containing box (for example, 50% along), and then the *y*-coordinate (for example, 60 px from the top) in relation to the top of the containing box. This gives you the ability to let things scale with percentages or use harder pixel values, depending on your requirements.

My favorite way to get started with a `clip-path` polygon is to use Bennett Feely's "Clippy" website: `https://bennettfeely.com/clippy/`.

There are a bunch of premade shapes to choose from, as well as a GUI for amending the shape. Highly recommended!

## clip-path with URL (clipping source)

You can also pass the `clip-path` a **clipping source** via a URL. The URL needs to be an SVG `clipPath` somewhere in the document.

I made a star shape as an SVG path and added an `id` of `starSymbol` to the `clipPath` element. With that in place, you can tell `clip-path` to use that path like this:

```
.clip-url {
  clip-path: url(#starSymbol);
}
```

*Figure 8.27: A clip-path applied with an SVG path*

You can view each of these `clip-path` examples in example_08-09.

## Animating clip-path

As if all this clipping malarkey wasn't interesting enough, you can also animate a `clip-path`, as long as there remains the same number of points in the shape. For example, you can animate a triangle into a different shaped triangle, but without some tricks, you can't convert that same triangle into a star. I say "without some tricks" because you can effectively do this by hiding a few points along the lines of the polygon so your triangle has enough points to animate into a star.

Here's a grab of an extra example I added, example_08-10. This is just to hopefully give you an idea of what can be done by adding a few of the things we have already learned and a few things we will learn in future chapters together:

*Figure 8.28: You can even animate clip-path*

This shows two elements with the same background image being masked with `clip-path`. You can also tint the image with an overlay like this:

```
background: linear-gradient(hsla(0, 0%, 0%, 0.4) 0, hsla(0, 0%, 0%, 0.4)
100%), url('image.jpg');
```

You may be wondering, if we wanted to tint the image with a color, why don't we just use a background color in the declaration?

The answer is that it doesn't work. When you set multiple backgrounds with the `background` property, it's not possible to use a `background-color`, even a semi-transparent one, above an image, and have the color let the image show through beneath.

However, one proven trick is to create a `background-image` using a `linear-gradient` with the same semi-opaque color at either end of the gradient, which creates the effect we are after.

We are then moving the main element around the page with one set of `keyframes` animations (we will get to animations in *Chapter 11, Transitions, Transformations, and Animations*) and animate the `clip-path` with another set.

I think once you start playing about with these techniques, you're going to surprise yourself with just what you can create with relative ease!

There may be occasions when you don't just want to clip what's in an element, and you actually want to overlay it with a mask. We can do that with CSS too! Let me show you.

## mask-image

You can also mask elements with images, from either an image source with transparency such as a PNG graphic, a `linear-gradient`, which we looked at earlier in this chapter, or an SVG `mask` element. You can read about all the possibilities afforded to us in the specification here: `https://www.w3.org/TR/css-masking-1/`.

In the meantime, we will just look at a fairly straightforward example so you can appreciate the kind of effect that is possible and how the syntax works to achieve it.

Suppose we have an image. I have one that NASA took of Mars. I'd get one I took myself but, you know, it's a bit of a jaunt.

Now, suppose we also have a PNG image that is transparent except for the word "MARS". We can use this PNG as a mask on top of our image element.

This is what we see in the browser:

*Figure 8.29: A mask image applied*

Here is our relevant HTML:

```
<img
  src="mars.jpg"
  alt="An image of Mars from space"
  class="mask-image-example"
/>
```

And here is our CSS:

```
.mask-image-example {
  display: block;
  height: 1024px;
  width: 1024px;
  margin: 0 auto;
  mask-image: url('mars-text-mask.png');
}
```

The only relevant part of the mask is the mask-image property, which tells the browser what we want to use as a mask on this element.

Now, the cynical among you might suggest the same effect could have just been achieved in a graphics package. I'd say you were right, but then raise you this:

```
.mask-image-example {
  display: block;
  height: 1024px;
  width: 1024px;
  margin: 0 auto;
  mask-image: url('mars-text-mask.png');
  animation: moveMask 6s infinite alternate;
}
@keyframes moveMask {
  0% {
    object-position: 0px 0px;
  }
  100% {
    object-position: 100px 100px;
  }
}
```

We will look at animations in *Chapter 11, Transitions, Transformations, and Animations*, but what we have done here is added an animation that moves the background image behind the mask so that the word "MARS" stays in position while the planet moves behind. Try doing that in Photoshop!

If we wanted to swap things around and have the mask move and the image of the planet stay put, it is as simple as swapping object-position in the animation for mask-position.

You can have a play with this example at example_08-11.

 Be aware that, to see this example and the next, you will need to view the file from a server. If you have Node installed, you can run npx serve on the Terminal from the root of the example folder to install and run a local server there.

There are quite a few related properties for mask-image that can alter the way the mask works. If you find yourself tasked with something mask-related, be sure to look through the specifications and see if there is anything in there that might aid your specific requirements.

Well, I don't know about you, but I'm almost exhausted with the visual CSS "cardio" we've just been through. Before you reach for the towel and water bottle, just let me tell you about mix-blend-mode.

## mix-blend-mode

One final, very visual, property I want to relate before we end this chapter is mix-blend-mode. This property lets you decide how you want one element to "blend" with the element it sits on top of.

Here are the possible blend modes: normal, multiply, screen, overlay, darken, lighten, color-dodge, color-burn, hard-light, soft-light, difference, exclusion, hue, saturation, color, and luminosity.

Static images don't really do this property justice, so I'd encourage you to open example_08-12 in a browser. We're using that same image of Mars from the last example but setting it as a fixed background for the body element.

Then, we add some text on top that you can scroll to see mix-blend-mode in effect. In this example, we have used overlay, for no reason other than I thought it worked best. If you open the example along with your developer tools, you can cycle through the other possibilities. It's perhaps redundant to say so, but the options themselves will have different effects, depending on the foreground and background they are being applied to.

 The specification for mix-blend-mode is the Compositing and Blending Level 1 specification: https://www.w3.org/TR/compositing-1/#mix-blend-mode.

# Summary

In this chapter, we've looked at a selection of the most useful CSS features for creating lightweight aesthetics in responsive web designs. CSS's background gradients curb our reliance on images for background effects.

We considered how they can be used to create infinitely repeating background patterns. We've also learned how to use text shadows to create simple text enhancements, and box shadows to add shadows to the outside and inside of elements.

We've also looked at CSS filters. They allow us to achieve even more impressive visual effects with CSS alone and can be combined for truly impressive results.

In the last part of this chapter, we looked at creating masking effects with both images and clipping paths.

We've added some considerable capabilities to our toolbelts! We will come back to the fancier CSS effects in *Chapter 11, Transitions, Transformations, and Animations*. But, before that...

In the next chapter, we're going to turn our attention to responsive images. If you work with image-heavy projects, you'll want to pay close attention. Using the right image for the right job can save users time and money. And using the right syntax to deliver the right image makes sure they get it!

# 9

# Responsive Images

We should always aim to build websites and applications to be as lean as possible. The benefits of faster sites are well documented for all meaningful metrics. As far back as 2009, Google was publishing its findings on the importance of page speed: `https://services.google.com/fh/files/blogs/google_delayexp.pdf`.

Images are by far the biggest contributor to website "weight," a significant contributor to web page speed, or lack thereof. Looking at the data from the 2021 Web Almanac at `https://almanac.httparchive.org/en/2021/page-weight#images`, we can see images accounting for almost twice as much weight as the next largest resource, JavaScript:

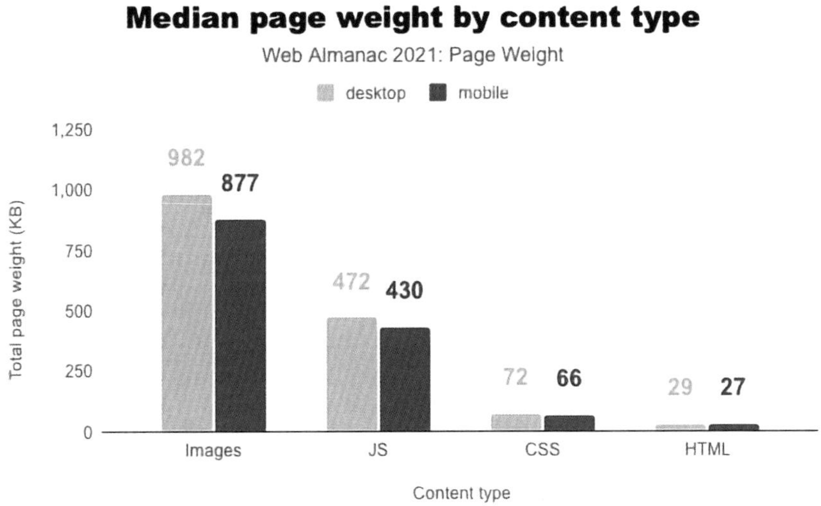

*Figure 9.1: A bar chart showing that images are far and away the largest resource*

Furthermore, research carried out by Google in 2017 suggested that "the probability of bounce increases 32% as page load time goes from 1 second to 3 seconds" and that "...53% of visits are abandoned if a mobile site takes longer than three seconds to load."

 Read more from that research here: `https://www.thinkwithgoogle.com/intl/en-gb/marketing-strategies/app-and-mobile/mobile-page-speed-new-industry-benchmarks/`.

As such, it is incumbent upon us to do everything in our power to make our images as lean, and relevant, for the screen viewing them as we can. This, in essence, is the aim of responsive images.

For the purpose of this chapter, let us make a distinction between the two different but related goals: how to serve the *leanest* image we can to our user, and how to serve the *most relevant* image to our user. While these two ideals overlap and sometimes share the same technical solution, the distinction may make digesting the ideas simpler.

In this chapter, we will be covering the following:

- Why we should use modern image formats where possible
- The AVIF image format
- The WebP image format
- How to progressively enhance modern image formats
- Understanding the responsive images problem space
- Using `srcset` for resolution switching
- How to achieve art direction with `picture`
- Practical considerations for responsive images

Let's begin by looking at image formats and how different formats alone can significantly reduce the amount of data our website needs to send down the wire.

## Modern image formats

Historically, it was simple to choose the correct image format to use in a given scenario.

If the image needed to animate and for some reason a video wasn't a viable option, you would opt for an animated GIF. If it was a photo, JPG was the logical choice, and if it was anything that needed transparency, it would be PNG as, unlike JPG, it supports alpha transparency.

However, if you want to save yourself and your users bandwidth, it is no longer so simple. Let's consider two newer image formats and where they might be applicable and advantageous to use.

AVIF and WebP are formats that, given the same image as a starting point, almost always produce a smaller file size and preferable quality than an equivalent JPG file.

## AVIF image format

AVIF, the image counterpart of AV1 video, is an open-source image format for still and, crucially, animated images. It supports an alpha channel, which JPG doesn't, and compresses data far more effectively than JPEG or even WebP (which we will look at shortly). It also supports greater color depth, allowing the use of wide gamut colors in images (you'll want to look at *Chapter 7, CSS Color*, for more info on color gamut). On top of that, it supports animations and "live" photos with image sequences.

If that wasn't enough, it almost always, to my eyes at least, produces a better-looking image when compared with, say, a JPG. So what's the catch? There are two. Firstly, the ease with which you can create an AVIF image, and then, secondly, the support in browsers for actually viewing them.

To create AVIF images you typically need a plugin for your graphic editor of choice; few graphic programs natively support AVIF currently. If you want a straightforward browser-based tool to do a conversion, look at Squoosh: `https://squoosh.app/`

When it comes to viewing AVIF images in the browser, as of 2022, there is only support for Chrome and Firefox. Not even Edge, itself with the same Chromium underpinnings as Chrome, supports it. Safari is also missing support on macOS. This is despite the fact that the WebKit engine Safari runs on is capable of using AVIF. This is because Safari uses the host operating system's image decoding capabilities – and macOS currently lacks support.

However, this doesn't mean we can't utilize AVIF; we just need to employ it where we can, and use a different format when we can't. We will come to the practicalities of doing that shortly. Before that, let's also consider WebP.

## WebP image format

WebP was a format created by Google. Roughly speaking, a WebP image will tend to give you a 25% file saving against a comparable PNG or JPG.

It also supports alpha and animation, so it can be a good replacement for GIF.

Making and viewing WebP is a little easier than AVIF, if only because it has been around for longer and, as such, enjoys wider support. All modern operating systems and browsers now support WebP. Even Mac-only graphics applications such as Sketch allow a native export to WebP.

While not offering quite the file savings of AVIF, WebP is a solid second choice. But, unless you only need to support the latest browsers, you will still need something in place for users on older systems.

# Image format comparisons

Let's consider an example to illustrate the possible savings. In the code that accompanies this chapter, you will find a file called `scones.jpg`. This is the same picture of scones we used in *Chapter 1, The Essentials of Responsive Web Design*, completely unmodified. On my computer, it tells me it has a file size of 199KB. If I load that file into the aforementioned Squoosh and leave the defaults, it tells me it can optimize the file down to a JPG of only 122KB. That file is in the code as `squoosh-scones.jpg`. That 39% saving in itself should be enough to show how much unneeded weight our images contain.

**How does image optimization work?**

By default, an image from an application like Photoshop or straight out of a camera contains heaps of extra information we just don't need when destined for the web. Things like the location the image was taken, the date and time, camera used, aperture and lens settings, focal depth, and heaps, heaps more. Plus, the image can almost always have its data rewritten in a more optimized manner. That by itself would be the general idea of **lossless** optimization. At this point, we would be taking no detail from the image. However, we can often go further, removing image data with no reduction in perceived quality. That process is known as **lossy** optimization.

The trick is to find the "sweet spot" where you are saving significant extra data but not diminishing the perceptual quality of the image. At the very least, for any serious work, you should be trying to automate lossless compression of images, where no human analysis of the output will be necessary.

Let's save that same file as a WebP file; this gives us a file of only 79.4KB, a 60% saving on the original file size. You can find that file as `squoosh-scones.webp`.

Lastly, let's save it as an AVIF file as shown in *Figure 9.2*. By default, Squoosh sets the quality slider on AVIF to only 30, but if I move the comparison line across onto the lovely strawberry jam of that image (gosh, this is making me hungry), we can see that some of the detail is being lost. But even if I move it up to a quality of 40, which I feel gives an acceptable visual, it still creates a file that is only 52.1KB, a 74% improvement on the original! You can find that file in the code as `squoosh-scones.avif`.

*Figure 9.2: The Squoosh app lets you see in real time the effect of your changes*

With our example file, with a few seconds' work, we were able to create a version of the image that was almost a quarter of the original size. This is but one image and one set of choices, but it should prove to you just how much unneeded data we are often serving up to our users.

And that brings us to how we actually serve up different file versions of an image. The answer is that we can use the `picture` element.

# Using the picture element to progressively enhance images

We will soon see how to use the picture element for "art direction," serving up different images for different situations. However, I have actually found the greatest practical utility in the picture element is for providing alternative image formats. Let's look at that first.

The most common use case I find myself currently needing is providing an AVIF version of an image, if possible, then a WebP version for users if they can't make use of AVIF, and then a JPG if a user can't make use of an AVIF or a WebP. Here is how we can do that with picture:

```
<picture>
    <source srcset="scone.avif" type="image/avif" />
    <source srcset="scone.webp" type="image/webp" />
    <img
        src="scone.jpg"
        alt="A delicious scone, baked to perfection"
        loading="lazy"
    />
</picture>
```

The essence of the picture element is wrapping a number of images up, with the preferred options first, and the browser chooses the first one it is able to make use of. If you have already read *Chapter 2* on *Writing HTML Markup*, you will recognize the source element from the *Providing alternate media sources* section. The principle is identical: we specify different versions of a piece of media, and the browser chooses the first one it can make use of.

In our example code above, we would prefer the browser to use the scone.avif image, but if it can't use that, it uses the scone.webp. If even that cannot be understood, it falls back to scone.jpg. Crucially, in this situation where all the images are of the same thing, you don't need to write the alt text for the image more than once. Whichever image the browser chooses, it will only download that one image.

In addition, back in *Chapter 2*, we covered the loading attribute, and noted that if we were happy for images to download in their own time, we could add loading="lazy" to them. The same is true here, but like the alt tag, you can see in our example code that we only have to specify it on the img tag; the two source elements in our picture are merely alternate src values for the img.

So that is how we can provide modern images for browsers that support them, and older, more broadly supported formats to those that don't, all the while providing solid accessibility and meaning with the alt tag in case the image doesn't load or the user can't make use of the visuals.

In the prior code, we are just dealing with a single image and different formats of it. That addresses our problem of file weight. Now let's look at how to deal with serving the best image given the situation. For that, we will put aside picture momentarily and make use of another tool, srcset. But first, let's be certain we understand the problem we are trying to solve.

# The inherent problem of responsive images

As an author, you cannot know about every possible device that may visit your site now or in the future. Only a browser knows the particulars of the device viewing a website; its screen size and device capabilities, for example.

Conversely, only the people making the website know what versions of an image we have at our disposal. We may have three versions of the same image: small, medium, and large, each with increasing dimensions to cater for the anticipated screen size and screen density eventualities. The browser does not know this. We have to tell it.

To summarize the conundrum, we, as the website authors, have only half of the solution, in that we know what images we have. The browser has the other half of the solution, in that it knows what device is visiting the site and what the most appropriate image dimensions and resolution would be.

How can we tell the browser what images we have at our disposal so that it may choose the most appropriate one for the user?

In the first few years of responsive web design, there was no specified way. Thankfully, now we have the Embedded content specification: https://html.spec.whatwg.org/multipage/embedded-content.html.

The Embedded content specification describes ways to deal with the simple resolution switching of images—to facilitate a user on a higher resolution screen receiving a higher resolution version of images. It also facilitates "art direction" situations for when authors want users to see a totally different image depending on a number of device characteristics (think media queries). For example, a close-up image of something on smaller viewports and then a wide-angle image of the same thing for larger viewports.

Demonstrating responsive image examples is tricky. It's not possible to appreciate on a single screen the different images that could be loaded with a particular syntax or technique. Therefore, just as when we looked at serving up different file versions of an image, the examples that follow will be mainly code, and you'll just have to trust me that it's going to produce the result you need in supporting browsers. Let's look at two further scenarios that you're likely to need responsive images for. These are switching one image for another when a different resolution is needed and changing an image entirely depending on the available viewport space.

## Simple resolution switching with srcset

Let's suppose you have three versions of the same image. One is suitable for standard pixel density displays, commonly referred to as "1x". Another image is higher resolution, to cater for higher density, or "1.5x" displays, and, finally, the third is a high "2x" resolution version for very high-density displays. Here is how we can let the browser know that we have these three versions available:

```
<img
  src="scones_small.jpg"
  srcset="scones_medium.jpg 1.5x, scones_large.jpg 2x"
  alt="a delicious looking baked scone"
/>
```

This is about as simple as things get with responsive images, so let's ensure that the syntax makes perfect sense.

First of all, the src attribute, which you will already be familiar with, has a dual role here; it's specifying the small 1x version of the image, and it also acts as a fallback image if the browser doesn't support the srcset attribute. That's why we are using it for the small image. This way, older browsers that will ignore the srcset information will get the smallest and best-performing image possible.

For browsers that understand srcset, with that attribute, we provide a comma-separated list of images that the browser can choose from. After the image name (such as scones_medium.jpg), we issue a simple hint.

I've specifically called it a hint rather than an instruction or a command, and you will see why in a moment. In this example 1.5x and 2x have been used, but any integer would be valid. For example, 3x or 4x would work too (providing you can find a suitably high-resolution screen).

However, there is an issue here; a device with a 1440px wide, 1x screen will get the same image as a 480px wide, 3x screen. That may or may not be the desired effect.

# Advanced switching with srcset and sizes

Let's consider another situation. In a responsive web design, it wouldn't be uncommon for an image to be the full viewport width on smaller viewports, but only half the width of the viewport at larger sizes. The main example in *Chapter 1, The Essentials of Responsive Web Design*, was a typical illustration of this. Here's how we can communicate these intentions to the browser:

```
<img
  srcset="scones-small.jpg 450w, scones-medium.jpg 900w"
  sizes="(min-width: 280px) 100vw, (min-width: 640px) 50vw"
  src="scones-small.jpg"
  alt="Lots of delicious scones"
/>
```

Inside the img tag, we are utilizing srcset again. However, this time, after specifying the images, we are adding a value with a w suffix. This tells the browser how wide the image is. In our example, we have a 450 px wide image (called scones-small.jpg) and a 900 px wide image (called scones-medium.jpg). It's important to note that this w-suffixed value isn't a "real" size. It's merely an indication to the browser, roughly equivalent to the width in "CSS pixels."

 What exactly defines a pixel in CSS? I wondered that myself. Then, I found the explanation at http://www.w3.org/TR/css3-values/#reference-pixel and wished I hadn't wondered.

This w-suffixed value makes more sense when we factor in the additional sizes attribute. The sizes attribute allows us to communicate the intentions for our images to the browser. In the example above, the first value is equivalent to "for devices that are at least 280px wide, I intend the image to be around 100vw wide."

If some of the units used, such as vh (where 1vh is equal to 1% of the viewport height) and vw (where 1vw is equal to 1% of the viewport width), don't make sense, be sure to read *Chapter 6, CSS Selectors, Typography, and More*.

The second part is, effectively, "Hi browser, for devices that are at least 640px wide, I only intend the image to be shown at 50vw." That may seem a little redundant until you factor in **dots per inch** (**DPI**) (or **DPR** for **device pixel ratio**). For example, on a 320px wide device with a 2x resolution (effectively requiring a 640px wide image, if shown at full width), the browser might decide the 900px wide image is actually a better match as it's the first option it has for an image that would be big enough to fulfill the required size.

## Did you say the browser "might" pick one image over another?

An important thing to remember is that the values given in the sizes attribute are merely hints to the browser. That doesn't necessarily ensure that the browser will always obey. This is a good thing. Trust me, it really is. It means that, in the future, if there is a reliable way for browsers to ascertain network conditions, it may choose to serve one image over another because it knows things at that point that we can't possibly know at this point as the author. Perhaps a user has a setting on their device to "only download 1x images" or "only download 2x images." In these scenarios, the browser can make the best call.

The alternative to the browser deciding is to use the picture element. Using this element ensures that the browser serves up the exact image you asked for. We looked at this element earlier in the chapter to solve the problem of serving the best image format for the user's needs. This time we are going to use it to serve different images in different scenarios. Let's take a look at how that works.

## Art direction with the picture element

The final scenario you may find yourself in is one in which you have different images that are applicable at different viewport sizes. For example, consider our cake-based example again from *Chapter 1*. Maybe on the smallest screens we would like a close-up of the scone with a generous helping of jam and cream on top. For larger screens, perhaps we have a wider image we would like to use. Perhaps it's a wide shot of a table loaded up with all manner of cakes. Finally, for larger viewports still, perhaps we want to see the exterior of a cake shop on a village street with people sitting outside eating cakes and drinking tea (I know, sounds like nirvana, right?).

We need three different images that are most appropriate at different viewport ranges. Here is how we could solve this with picture:

```
<picture>
  <source media="(min-width: 480px)" srcset="cake-table.jpg" />
  <source media="(min-width: 960px)" srcset="cake-shop.jpg" />
  <img src="scones.jpg" alt="Lots of cakes" />
</picture>
```

Be aware that when you use the picture element, it is merely a wrapper to facilitate other images making their way to the img tag within. If you want to style the images in any way, it's the img tag that should get your attention. Similarly, you can't change the alt tag contents by depending on which image gets loaded, so make sure you provide text that covers all eventualities as best you can.

Secondly, the `srcset` attribute here works exactly the same as in the previous example.

Thirdly, the `img` tag provides your fallback image and also the image that will be displayed if a browser understands `picture` but none of the media definitions match.

 Just to be crystal clear, do not omit the `img` tag from within a `picture` element or things won't end well!

The key difference with `picture` is that we have a `source` tag. Here, we can use media query-style expressions to explicitly tell the browser which asset to use in a matching situation. Our first one in the preceding example is telling the browser, "Hey you, if the screen is at least 480 px wide, load in the `cake-table.jpg` image instead." As long as the conditions match, the browser will dutifully obey.

## A practical note on providing alternate image formats and sizes

Writing a `picture` element every time you want to include alternate versions of an image on a page is an awful lot of boilerplate code. As such, many content management systems and static site generator tools will add responsive image code for you behind the scenes. For example, when you upload an image into WordPress for use in a blog post, it automatically makes alternate sizes and serves those up as options in a `srcset` attribute inside an `img` tag:

```
▼<figure id="attachment_4410" aria-describedby="caption-attachment-4410" class="wp-caption alignnon
e">
    <img width="1920" height="1080" src="https://benfrain.com/assets/00034.jpg" alt="comparing Raise t
    o the Moonlander" class="size-full wp-image-4410" srcset="https://benfrain.com/assets/00034.jpg 19
    20w, https://benfrain.com/assets/00034-300x169.jpg 300w, https://benfrain.com/assets/00034-1024x57
    6.jpg 1024w, https://benfrain.com/assets/00034-100x56.jpg 100w, https://benfrain.com/assets/00034-
    768x432.jpg 768w, https://benfrain.com/assets/00034-1536x864.jpg 1536w" sizes="(max-width: 1920px)
    100vw, 1920px"> == $0
    <figcaption id="caption-attachment-4410" class="wp-caption-text">The Raise alongside a Sofle and
    Moonlander</figcaption>
</figure>
```

*Figure 9.3: The kind of markup WordPress adds when I insert an image into my blog*

# Summary

Hopefully, the terminology, techniques, and appropriate applications for responsive images are now a little clearer.

In this chapter, we looked at new image formats like AVIF and WebP, and the massive economies they can offer in terms of file size. We considered their shortcomings in terms of support and looked at how we can use the `picture` element to serve up both those image types alongside a suitable fallback.

We also looked at `srcset` and how that allows us to provide the browser with a number of possibilities alongside our preference, enabling the browser to make an informed choice about which to use.

We then looked at `picture` again, considering how to use it to serve entirely different images based on things like viewport width.

The techniques we have covered in this chapter apply to bitmap images — photos and such. But that's just one side of the image coin. In the next chapter, we will take a deep dive into Scalable Vector Graphics (SVG), and how to embrace the vector `image` format made for the web.

# Join our book's Discord space

Need clarity on using the leanest, most relevant images? Join the book's Discord workspace to discuss all your responsive web design concerns directly with the author and interact with other readers:

https://packt.link/RWD4e

# 10

# SVG

SVG is an important technology for responsive web design as it provides pin-sharp and future-proof graphical assets for all screen resolutions.

Images on the web, with formats such as JPEG, GIF, or PNG, have their visual data saved as set pixels. If you save a graphic in any of those formats with a set width and height and zoom the image to twice its original size or more, their limitations can be easily exposed.

Here's a screen grab of just that; a PNG image I've zoomed into in the browser:

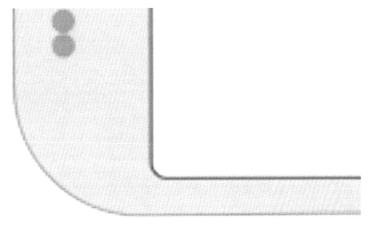

*Figure 10.1: The shortcomings of raster images are easy to see on today's high-definition screens*

Can you see how the image looks obviously pixelated? Here is the exact same image saved as a vector image, in SVG format, and zoomed to a similar level:

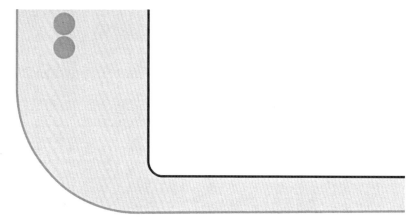

*Figure 10.2: An SVG looks sharp, regardless of the display size*

Hopefully, the difference is obvious.

Unless you are dealing with photographic imagery, using SVG rather than JPEG, GIF, or PNG for any kind of vector artwork will produce resolution-independent graphics that require far smaller file sizes.

While we will touch upon many aspects of SVG in this chapter, the focus will be on how to integrate them into your workflow, while also providing an overview of what is possible with SVG.

In this chapter, we will cover:

- SVG, a brief history, and an anatomy of a basic SVG document
- Creating SVGs with popular image editing packages and services
- Inserting SVGs into a page with `img` and `object` tags
- Inserting SVGs as background images
- Inserting SVGs directly (inline) into HTML
- Reusing SVG symbols
- Referencing external SVG symbols
- What capabilities are possible with each insertion method
- Animating SVGs with SMIL
- Styling SVGs with an external style sheet

- Styling SVGs with internal styles

- Re-coloring and animating SVGs with CSS

- Media queries and SVGs

- Optimizing SVGs

- Using SVGs to define filters for CSS

- Manipulating SVGs with JavaScript and JavaScript libraries

- Implementation tips

- Further resources

SVG is a dense subject. Which portions of this chapter are most relevant to your needs will depend on what you actually need from SVG. Hopefully, I can offer a few shortcuts right up front.

If you simply want to replace static graphical assets on a website with SVG versions, for sharper images and/or smaller file sizes, then look at the shorter sections on using SVG as background images and within img tags.

If you're curious about what applications and services can help you generate and manage SVG assets, skip to the *Creating SVGs with popular image editing packages and services* section for some useful links and pointers.

If you want to understand SVG more fully, or animate and manipulate SVG, you better get yourself comfy and get a double size of your favorite beverage, as this may take a while.

To begin our journey of understanding, step back with me into 2001.

# A brief history of SVG

The first release of SVG was in 2001. That was not a typo. SVG has been "a thing" since 2001. While it gained traction along the way, it's only since the advent of high-resolution devices that SVGs have received widespread interest and adoption. Here is the introduction to SVGs from the 1.1 specification (https://www.w3.org/TR/SVG11/intro.html):

> *SVG is a language for describing two-dimensional graphics in XML [XML10]. SVG allows for three types of graphic objects: vector graphic shapes (for paths consisting of straight lines and curves), images, and text.*

As the name implies, Scalable Vector Graphics allow two-dimensional images to be described in code as vector points. This makes them a great candidate for icons, line drawings, and charts.

As vectors describe relative points, they can scale to any size, without loss of fidelity. Furthermore, in terms of data, as SVGs are described as vector points, it tends to make them tiny, compared to a comparably sized JPEG, GIF, or PNG file.

Browser support for SVG is now widespread: `https://caniuse.com/#search=svg`.

# An image that is also a readable web document

Ordinarily, if you view the code of an image file in a text editor, the resultant text is completely unintelligible.

Where SVG graphics differ is that they are actually described in a markup style language. SVG is written in **Extensible Markup Language (XML)**, a close relative of HTML. Although you may not realize it, XML is everywhere on the internet. Do you use an RSS reader? That's XML right there. XML is the language that wraps up the content of an RSS feed and makes it consumable to a variety of tools and services.

So, not only can machines read and understand SVG graphics, but we can too.

Let me give you an example. Take a look at this star graphic:

*Figure 10.3: A basic SVG*

This is an SVG graphic, called `Star.svg`, inside `example_10-01`. You can either open this example in the browser where it will appear as the star, or you can open it in a text editor, and you can see the code that generates it. Consider this:

```
<?xml version="1.0" encoding="UTF-8" standalone="no"?>
<svg
  width="198px"
  height="188px"
```

```
      viewBox="0 0 198 188"
      version="1.1"
      xmlns="http://www.w3.org/2000/svg"
      xmlns:xlink="http://www.w3.org/1999/xlink"
      xmlns:sketch="http://www.bohemiancoding.com/sketch/ns"
   >
      <!-- Generator: Sketch 3.2.2 (9983) - http://www.bohemiancoding.com/
      sketch -->
      <title>Star 1</title>
      <desc>Created with Sketch.</desc>
      <defs></defs>
      <g
        id="Page-1"
        stroke="none"
        stroke-width="1"
        fill="none"
        fill-rule="evenodd"
        sketch:type="MSPage"
      >
        <polygon
          id="Star-1"
          stroke="#979797"
          stroke-width="3"
          fill="#F8E81C"
          sketch:type="MSShapeGroup"
          points="99 154 40.2214748 184.901699 51.4471742 119.45085 3.89434837
          73.0983006 69.6107374 63.5491503 99 4 128.389263 63.5491503
          194.105652 73.0983006 146.552826 119.45085 157.778525 184.901699 "
        ></polygon>
      </g>
   </svg>
```

That is the entirety of the code needed to generate that star as an SVG graphic.

Now, ordinarily, if you've never looked at the code of an SVG graphic before, you may be wondering why you would ever want to. If all you want is vector graphics displayed on the web, you certainly don't need to. Just find a graphics application that will save your vector artwork as an SVG and you're done.

We will list a few of those packages in the coming pages. However, although it's certainly common and possible to only work with SVG graphics from within a graphics editing application, understanding exactly how an SVG fits together and how you can tweak it to your exact will can become very useful if you need to start manipulating and animating an SVG.

So, let's take a closer look at that SVG markup and get an appreciation of what exactly is going on in there. I'd like to draw your attention to a few key things.

## The root SVG element

The root SVG element here has attributes for `width`, `height`, and `viewBox`:

```
<svg width="198px" height="188px" viewBox="0 0 198 188"
```

Each of these plays an important role in how an SVG is displayed.

Hopefully, at this point, you understand the term **viewport**. It's been used in most chapters of this book to describe the area of a device through which content is viewed. For example, a mobile device might have a 320 px by 480 px viewport. A desktop computer might have a 1,920 px by 1,080 px viewport.

The `width` and `height` attributes of the SVG effectively create a viewport. Through this defined viewport, we can peek in to see the shapes defined inside the SVG. Just like a web page, the contents of the SVG may be bigger than the viewport, but that doesn't mean the rest isn't there; it's merely hidden from our current view.

The `viewBox`, on the other hand, defines the coordinate system in which all the shapes of the SVG are governed. You can think of the `viewBox` values `0 0 198 188` as describing the top-left and bottom-right areas of a rectangle. The first two values, known technically as `min-x` and `min-y`, describe the top-left corner, while the second two, known technically as width and height, describe the bottom-right corner. Having the `viewBox` attribute allows you to do things like zoom an image in or out. For example, if you halve the `width` and `height` in the `viewBox` attribute like this:

```
<svg width="198px" height="188px" viewBox="0 0 99 94"
```

The shape, which is half the size of the SVG, will "zoom" up to fill the size of the SVG width and height.

To really understand `viewBox` and the SVG coordinate system and the opportunities it presents, I recommend this post by Sara Soueidan: `https://sarasoueidan.com/blog/svg-coordinate-systems/` and this post by Jakob Jenkov: `https://jenkov.com/tutorials/svg/index.html`.

## Namespace

This SVG has an additional namespace defined for the Sketch graphics program that generated it (`xmlns` is short for **XML namespace**):

```
xmlns:sketch="http://www.bohemiancoding.com/sketch/ns"
```

These namespace references tend to only be used by the program that generated the SVG, so they are often not needed when the SVG is bound for the web. Optimization processes for reducing the size of SVGs will often strip them out.

## The title and desc tags

There are `title` and `desc` tags that make an SVG document highly accessible:

```
<title>Star 1</title>
    <desc>Created with Sketch.</desc>
```

These tags can be used to describe the contents of the graphics when they cannot be seen. However, when SVG graphics are used for background graphics, these tags can be stripped to further reduce the file size.

## The defs tag

There is an empty `defs` tag in our example code:

```
<defs></defs>
```

Despite being empty in our example, this is an important element. It is used to store definitions of all manner of reusable content, such as gradients, symbols, paths, and more.

# The g element

The g element is used to group other elements together. For example, if you were drawing an SVG of a car, you might group the shapes that make up an entire wheel inside a g tag:

```
<g id="Page-1" stroke="none" stroke-width="1" fill="none" fill-
rule="evenodd" sketch:type="MSPage">
```

In our g tag, we can see the earlier namespace of Sketch being reused here. It will help that graphics application open this graphic again, but it serves no further purpose should this image be bound for elsewhere.

# SVG shapes

The innermost node in this example is a polygon:

```
<polygon id="Star-1" stroke="#979797" stroke-width="3" fill="#F8E81C"
sketch:type="MSShapeGroup" points="99 154 40.2214748 184.901699 51.4471742
119.45085 3.89434837 73.0983006 69.6107374 63.5491503 99 4 128.389263
63.5491503 194.105652 73.0983006 146.552826 119.45085 157.778525
184.901699 "></polygon>
```

SVGs have a number of ready-made shapes available: path, rect, circle, ellipse, line, polyline, and polygon.

# SVG paths

SVG paths differ from the shapes of SVGs as they are composed of any number of connected points, giving you the freedom to create any shape you like.

For example, take a look at this path, which describes the same star as before but with the shape described as a path instead of a polygon. Pay particular attention to the d attribute:

```
<path d="M99 154l-58.78 30.902 11.227-65.45L3.894 73.097l65.717-9.55L99
4l29.39 59.55 65.716 9.548-47.553 46.353 11.226 65.45z" />
```

So, those are the guts of an SVG file, and hopefully now you have a high-level understanding of what's going on. While some will relish the opportunity to handwrite or edit SVG files in code, a great many more would rather generate SVGs with a graphics package. Let's consider some of the more popular choices.

# Creating SVGs with popular image editing packages and services

While SVGs can be opened, edited, and written in a text editor, there are plenty of applications offering a **Graphical User Interface (GUI)** that make authoring complex SVG graphics easier. Perhaps the most obvious choice is Adobe's Illustrator (PC/Mac). However, it is expensive for casual users, so my own preference is either Bohemian Coding's Sketch (Mac only: `https://www.sketch.com/`), which still isn't cheap at $99 a year, or Figma, which is cross-platform and also uses a subscription-based model that is currently free for the starter plan. Check out Figma at `https://www.figma.com/`.

If you use Windows/Linux and/or are looking for cheap options, consider the free and open source Inkscape (`https://inkscape.org/en/`). It's by no means the prettiest tool to work with, but it is very capable (if you want any proof, view the Inkscape gallery: `https://inkscape.org/en/community/gallery/`).

Finally, there are a few online editors. Google has svg-edit (`https://github.com/SVG-Edit/svgedit`). There is also DRAW SVG (`https://www.drawsvg.org/`) and Method Draw, an arguably better-looking fork of svg-edit (`https://editor.method.ac/`).

## Saving time with SVG icon services

The aforementioned applications all give you the capability to create SVG graphics from scratch. However, if it's icons you're after, you can probably save a lot of time (and, for me, get better results) by downloading SVG versions of icons from an online icon service.

My personal favorite is `https://icomoon.io`, although `https://fontastic.me` is also great. To quickly illustrate the benefits of an online icon service, loading the `https://icomoon.io` application gives you a searchable library of icons (some free, some paid):

*Figure 10.4: Online services can make it simple to get started incorporating SVGs*

You select the ones you want and then click **Download**. The resultant file contains the icons as SVGs, PNGs, and also SVG symbols for placement in the `defs` element (remember that the `defs` element is a container element for referenced elements).

To see for yourself, open `example_10-02`. You can see the resultant downloaded files after I'd chosen five icons from `https://icomoon.io`.

# Inserting SVGs into your web pages

There are a number of things that you can do with SVG images that you can't do with normal image formats (JPEG, GIF, and PNG). The range of what's possible is largely dependent on the way that the SVG is inserted into the page.

So, before we get to what we can actually do with SVGs, we'll consider the various ways we can actually get them on the page in the first place.

# Using an img tag

The most straightforward way to use an SVG graphic is exactly how you would insert any image into an HTML document. We just use a good ol' `img` tag:

```
<img src="mySconeVector.svg" alt="Amazing line art of a scone" />
```

This makes the SVG behave more or less like any other image. There isn't much else to say about that.

# Using an object tag

The `object` tag is the container recommended by the W3C for holding non-HTML content in a web page (the specification for `object` is here: `https://html.spec.whatwg.org/multipage/iframe-embed-object.html#the-object-element`). We can make use of it to insert an SVG into our page like this:

```
<object data="img/svgfile.svg" type="image/svg+xml">
    <span class="fallback-info">Your browser doesn't support SVG</span>
</object>
```

Either a `data` or `type` attribute is required, although I would always recommend adding both. The `data` attribute is where you link out to the SVG asset in the same manner you would link to any other asset. The `type` attribute describes the MIME (internet media type) type relevant to the content. In this instance, `image/svg+xml` is the MIME type to indicate that the data is SVG. You can add a `width` and `height` attribute too if you want to constrain the size of the SVG with this container.

An SVG inserted into the page via an `object` tag is also accessible with JavaScript, so that's one reason to insert them this way. However, an additional bonus of using the `object` tag is that it provides a simple mechanism for when a browser doesn't understand the data type.

For example, imagine a dreadful scenario where you have to support an incredibly old browser like Internet Explorer 8, which has no support for SVG. Opening that `object` there, the `object` would simply see the message "Your browser doesn't support SVG." You can use this space to provide a fallback image in an `img` tag. However, be warned that from my cursory testing, the browser will always download the fallback image, regardless of whether it actually needs it. Therefore, if you want your site to load in the shortest possible time (you do, trust me), this might not actually be the best choice.

An alternative approach to providing a fallback would be to add a `background-image` via the CSS. For example, in our previous example, our fallback span has a `class` of `.fallback-info`. We could make use of this in CSS to link to a suitable `background-image`. That way, the background image will only be downloaded if required.

## Inserting an SVG as a background image

SVGs can be used as background images in CSS, much the same as any other image format (PNG, JPG, or GIF). There's nothing special about the way you reference them:

```
.item {
  background-image: url('image.svg');
}
```

If you find yourself in the unlikely situation of needing to support browsers that don't support SVG (Android 2 and Internet Explorer 8, for example), you can use CSS feature queries, which we looked at in *Chapter 6, CSS Selectors, Typography, and More*:

```
.item {
  background-image: url('image.png');
}
@supports (fill: black) {
  .item {
    background-image: url('image.svg');
  }
}
```

The `@supports` rule works here because `fill` is an SVG property, so if the browser understands that, it will take the lower rule over the first.

If your needs for SVG are primarily static background images, perhaps for icons and the like, I highly recommend implementing SVGs as background images. That's because there are a number of tools that will automatically create image sprites or style sheet assets (which means including the SVGs as data URIs), fallback PNG assets, and requisite style sheets from any individual SVGs you create. Using SVGs this way is very well supported; the images themselves cache well (so performance-wise, they work very well), and it's simple to implement.

## A brief aside on data URIs

After reading the previous section, you might wonder what on earth a **Data Uniform Resource Identifier** (URI) is. In relation to CSS, it's a means of embedding what would ordinarily be an external asset, such as an image, within the CSS file itself.

Therefore, where we might ordinarily do this to link to an external image file:

```
.external {
  background-image: url('Star.svg');
}
```

We could include the image inside our style sheet with a data URI, like this:

```
.data-uri {
  background-image: url(data:image/svg+xml,%3C%3Fxml%20
  version%3D%221.0%22%20encoding%3D%22UTF-8%22%20
  standalone%3D%22no%22%3F%3E%0A%3Csvg%20width%3D%22198px%22%20
  height%3D%22188px%22%20viewBox%3D%220%200%20198%20
  188%22%20version%3D%221.1%22%20xmlns%3D%22http%3A%2F%2Fwww.
  w3.org%2F2000%2Fsvg%22%20xmlns%3Axlink%3D%22http%3A%2F%2Fwww.
  w3.org%2F1999%2Fxlink%22%20xmlns%3Asketch%3D%22http%3A%2F%2Fwww.
  bohemiancoding.com%2Fsketch%2Fns%22%3E%0A%20%20%20%20%3C%21--%20
  Generator%3A%20Sketch%203.2.2%20%28899893%29%20-%20http%3A%2F%2Fwww.
  bohemiancoding.com%2Fsketch%20--%3E%0A%20%20%20%20%3Ctitle%3EStar%20
  1%3C%2Ftitle%3E%0A%20%20%20%20%3Cdesc%3ECreated%20with%20
  Sketch.%3C%2Fdesc%3E%0A%20%20%20%20%3Cdefs%3E%3C%2Fdefs%3E%0A%20
  %20%20%20%3Cg%20id%3D%22Page-1%22%20stroke%3D%22none%22%20stroke-
  width%3D%221%22%20fill%3D%22none%22%20fill-rule%3D%22evenodd%22%20
  sketch%3Atype%3D%22MSPage%22%3E%0A%20%20%20%20%20%20%20%20%3Cpolygon%20
  id%3D%22Star-1%22%20stroke%3D%22%233979797%22%20stroke-width%3D%223%22%20
  fill%3D%22%23F8E81C%22%20sketch%3Atype%3D%22MSShapeGroup%22%20
  points%3D%2299%20154%2040.2214748%20184.901699%2051.4471742%20
  119.45085%203.89434837%2073.0983006%2069.6107374%2063.5491503%2099%20
  4%20128.389263%2063.5491503%20194.105652%2073.0983006%20146.552826%20
  119.45085%20157.778525%20184.901699%20%22%3E%3C%2Fpolygon%3E%0A%20%20%20
  %20%3C%2Fg%3E%0A%3C%2Fsvg%3E);
}
```

It's not pretty, but it provides us with a way to negate a separate request over the network. There are different encoding methods for data URIs and plenty of tools available to create data URIs from your assets.

If you're encoding SVGs in this manner, I would suggest avoiding the Base64 method as it doesn't compress as well as text for SVG content.

## Generating image sprites

My personal recommendation, tool-wise, for generating image sprites or data URI assets, is iconizr (`https://iconizr.com`). It gives you complete control over how you would like your resultant SVG and fallback PNG assets. You can have the SVGs and fallback PNG files output as data URIs or image sprites, and it even includes the requisite JavaScript snippet for loading the correct asset if you opt for data URIs. This is highly recommended.

While I'm a big fan of SVGs as background images, if you want to animate them dynamically, or inject values into them via JavaScript, then it will be best to opt for inserting SVG data "inline" into the HTML.

## Inserting an SVG inline

As SVG is merely an XML document, you can insert it directly into the HTML. For example:

```
<div>
    <h3>Inserted 'inline':</h3>
    <span class="inlineSVG">
        <svg id="svgInline" width="198" height="188" viewBox="0 0 198 188"
        xmlns="http://www.w3.org/2000/svg" xmlns:xlink="http://www.
        w3.org/1999/xlink">
        <title>Star 1</title>
            <g class="star_Wrapper" fill="none" fill-rule="evenodd">
                <path id="star_Path" stroke="#979797" stroke-width="3"
                fill="#F8E81C" d="M99 154l-58.78 30.902 11.227-65.45L3.894
                73.097l65.717-9.55L99 4l29.39 59.55 65.716 9.548-47.553
                46.353 11.226 65.452z" />
            </g>
        </svg>
    </span>
</div>
```

There is no special wrapping element needed; you literally just insert the SVG markup inside the HTML markup. It's also worth noting that if you remove any width and height attributes on the svg element, the SVG will scale fluidly to fit the containing element.

Inserting SVG as markup into your documents is probably the most versatile option in terms of accessing the broadest range of SVG features.

Let's consider some of those features that inserting SVGs inline allows next.

# Reusing graphical objects from symbols

Earlier in this chapter, I mentioned that I had picked and downloaded some icons from IcoMoon (https://icomoon.io). They were icons depicting touch gestures: swipe, pinch, drag, and more. Suppose, in a website you are building, you need to make use of them multiple times. Remember I mentioned that there was a version of those icons as SVG symbol definitions? That's what we will make use of now.

In example_10-03, we insert the various symbol definitions inside the defs element of an SVG in the page. You'll notice that, on the svg element, an inline style is used, display:none, and the height and width attributes have both been set to 0 (those styles could be set in CSS if you prefer). This is so that this SVG takes up no space. We are only using this SVG to house symbols of the graphical objects we want to use elsewhere. So, our markup starts like this:

```
<body>
    <svg display="none" width="0" height="0" version="1.1" xmlns="http://
    www.w3.org/2000/svg" xmlns:xlink="http://www.w3.org/1999/xlink">
    <defs>
    <symbol id="icon-drag-left-right" viewBox="0 0 1344 1024">
        <title>drag-left-right</title>
        <path class="path1" d="M256 192v-160l-224 224 224 224v-160h256v-
        128z"></path>
```

Notice the symbol element inside the defs element? This is the element to use when we want to define a shape for later reuse.

 You can create symbols for use inside the defs tag by taking an existing SVG, changing the svg tag to symbol, removing the namespace attribute, and then nesting it inside the defs tag.

After the SVG has defined all necessary symbols for our work, we have all our "normal" HTML markup. Then, when we want to make use of one of those symbols, we can do this:

```
<svg class="icon-drag-left-right">
  <use xlink:href="#icon-drag-left-right"></use>
</svg>
```

That will display the drag left and right icon:

*Figure 10.5: With SVGs inserted inline, it's possible to reuse graphics*

The magic here is the use element. As you might have guessed from the name, it's used to make use of existing graphical objects that have already been defined elsewhere. The mechanism for choosing what to reference is the xlink attribute, which, in this case, is referencing the symbol ID of the "drag left and right" icon (#icon-drag-left-right) we have inline at the beginning of the markup.

When you reuse a symbol, unless you explicitly set a size (either with attributes on the element itself or with CSS), use will be set to a width and height of 100%. So, to resize our icon, we could do this:

```
.icon-drag-left-right {
  width: 2.5rem;
  height: 2.5rem;
}
```

The use element can be used to reuse all sorts of SVG content: gradients, shapes, symbols, and more.

## Inline SVGs allow different colors in different contexts

With inline SVGs, you can also do useful things like change colors based on context, and that's great when you need multiple versions of the same icon in different colors:

```
.icon-drag-left-right {
  fill: #f90;
}
.different-context .icon-drag-left-right {
  fill: #ddd;
}
```

## Making dual-tone icons that inherit the color of their parent

With inline SVGs, you can also have some fun and create two-tone effects from a single color icon (as long as the SVG is made up of more than one path) with the use of currentColor, the oldest CSS variable. To do this, inside the SVG symbol, set the fill of the path you want to be one color as currentColor. Then, use the color value in your CSS to color the element. For the paths in the SVG symbol without the fill, set them as currentColor; they will receive the fill value. To exemplify this:

```
.icon-drag-left-right {
  width: 2.5rem;
  height: 2.5rem;
  fill: #f90;
  color: #ccc; /* this gets applied to the path that has its fill
  attribute set to currentColor in the symbol */
}
```

Here's that same symbol reused three times, each with different colors and sizes:

*Figure 10.6: Making dual-color SVGs by inheriting colors*

Remember, you can dig around the code in example_10-03. It's also worth noting that the color doesn't have to be set on that element itself—it can be on any parent element; currentColor will inherit a value from up the DOM tree to the nearest parent with a color value set.

## Re-coloring SVGs with CSS custom properties

Nowadays, I find the most effective way to recolor the same SVG or symbol is by using CSS custom properties. We explore them fully in *Chapter 12, Custom Properties and CSS Functions*, but for now, we will just consider how they can help us with SVG. The following example can be found at example_10-04.

I have made a pentagon shape using two paths. Each path has a fill and a stroke value. Here is the SVG:

```
<svg class="shape" width="268" height="254" xmlns="http://www.w3.org/2000/
svg">
  <g fill="none" fill-rule="evenodd" stroke-width="10">
    <path d="M134 6.18L6.73 98.647l48.613 149.615h157.314L261.27 98.647
    134 6.18z" stroke="var(--stroke1)" fill="var(--fill1)"/>
    <path d="M134 36.18l-98.738 71.738 37.714 116.074h122.048l37.714-
    116.074L134 36.18z" stroke="var(--stroke2)" fill="var(--fill2)"/>
  </g>
</svg>
```

Notice how for each path element, both the stroke and fill values have been set to a CSS custom property. With those values in place, I can then set any colors I want for that SVG with CSS, JavaScript, or a combination of the two!

In our example, I have set default colors and hover colors, like this:

```
.shape {
  display: block;
  --stroke1: #ddd;
  --fill1: #444;
  --stroke2: #f90;
  --fill2: #663d00;
}
.shape:hover {
  --stroke1: #333;
  --fill1: #444;
```

```
    --stroke2: #fff;
    --fill2: #ffc266;
  }
```

Sadly, grayscale images fail us a little here, but this is the default coloring (I made the example document background dark just to make it clearer):

*Figure 10.7: CSS custom properties make recoloring SVGs simple*

Then, to prove how easy it is to amend it further still, if you open the example, you will see a button that uses a tiny bit of JavaScript to toggle a class on the page, adding or removing the .amended class. This allows us to have two further sets of colors for this shape:

```
  .amended .shape {
    --stroke1: #080b2b;
    --fill1: #141a67;
    --fill2: #192183;
    --stroke2: #2d3ad7;
  }
  .amended .shape:hover {
    --stroke1: #092b08;
    --fill1: #125610;
    --fill2: #2dd728;
    --stroke2: #1b8118;
  }
```

This results in four blue colors ordinarily and four green colors when hovered over:

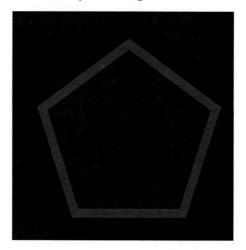

*Figure 10.8: CSS custom properties create near limitless possibilities*

As you can see, there are a lot of positives to placing SVGs inside the markup. The only downside is that it's necessary to include the same SVG data on every page where you want to use the icons. Sadly, this is bad for performance, as the assets (the SVG data) aren't going to be cached easily. However, there is another option.

## Reusing graphical objects from external sources

Rather than paste an enormous set of SVG symbols in each page, while still using the use element, it's possible to link out to external SVG files and grab the portion of the document you want to use. Take a look at example_10-05 and the same three icons as we had in example_10-03, which are put on the page in this manner:

```
<svg class="icon-drag-left-right">
  <use xlink:href="defs.svg#icon-drag-left-right"></use>
</svg>
```

Be aware that some of these examples need running on a server. Two simple solutions: either use something like BrowserSync or npx serve to create a simple local server, or paste the code into a service like https://codepen.io/.

The important part to understand is href. We are linking to an external SVG file (the defs.svg part) and then specifying the ID of the symbol within that file we want to use (the #icon-drag-left-right part). The benefits of this approach are that the asset is cached by the browser (just like any other external image would/could be) and it saves littering our markup with an SVG full of symbol definitions. The downside is that, unlike when defs are placed inline, any dynamic changes to defs.svg (for example, if a path was being manipulated by JavaScript) won't be updated in the use tags.

# What you can do with each SVG insertion method (inline, object, background-image, and img)

As mentioned previously, SVGs differ from other graphical assets. They can behave differently depending on the way they are inserted into a page. As we have seen, there are four main ways in which to place SVG onto the page:

- Inside an img tag
- Inside an object tag
- As a background-image
- Inline

And depending on the insertion method, certain capabilities will or will not be available to you. As we go on to look at some of these capabilities, it may be useful to refer back to this table, which covers what's possible with each insertion method:

| Feature | img | object | inline | bg image |
|---|---|---|---|---|
| SMIL | Y | Y | Y | Y |
| External CSS | N | ⋆[1] | Y | N |
| Internal CSS | Y | Y | Y | Y |
| Access via JS | N | Y | Y | N |
| Cacheable | Y | Y | ⋆[2] | Y |
| MQ in SVG | Y | Y | ⋆[3] | Y |
| Use possible | N | Y | Y | N |

*Figure 10.9: Depending on the insertion method, differing capabilities are possible*

Now, there are caveats to consider, marked within numbers:

1.  When using an SVG inside an object, you can use an external style sheet to style the SVG, but you have to link to that style sheet from within the SVG.

2.  You can use SVGs in an external asset (which is cacheable), although those external assets cannot be manipulated by JavaScript.

3.  A media query inside the styles section of an "inlined" SVG works on the size of the document it lives in (not the size of the SVG itself).

Be aware that browser implementations of SVG also vary. Therefore, just because those things should be possible (as indicated previously) doesn't mean they will be in every browser, or that they will behave consistently!

The results in the preceding table are based on the test page in `example_10-06`.

The behavior of the test page is comparable in the latest versions of Firefox, Chrome, and Safari.

# Extra SVG capabilities and oddities

Let's put aside the foibles of browsers for a moment and consider what some of these features in the table actually allow, and why you may or may not want to make use of them.

SVGs will always render as sharp as the viewing device will allow and regardless of the manner of insertion. For most practical situations, resolution independence is usually reason enough to use SVG. It's then just a question of choosing whichever insertion method suits your workflow and the task at hand.

However, there are other capabilities and oddities that are worth knowing about, such as SMIL animation, different ways to link to external style sheets, marking internal styles with character data delimiters, amending an SVG with JavaScript, and making use of media queries within an SVG. Let's cover those next.

## SMIL animation

SMIL animations (`https://www.w3.org/TR/smil-animation/`) are a way to define animations for an SVG within the SVG document itself. SMIL (pronounced "smile," in case you were wondering) stands for Synchronized Multimedia Integration Language and was developed as a method of defining animations inside an XML document (remember, SVG is XML-based).

Here's an example of how to define a SMIL-based animation:

```
<g class="star_Wrapper" fill="none" fill-rule="evenodd">
```

```
<animate
  xlink:href="#star_Path"
  attributeName="fill"
  attributeType="XML"
  begin="0s"
  dur="2s"
  fill="freeze"
  from="#F8E81C"
  to="#14805e"
/>
<path
  id="star_Path"
  stroke="#979797"
  stroke-width="3"
  fill="#F8E81C"
  d="M99 154l-58.78 30.902 11.227-65.45L3.894 73.097l65.717-9.55L99
  4l29.39 59.55 65.716 9.548-47.553 46.353 11.226 65.452z"
/>
</g>
```

I've grabbed a section of the earlier SVG we looked at. The g is a grouping element in SVG, and this one includes both a star shape (the path element with id="star_Path") and the SMIL animation within the animate element. That simple animation tweens the fill color of the star from yellow to green in 2 seconds.

### Tweening

 In case you didn't already know (I didn't), "tweening" as a term is simply a shortening of "inbetweening," as it merely indicates all the in-between stages from one animation point to another.

What's more, it does that whether the SVG is put on the page in an img, object, background-image, or inline (honestly, open up example_10-06 in any recent browser to see).

Wow! Great, right? Well, kind of. Despite being a standard for some time, SMIL remains on shaky ground. In the second edition of this book, released in August 2015, it looked like the Chrome browser was going to deprecate SMIL in Chrome.

However, like a phoenix from the flames, Chrome provided a "stay of execution" of their intention to deprecate SMIL in August 2016: `https://groups.google.com/a/chromium.org/d/msg/blink-dev/5o0yiO440LM/YGEJBsjUAwAJ`.

So, while theoretically, SMIL is good to use for some use cases, I tend to quarantine it mentally in a "use as a last resort" technique.

However, if you still have a need to use SMIL, Sara Soueidan wrote an excellent, in-depth article about SMIL animations here: `https://css-tricks.com/guide-svg-animations-smil/`.

## Styling an SVG with an external style sheet

It's possible to style an SVG with CSS. This can be CSS enclosed in the SVG itself, or in the CSS style sheets you would write all your "normal" CSS in.

Now, if you refer back to our features table from earlier in this chapter, you can see that styling SVG with external CSS isn't possible when the SVG is included via an img tag or as a `background-image` (apart from in Internet Explorer). It's only possible when SVGs are inserted via an object tag or inline.

There are two syntaxes for linking to an external style sheet from an SVG. The most straightforward way is like this (you would typically add this in the `defs` section):

```
<link href="styles.css" type="text/css" rel="stylesheet"/>
```

It's akin to the way we used to link to style sheets prior to HTML5 (for example, note the type attribute is no longer necessary in HTML5). However, despite this working in many browsers, it isn't the way the specifications define how external style sheets should be linked in SVG (`https://www.w3.org/TR/SVG/styling.html#ReferencingExternalStyleSheets`). Here is the correct/official way, actually defined for XML back in 1999 (`https://www.w3.org/1999/06/REC-xml-stylesheet-19990629/`):

```
<?xml-stylesheet href="styles.css" type="text/css"?>
```

You need to add this above the opening SVG element in your file. For example:

```
<?xml-stylesheet href="styles.css" type="text/css"?>
<svg
  width="198"
  height="188"
  viewBox="0 0 198 188"
```

```
    xmlns="http://www.w3.org/2000/svg"
    xmlns:xlink="http://www.w3.org/1999/xlink"
></svg>
```

You don't have to use an external style sheet; you can use inline styles directly in the SVG itself if you would rather.

## Styling an SVG with internal styles

You can place styles for an SVG within the SVG itself. They should be placed within the `defs` element. As SVG is XML-based, it's safest to include the **Character Data marker** (**CDATA**). The Character Data marker simply tells the browser that the information within the Character Data delimited section could ordinarily be interpreted as XML markup, but should not be. The syntax is like this:

```
<defs>
  <style type="text/css">
    <![CDATA[
        #star_Path {
            stroke: red;
        }
    ]]>
  </style>
</defs>
```

## SVG properties and values within CSS

Notice the `stroke` property in the prior code block? This isn't a CSS property; it's an SVG property. There are quite a few specific SVG properties you can use in styles (regardless of whether they are declared inline or via an external style sheet). For example, with an SVG, as you have seen in an earlier example, you don't specify a `background-color`; instead, you specify a `fill`. You don't specify a `border`; you specify a `stroke-width`.

For the full list of SVG-specific properties, take a look at the specification here: `https://www.w3.org/TR/SVG/styling.html`.

With either inline or external CSS, it's possible to do all the "normal" CSS things you would expect: change an element's appearance, animate and transform elements, and so on.

## Animating an SVG with CSS

Let's consider a quick example of adding a CSS animation inside an SVG (remember, these styles could just as easily be in an external style sheet too). Let's take the star example we have looked at throughout this chapter and make it spin. You can look at the finished example in example_10-07:

```
<div class="wrapper">
  <svg
    width="198"
    height="188"
    viewBox="0 0 220 200"
    xmlns="http://www.w3.org/2000/svg"
    xmlns:xlink="http://www.w3.org/1999/xlink"
  >
    <title>Star 1</title>
    <defs>
      <style type="text/css">
        <![CDATA[
        @keyframes spin {
            0% {
                transform: rotate(0deg);
            }
            100% {
                transform: rotate(360deg);
            }
        }
        .star_Wrapper {
            animation: spin 2s 1s;
            transform-origin: 50% 50%;
        }
        .wrapper {
            padding: 2rem;
            margin: 2rem;
        }
        ]]>
      </style>
      <g id="shape">
        <path fill="#14805e" d="M50 50h50v50H50z" />
```

```
          <circle fill="#ebebeb" cx="50" cy="50" r="50" />
        </g>
      </defs>
      <g class="star_Wrapper" fill="none" fill-rule="evenodd">
        <path
          id="star_Path"
          stroke="#333"
          stroke-width="3"
          fill="#F8E81C"
          d="M99 154l-58.78 30.902 11.227-65.45L3.894 73.097l65.717-9.55L99
          4l29.39 59.55 65.716 9.548-47.553 46.353 11.226 65.453z"
        />
      </g>
    </svg>
  </div>
```

If you load that example in the browser, after a 1-second delay, the star will spin a full circle over the course of 2 seconds.

Notice how a transform-origin of 50% 50% has been set on the SVG? This is because, unlike CSS, the default transform-origin of an SVG is not 50% 50% (center in both axis); it's actually 0 0 (top left). Without that property set, the star would rotate around the top-left point.

You can get quite far animating SVGs with CSS animations. However, when you want to add interactivity or synchronize several events, it's generally best to lean on JavaScript. And the good news is that there are great libraries that make animating SVGs really easy. Let's look at an example of that now.

## Animating SVG with JavaScript

With an SVG inserted into the page via an object tag or inline, it's possible to manipulate the SVG directly or indirectly with JavaScript. By indirectly, I mean it's possible with JavaScript to change a class on or above the SVG that would cause a CSS animation to start. For example:

```
svg {
  /* no animation */
}
.added-with-js svg {
  /* animation */
}
```

However, it's also possible to animate an SVG via JavaScript directly.

If you're animating just one or two things independently, it's probable things would be lighter, code-wise, if you wrote the JavaScript by hand. However, if you need to animate lots of elements or synchronize the animation of elements as if on a timeline, JavaScript libraries can really help. Ultimately, you will need to judge whether the weight of including the library in your page can be justified for the goal you are trying to achieve.

My recommendation for animating SVGs via JavaScript is the GreenSock Animation Platform (`https://greensock.com`). For the next example, we'll cover a very simple example using Green-Sock.

## A simple example of animating an SVG with GreenSock

Suppose we want to make an interface dial that animates when we click a button from zero to whatever value we input. We want not only the stroke of the dial to animate in both length and color but also the number from zero to the value we input. You can view the completed implementation in `example_10-08`.

So, if we entered a value of 75 and clicked **Animate!!**, the dial would fill around to look like this:

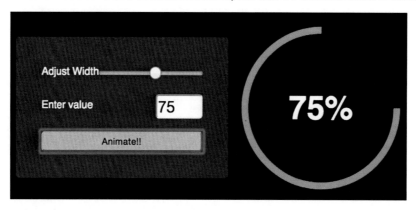

*Figure 10.10: Animation libraries make animating SVGs simpler*

Instead of listing out the entire JavaScript file (which is heavily commented, so it should make some sense to read in isolation), for brevity's sake, we'll just consider the key points.

The basic idea is that we have made a circle as an SVG `<path>` (rather than a `<circle>` element). As it's a path, it has a stroke. SVG has a property called `stroke-dashoffset`. This value lets you control where the dash applied to a path starts. Because of this, the `stroke-dasharray`, which is the actual pattern of the dash, can be offset an amount equal to the length of the path itself.

This allows us to animate those properties and the result is as if the path is being drawn.

There's more info on this technique in the boxed-out section below.

In case you haven't come across the SVG "line drawing" technique before, it was popularized by Polygon magazine when Vox Media animated a couple of line drawings of the Xbox One and PlayStation 4 games consoles. You can read the original post here: `https://product.voxmedia.com/2013/11/25/5426880/polygon-feature-design-svg-animations-for-fun-and-profit`.

There's also an excellent and more thorough explanation of the technique by Jake Archibald here: `https://jakearchibald.com/2013/animated-line-drawing-svg/`.

If the value to animate dasharray was a static, known value, this effect would be relatively simple to achieve with a CSS animation and a little trial and error (more on CSS animations in the next chapter). However, besides a dynamic value, at the same time as we are "drawing" the line, we want to fade in the stroke color from one value to another and visually count up to the input value in the text node. This is an animation equivalent to patting our heads, rubbing our tummies, and counting backward from 10,000. GreenSock makes those things easy (the animation part; it won't rub your tummy or pat your head, although it can count back from 10,000, should you need it to).

Here are the lines of JavaScript needed to make GreenSock do all three:

```
// Animate the drawing of the line and color change
TweenLite.to(circlePath, 1.5, {
  'stroke-dashoffset': '-' + amount,
  stroke: strokeEndColour,
});
// Set a counter to zero and animate to the input value
var counter = {var: 0};
TweenLite.to(counter, 1.5, {
  var: inputValue,
  onUpdate: function() {
    text.textContent = Math.ceil(counter.var) + '%';
  },
  ease: Circ.easeOut,
});
```

In essence, with the `TweenLite.to()` function, you pass in the thing you want to animate, the time over which the animation should occur, and then the values you want to change (and what you want them to change to).

The GreenSock site has excellent documentation and support forums, so if you find yourself needing to synchronize a number of animations at once, be sure to clear a day from your diary and familiarize yourself with GreenSock.

## Using SVGs as filters

In *Chapter 8, Stunning Aesthetics with CSS*, we looked at the CSS filter effects. With help from SVG, we can create even more filters. In `example_10-09`, we have a page with the following markup inside the body:

```
<img class="HRH" src="queen@2x-1024x747.png" />
```

It's an image of Queen Elizabeth II of the United Kingdom. Ordinarily, it looks like this:

*Figure 10.11: An image with no SVG filter applied*

Now, also in that example folder, is an SVG with a filter defined in the defs elements. The SVG markup looks like this:

```
<svg xmlns="http://www.w3.org/2000/svg" version="1.1">
  <defs>
    <filter id="myfilter" x="0" y="0">
      <feColorMatrix
        in="SourceGraphic"
        type="hueRotate"
        values="90"
        result="A"
      />
      <feGaussianBlur in="A" stdDeviation="6" />
    </filter>
  </defs>
</svg>
```

Within the filter, we are first defining a hue rotation of 90 (using feColorMatrix), and then passing that effect, via the result attribute, to the next filter (feGaussianBlur) with a blur value of 6. Be aware that I've been deliberately heavy-handed here. This doesn't produce a nice aesthetic, but it should leave you in no doubt that the effect has worked!

Now, rather than add that SVG markup to the HTML, we can leave it where it is and reference it using the same CSS filter syntax we saw in the previous chapter:

```
.HRH {
  filter: url('filter.svg#myfilter');
}
```

And this is the effect in the browser:

*Figure 10.12: An image with an SVG filter applied*

So, it's possible with SVG to create yourself an entirely bespoke filter. Just one more string to SVG's bow!

## A note on media queries inside SVGs

All browsers that understand SVG should respect the CSS media queries defined inside. However, when it comes to media queries inside SVGs, there are a few things to remember.

For example, suppose you insert a media query inside an SVG, like this:

```
<style type="text/css"><![CDATA[
    #star_Path {
        stroke: red;
    }
    @media (min-width: 800px) {
        #star_Path {
```

```
            stroke: violet;
        }
    }
]]></style>
```

And that SVG is displayed on the page at a width of 200 px, inside a browser viewport that is 1,200 px wide.

We might expect the stroke of the star to be violet when the screen is 800 px and above. After all, that's what we have our media query set to. However, when the SVG is placed on the page via an img tag, as a background image, or inside an object tag, it has no knowledge of the outer HTML document. Hence, in this situation, min-width means the minimum width of the SVG itself. So, unless the SVG itself is displayed on the page at a width of 800 px or more, the stroke won't be violet.

Conversely, when you insert an SVG inline, it merges (in a manner of speaking) with the outer HTML document. The min-width media query here is looking to the viewport (as is the HTML) to decide when the media query matches.

To solve this particular problem and make the same media query behave consistently, we could amend our media query to this:

```
@media (min-device-width: 800px) {
  #star_Path {
    stroke: violet;
  }
}
```

That way, regardless of the SVG size or how it is embedded, it is looking to the device width (effectively the viewport).

## Optimizing SVGs

As conscientious developers, we want to ensure that assets are as small as possible. The easiest way to do this with SVGs is to make use of automation tools that can optimize various particulars of SVG documents. Besides obvious economies such as removing elements (for example, stripping the title and description elements), it's also possible to perform a raft of micro-optimizations that, when added up, make for far leaner SVG assets. Presently, for this task, I would recommend SVGO (https://github.com/svg/svgo).

If you have never used SVGO before, I would recommend starting with SVGOMG (https://jakearchibald.github.io/svgomg/). It's a browser-based version of SVGO that enables you to toggle the various optimization plugins and get instant feedback on the file savings. Remember our example star SVG markup from the beginning of this chapter? By default, that simple SVG is 489 bytes in size. By passing that through SVGO, it's possible to get the size down to just 218 bytes, and that's leaving the viewBox in. That's a saving of 55.42%. If you're using a raft of SVG images, these savings can really add up. Here's what the optimized SVG markup looks like:

```
<svg
  width="198"
  height="188"
  viewBox="0 0 198 188"
  xmlns="http://www.w3.org/2000/svg"
>
  <path
    stroke="#979797"
    stroke-width="3"
    fill="#F8E81C"
    d="M99 154l-58.78 30.902 11.227-65.45L3.894 73.097l65.717-9.55L99
    4l29.39 59.55 65.716 9.548-47.553 46.353 11.226 65.454z"
  />
</svg>
```

Before you spend too long with SVGO, be aware that, such is the popularity of SVGO, plenty of other SVG tools also make use of it. For example, the aforementioned iconizr (https://iconizr.com) tool runs your SVG files through SVGO by default anyway, before creating your assets, so ensure you aren't unnecessarily double optimizing.

# SVG implementation tips

We're almost at the end of this chapter now and there is still so much we could talk about regarding SVG. Therefore, at this point, I'll just list a few unrelated considerations. They aren't necessarily worthy of protracted explanations, but I'll list them here in note form in case they save you from hours of searching Stack Overflow:

- If you have no need to animate your SVGs, opt for an image sprite of your assets or a data URI style sheet. It's far easier to provide fallback assets and they almost always perform better from a performance perspective.

- Automate as many steps in the asset creation process as possible; this reduces human error and produces predictable results faster.

- To insert static SVGs in a project, pick a single delivery mechanism and stick to it (image sprite, data URI, or inline). It can become a burden to produce some assets one way and some another and maintain the various implementations.

- There is no easy "one size fits all" choice with SVG animation. For occasional and simple animations, use CSS. For complex interactive or timeline-style animations, lean on a proven library such as GreenSock. Or, look at using the JavaScript Web Animations API.

These are just guides, not gospel. There will be times when you need to make a choice that may seem counter-intuitive to conventional wisdom. But at least if you have taken in the details here, you will be able to make informed choices when it comes to working with SVG.

## Summary

This has been a dense chapter. We have covered a lot of the essential information needed to start making sense of and implementing SVGs in a responsive project. We have considered the different graphics applications and online solutions available to create SVG assets, then the various insertion methods possible and the capabilities each allows, along with the various browser peculiarities to be aware of.

We've also considered how to link to external style sheets and reuse SVG symbols from within the same page and when referenced externally. We even looked at how we can make filters with SVG that can be referenced and used in CSS.

Finally, we considered how to make use of JavaScript libraries to aid animating SVGs, as well as how to optimize SVGs with the aid of the SVGO tool.

In the next chapter, we'll be looking at CSS transitions, transforms, and animations. It's also worth reading that chapter in relation to SVG, as many of the syntaxes and techniques can be used and applied in SVG documents too.

## Further resources

As I mentioned at the start of this chapter, I have neither the space nor the knowledge to impart all there is to know about SVG. Therefore, I'd like to make you aware of the following excellent resources, which provide additional depth and range on the subject:

- *SVG Essentials, 2nd Edition*, by J. David Eisenberg and Amelia Bellamy-Royds: `https://www.oreilly.com/library/view/svg-essentials-2nd/9781491945308/`

- "A Guide to SVG Animations (SMIL)" by Sara Soueidan: `https://css-tricks.com/guide-svg-animations-smil/`

- *Testing media queries inside SVGs*, by Jeremie Patonnier: `http://jeremie.patonnier.net/experiences/svg/media-queries/test.html`

- *An SVG Primer for Today's Browsers*: `https://www.w3.org/Graphics/SVG/IG/resources/svgprimer.html`

- "Understanding SVG Coordinate Systems and Transformations (Part 1)" by Sara Soueidan: `https://sarasoueidan.com/blog/svg-coordinate-systems/`

- "Hands On: SVG Filter Effects": `https://testdrive-archive.azurewebsites.net/Graphics/hands-on-css3/hands-on_svg-filter-effects.htm`

- The full set of SVG tutorials by Jakob Jenkov: `https://jenkov.com/tutorials/svg/index.html`

# 11

# Transitions, Transformations, and Animations

CSS can handle the majority of motion requirements using CSS transitions and transforms, or CSS animations.

To clearly understand what transitions, transforms, and animations do, I will offer this, perhaps overly simplistic, summary:

- A CSS **transition** is used to define how one visual state should move (transition) to another, differing visual state.
- A CSS **transform** is used to take an existing element and transform it into something or someplace else without affecting any other elements on the page. For example, "make this twice as big" and "move this 100 px to the right" are plain text descriptions of tasks we can achieve with CSS transforms. However, the transform doesn't control *how* the element makes that change; that is the job of the transition.
- A CSS **animation** is typically used to make a series of changes to an element.

If those differences seem a little vague at this point, hopefully, by the end of this chapter, they won't.

In this chapter, we'll cover:

- What CSS transitions are and how to use them
- Writing CSS transitions and understanding the shorthand syntax
- CSS transition timing functions (ease, `cubic-bezier`, and so on)
- What CSS transforms are and how to use them

- Understanding different 2D transforms (`scale`, `rotate`, `skew`, `translate`, and `matrix`)
- Understanding 3D transforms
- How to animate with CSS using keyframes

Let's get started with an introduction to CSS transitions.

# What CSS transitions are and how we can use them

Transitions are the simplest way to create some visual "effect" between one state and another with CSS. Let's consider a simple example: an element that transitions from one state to another when hovered over.

When styling hyperlinks in CSS, it's common practice to create a hover state: an obvious way to make users aware that the item they are hovering over can be interacted with. Hover states are of little relevance to the growing number of touchscreen devices, but for mouse users, they're a great and simple interaction between website and user. They're also handy for illustrating transitions, so that's what we will start with.

Traditionally, using only CSS, hover states are an on/off affair. There is one set of properties and values on an element as the default, and when a pointer is hovered over that element, the properties and values are instantly changed. However, CSS transitions, as the name implies, allow us to transition between one or more properties and values to other properties and values.

A couple of important things to know upfront. Firstly, you can't transition from `display: none;`. When something is set to `display: none;` it isn't actually "painted" on the screen, so it has no existing state you can transition from.

 Although you can't transition from `display: none`, it is possible to run an animation on an element as soon as its `display` property is changed. So, you could, for example, change an element's `display` property from `display: none` and then run an animation to fade it in from 0% opacity. We'll cover animations later in this chapter.

In order to create the effect of something fading in, you would have to transition opacity or position values. Secondly, not all properties can be transitioned. To ensure you're not attempting the impossible, here is the list of transitionable (I know, it's not even a word) properties: `https://developer.mozilla.org/en-US/docs/Web/CSS/CSS_animated_properties`.

If you open up example_11-01, you'll see a few links in a nav. Here's the relevant markup:

```
<nav>
  <a href="#">link1</a>
  <a href="#">link2</a>
  <a href="#">link3</a>
  <a href="#">link4</a>
  <a href="#">link5</a>
</nav>
```

And here's the relevant CSS:

```
a {
  font-family: sans-serif;
  color: #fff;
  text-indent: 1rem;
  background-color: #ccc;
  display: inline-flex;
  flex: 1 1 20%;
  align-self: stretch;
  align-items: center;
  text-decoration: none;
  transition: box-shadow 1s;
}
a + a {
  border-left: 1px solid #aaa;
}
a:hover {
  box-shadow: inset 0 -3px 0 #cc3232;
}
```

And here are the two states; first, the default:

*Figure 11.1: Two links, in their default state*

And then here's the hover state:

*Figure 11.2: When hovered, we underline the link*

Ordinarily, hovering over the link snaps from the first state (no red line) to the second (red line); it's an on/off affair. However, this line:

```
transition: box-shadow 1s;
```

adds a transition to the box-shadow from the existing state to the hover state over 1 second.

 You'll notice in the CSS of the preceding example that we're using the adjacent sibling selector +. You'll remember this selector from *Chapter 6, CSS Selectors, Typography, and More*. This means if an element (an anchor tag in our example) directly follows another element (another anchor tag), then apply the enclosed styles. It's useful here as we don't want a left border on the first element.

The transition property is applied on the "from" state, not the "to" state of a selector. In our case, we add the transition property and values on the element in its default state, not the hover state. You could add a transition property to the hover state too, but this would apply when you transition away from the hover state and back to default. This implementation is so that multiple different states such as :active, :focus, :hover, and more can also have different styles set and enjoy the same transition to them.

## The properties of a transition

A transition can be declared using up to four properties:

- transition-property: The name of the CSS property to be transitioned (such as background-color, text-shadow, or all to transition every possible property).

- transition-duration: The length of time over which the transition should occur (defined in seconds, for example, .3s, 2s, or 1.5s).

- transition-timing-function: How the transition changes speed during the duration (for example, ease, linear, ease-in, ease-out, ease-in-out, or cubic-bezier).

- transition-delay: An optional value to determine a delay before the transition commences. Alternatively, a negative value can be used to commence a transition immediately but part way through its transition "journey." It's defined in seconds, for example, .3s, 1s, or 2.5s.

 For any duration defined in seconds with s in CSS, you can also define it in milliseconds, if you prefer. For example, instead of 0.5s for half a second, you could write 500ms. It's purely a preference thing, but for predictability, I would advise you to choose one or the other and stick to it throughout a project.

Used separately, the various transition properties can be used to create a transition like this:

```
.style {
  /*...(more styles)...*/
  transition-property: all;
  transition-duration: 1s;
  transition-timing-function: ease;
  transition-delay: 0s;
}
```

This particular rule effectively says, "Transition any transitionable property on this element over 1 second with no delay using the ease timing function."

## The transition shorthand property

We can roll these individual declarations into a single, shorthand version:

```
transition: all 1s ease 0s;
```

One important point to note when writing the shorthand version is that the first time-related value provided is always parsed to be the transition-duration. The second time-related value is parsed to be the transition-delay. The shorthand version is the one I favor, as I generally only need to define the duration of the transition and the properties that should be transitioned.

To exemplify, suppose I wanted the background-color to transition over 2 seconds:

```
transition: background-color 2s;
```

If no timing function is provided, the default timing function of ease is applied.

I would also advise only defining the property or properties you actually need to transition. It's really handy to just set all, but, for example, if you only need to transition opacity, then only define opacity as the transition property. When you set all, there is a chance you will be inadvertently transitioning properties you don't want to, which can possibly lead to bugs for yourself or others down the line.

## Transitioning different properties over different periods of time

Where a rule has multiple properties declared, you don't have to transition all of them in the same way. Consider this rule:

```
.style {
  /* ...(more styles)... */
```

```
    transition-property: border, color, text-shadow;
    transition-duration: 2s, 3s, 8s;
}
```

Here, we have specified with `transition-property` that we'd like to transition the border, `color`, and `text-shadow`. Then, with the `transition-duration` declaration, we are stating that the border should transition over 2 seconds, the `color` over 3 seconds, and the `text-shadow` over 8 seconds. The comma-separated durations match the comma-separated order of the transition properties.

You can also perform the same job with the shorthand syntax, and again this is my preferred way to do it:

```
.style {
    transition: border 2s, color 3s, text-shadow 8s;
}
```

I think it is far easier to reason about each property and its timing when they are written next to each other.

So far, we have dealt with transitioning different properties over different durations. However, there is also a fairly limitless number of timing functions that change how an element property changes over a duration.

## Understanding timing functions

When you declare a `transition`, the properties, durations, and delays are relatively simple to understand. However, understanding what each timing function does can be a little trickier. Just what do `ease`, `linear`, `ease-in`, `ease-out`, `ease-in-out`, and `cubic-bezier` actually do? Each of them is actually a predefined `cubic-bezier` curve, essentially the same as an easing function. Or, more simplistically, a mathematical description of how the transition should look. It's generally easier to visualize these curves, so I recommend you head over to `https://cubic-bezier.com/` or `https://easings.net`.

Both these sites let you compare timing functions and see the difference each one makes. Here is a screenshot of `https://easings.net`—on the website, you can hover over each line for a demonstration of the easing function:

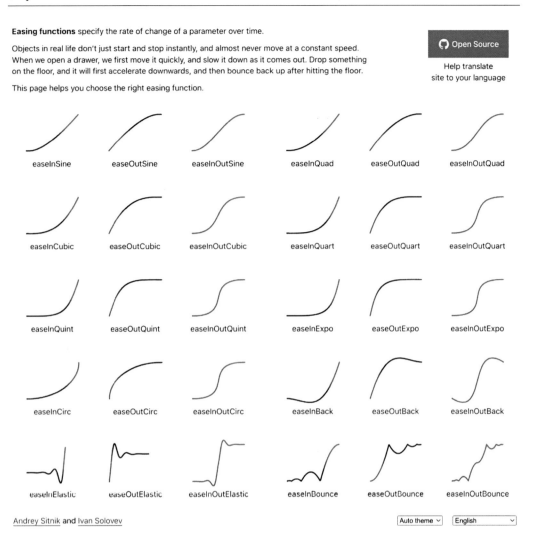

Easing functions specify the rate of change of a parameter over time.

Objects in real life don't just start and stop instantly, and almost never move at a constant speed. When we open a drawer, we first move it quickly, and slow it down as it comes out. Drop something on the floor, and it will first accelerate downwards, and then bounce back up after hitting the floor.

This page helps you choose the right easing function.

Open Source

Help translate
site to your language

easeInSine  easeOutSine  easeInOutSine  easeInQuad  easeOutQuad  easeInOutQuad

easeInCubic  easeOutCubic  easeInOutCubic  easeInQuart  easeOutQuart  easeInOutQuart

easeInQuint  easeOutQuint  easeInOutQuint  easeInExpo  easeOutExpo  easeInOutExpo

easeInCirc  easeOutCirc  easeInOutCirc  easeInBack  easeOutBack  easeInOutBack

easeInElastic  easeOutElastic  easeInOutElastic  easeInBounce  easeOutBounce  easeInOutBounce

Andrey Sitnik and Ivan Solovev

Auto theme ⌄   English ⌄

*Figure 11.3: Easings.net provides a handy visualization of a number of different timing functions*

However, even if you can write your own cubic-bezier curves blindfolded, the likelihood is, for most practical situations, it makes little difference. The reason for this is that, like any visual flourish, it's necessary to employ transition effects subtly. For real-world implementations, transitions that occur over too great a period of time tend to make a site feel slow. For example, navigation links that take 5 seconds to transition are going to frustrate rather than wow your users. The perception of speed is incredibly important for our users, and you and I must concentrate on making websites and applications feel as fast as possible.

Therefore, unless there is a compelling reason to do so, using the default transition (ease) over a short interval is often best; a maximum of 1 second is my own preference, and usually as little as 0.2s.

**Fun transitions for responsive websites**

Did you ever have one of those occasions growing up when one parent was out for the day and the other parent said something to the effect of, "OK, while your mom/dad is out, we're going to put sugar all over your breakfast cereal, but you have to promise not to tell them when they come back." I'm certainly guilty of that with my little ankle biters. So, here's the thing. While no one is looking, let's have a bit of fun. I don't recommend this for production, but try adding this to your responsive project:

```
* {
    transition: all 1s;
}
```

Here, we are using the CSS universal selector * to select everything and then setting a transition on all properties for 1 second (1s). As we have omitted to specify the timing function, ease will be used by default and there will be no delay as, again, a default of 0 is assumed if an alternative value is not added. The effect? Well, try resizing your browser window and most things (links, hover states, and the like) behave as you would expect. However, because everything transitions, it also includes any rules within media queries, so as the browser window is resized, elements sort of flow from one state to the next. Is it essential? Absolutely not! Is it fun to watch and play around with? Certainly! Now, remove that rule before your mom sees it!

Right, hopefully, we have transitions licked. Now we can have some fun, because we are going to learn how to effortlessly move elements around the screen with transforms. There are 2D and 3D variants; we will start with 2D and if that gets a bit flat (see what I did there? No? I'll see myself out) then we will move on to 3D.

# CSS 2D transforms

Despite sounding similar to CSS transitions, CSS transforms are entirely different. As we already established, transitions deal with the transition from one state to another. Transforms, on the other hand, are a means of defining what the state should actually be.

My own (admittedly childish) way of remembering the difference is like this: imagine a Transformer robot like Optimus Prime. When he has changed into a truck, he has transformed.

However, the period between robot and truck is a transition (he's transitioning from one state to another). Obviously, if you have no idea who or what Optimus Prime even is, feel free to mentally discard the last few sentences. Hopefully, all will become clear when we get to the examples in a moment.

There are two groups of CSS transforms available: 2D and 3D. 2D variants are probably a little more straightforward, so let's look at those first. The CSS 2D Transforms Module allows us to use the following transforms:

- `scale`: Scale an element (larger or smaller)
- `translate`: Move an element on the screen (up, down, left, and right)
- `rotate`: Rotate the element by a specified amount (defined in degrees or turns)
- `skew`: Skew an element with its *x* and *y* coordinates
- `matrix`: Allows you to move and shape transformations in multiple ways

An essential concept to understand is that transforms occur *outside of the document flow*. More simply, any element that is transformed will not affect the position of any other element that is not a child of it. This is quite different from adding a transition to an element when you change the margin, height, or other transitionable/animatable property.

Open `example_11-02` and you will see two sentences; the first has `margin-left: 10px` applied to the bold word **item** on hover, while the second sentence has `transform: translateX(10px)` applied to the same word on hover. Both have a transition of 1 second applied.

With nothing hovered over, they look like this:

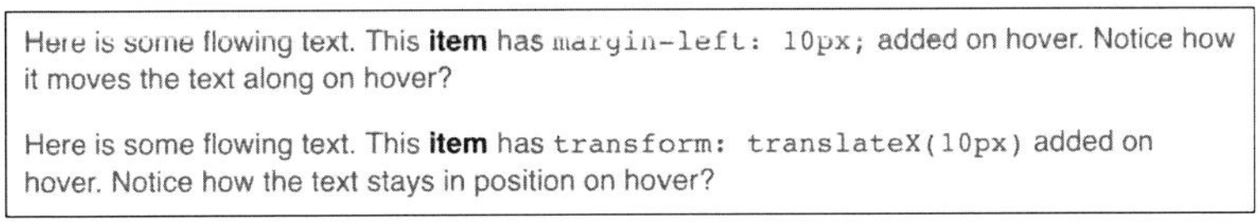

> Here is some flowing text. This **item** has margin-left: 10px; added on hover. Notice how it moves the text along on hover?
>
> Here is some flowing text. This **item** has transform: translateX(10px) added on hover. Notice how the text stays in position on hover?

*Figure 11.4: Two paragraphs in their default state*

Hover over **item** in the first paragraph and the following happens; notice the text after that word has been shunted along?

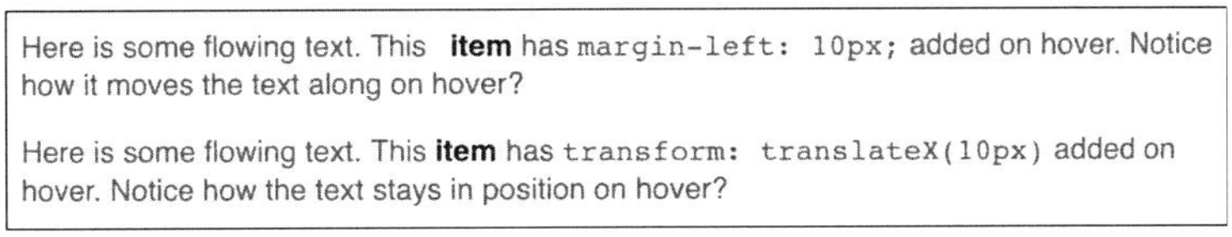

> Here is some flowing text. This  **item** has margin-left: 10px; added on hover. Notice how it moves the text along on hover?
>
> Here is some flowing text. This **item** has transform: translateX(10px) added on hover. Notice how the text stays in position on hover?

*Figure 11.5: When the first paragraph is hovered over, "item" gets a margin applied, moving all the text after it too*

Now, hover over **item** in the second paragraph and notice how just that word moves. The words around it are unaffected.

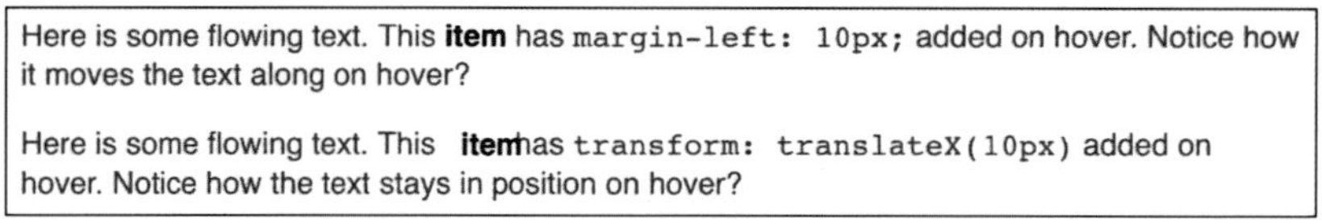
Here is some flowing text. This **item** has margin-left: 10px; added on hover. Notice how it moves the text along on hover?
Here is some flowing text. This **item**has transform: translateX(10px) added on hover. Notice how the text stays in position on hover?

*Figure 11.6: In the second paragraph, "item" is transformed, moving to the right without affecting anything else*

So, transforms, either 2D or 3D, do not affect document flow.

Let's try out the various 2D transforms. You can test each of these out by opening `example_11-03` in the browser. There's a transition applied to all of the transforms so that you get a better idea of what's happening.

## Scale

Here's the syntax for `scale`:

```
.scale:hover {
  transform: scale(1.4);
}
```

Hovering over the **scale** link in our example produces this effect:

scale(1.4)
ranslate(-20px, -20px)
rotate(30deg)

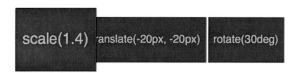

*Figure 11.7: You can scale elements up or down in size*

We've told the browser that when this element is hovered over, we want the element to scale to 1.4 times its original value.

Besides the values we've already used to enlarge elements, by using values below 1, we can shrink elements; the following will shrink the element to half its size:

```
transform: scale(0.5);
```

You can also apply a scale only on a single axis. Horizontal is `scaleX` and vertical is `scaleY`. So, if you wanted to scale something to twice its width, you'd use:

```
transform: scaleX(2);
```

# Translate

Here's the syntax for `translate`:

```
.translate:hover {
  transform: translate(-20px, -20px);
}
```

Here's the effect that rule has on our example:

*Figure 11.8: translate lets you move an element anywhere on the x or y axis*

The `translate` property tells the browser to move an element by an amount, defined by a length (for example, vw, px, %, and so on). The first value is the *x* axis and the second value is the *y* axis. Positive values given within parentheses move the element right or down; negative values move it left or up. If you only pass one value, then it is applied to the *x* axis.

If you want to specify just one axis to translate an element, you can also use `translateX(-20px)`, which, in this instance, would move the element left 20 px, or you could use `translateY(-20px)`, which, in this case, would move the element 20 px up.

## Using translate to center absolutely positioned elements

`translate` provides a really useful way to center absolutely positioned elements within a relatively positioned container. You can view this example at `example_11-04`.

Consider this markup:

```
<div class="outer">
  <div class="inner"></div>
</div>
```

And then this CSS:

```
.outer {
  position: relative;
  height: 400px;
  background-color: #f90;
```

```
}
.inner {
  position: absolute;
  height: 200px;
  width: 200px;
  margin-top: -100px;
  margin-left: -100px;
  top: 50%;
  left: 50%;
}
```

You've perhaps done something similar to this yourself. When the dimensions of the absolutely positioned element are known (200 px × 200 px in this case), we can use negative margins to "pull" the item back to the center. However, what happens when you want to include content and have no way of knowing how tall it will be?

For example, let's add some random content to the inner box:

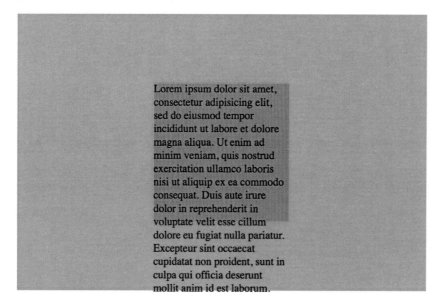

*Figure 11.9: Text overflowing our box can be fixed with transform*

Yes, that problem! Right, let's use transform to sort this mess out:

```
.inner {
  position: absolute;
```

```
    width: 200px;
    background-color: #999;
    top: 50%;
    left: 50%;
    transform: translate(-50%, -50%);
}
```

And here is the result:

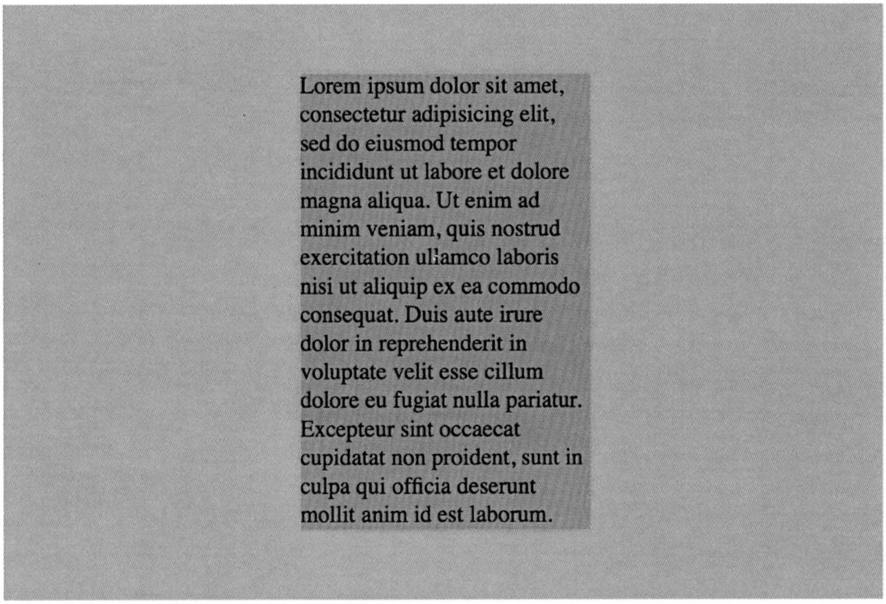

Lorem ipsum dolor sit amet, consectetur adipisicing elit, sed do eiusmod tempor incididunt ut labore et dolore magna aliqua. Ut enim ad minim veniam, quis nostrud exercitation ullamco laboris nisi ut aliquip ex ea commodo consequat. Duis aute irure dolor in reprehenderit in voluptate velit esse cillum dolore eu fugiat nulla pariatur. Excepteur sint occaecat cupidatat non proident, sunt in culpa qui officia deserunt mollit anim id est laborum.

*Figure 11.10: With a smart application of transform, overflow issues are avoided*

Here, top and left are positioning the inner box inside its container so that the top-left corner of the inner box starts at a point 50% along and 50% down the outer box. Then, transform is working on the inner element and positioning it negatively in those axes by half (-50%) of its own width and height. Nice!

 One aspect of what we learned here bears repeating. When using percentages in transforms, remember that they are a percentage of *the element being transformed*, not its parent.

# Rotate

The rotate transform allows you to rotate an element. Here's the syntax:

```
.rotate:hover {
  transform: rotate(30deg);
}
```

In the browser, here's what happens:

*Figure 11.11: Rotating elements is straightforward with a transform*

The value in parentheses should always be an angle. The angle can be expressed in degrees, gradians, radians, or turns. Personally, I default to using degrees (for example, 90deg), but all units are equally valid. While positive angle values always apply clockwise, using negative values will rotate the element counter-clockwise.

Pass an angle greater than a full revolution and the element will keep turning until it has turned around to the required degree. Therefore, you can also go crazy and make elements spin by specifying a value like the following:

```
transform: rotate(3600deg);
```

This will rotate the element 10 times in a complete circle. Practical uses for this particular value are few and far between but, you know, if you ever find yourself designing websites for a windmill company, it may come in handy.

# Skew

If you've spent any time working in Photoshop, you'll have a good idea of what skew does. It allows an element to be skewed on either or both of its axes. Here's the code for our example:

```
.skew:hover {
  transform: skew(40deg, 12deg);
}
```

Setting this on the hover state produces the following effect on hover:

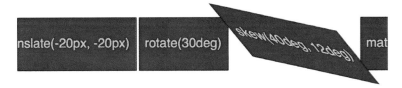

*Figure 11.12: Just like it sounds, a skew can produce some dramatic effects*

The first value is the skew applied to the *x* axis (in our example, 40deg), while the second (12deg) is for the *y* axis. Omitting the second value means any value will merely be applied to the *x* axis (horizontal). For example:

```
transform: skew(10deg);
```

Just like with translate, you can apply skews to just one axis with skewX() and skewY().

## Matrix

Did somebody mention a completely overrated film? No? What's that? You want to know about the CSS matrix, not the film? Oh, okay.

The matrix transform syntax looks rather impenetrable. Here's our example code:

```
.matrix:hover {
    transform: matrix(1.178, -0.256, 1.122, 1.333, -41.533, -1.989);
}
```

The matrix is a mathematical description. It essentially allows you to combine a number of other transforms (scale, rotate, skew, and so on) and express it as a single declaration. The preceding declaration results in the following effect in the browser:

*Figure 11.13: Not for the faint-hearted, the matrix value*

If you find yourself doing work with animations in JavaScript without the help of an animation library, you'll probably need to become a little more acquainted with `matrix`. It's the syntax all the other transforms get computed into behind the scenes, so if you're grabbing the current state of an animation with JavaScript, it will be the `matrix` value you will need to inspect and understand.

Now, I like a challenge (unless, you know, it's sitting through the Marvel Cinematic Universe back catalog), but I think the majority of us would agree that that syntax is a bit testing. The specification doesn't exactly clear matters up: `https://www.w3.org/TR/css-transforms-1/#mathematical-description`.

However, the truth is I can count on the fingers of one hand how many times I've needed to write or understand a CSS transform described as a `matrix`, so it likely isn't something to concern yourself with.

If you do find yourself needing to create one, I'd suggest heading over to `https://www.useragentman.com/matrix/`. The Matrix Construction Set website allows you to drag and drop the element exactly where you want it and includes good ol' copy-and-paste code for your CSS file.

## The transform-origin property

Notice how, with CSS, the default transform origin—the point the browser uses as the center for the transform—is in the middle: 50% along the *x* axis and 50% along the *y* axis of the element. This differs from SVG, which defaults to the top left (or `0 0`).

Using the `transform-origin` property, we can amend the point from which transforms originate.

Consider our earlier `matrix` transform. The default `transform-origin` is `50% 50%` (the center of the element). The Firefox developer tools show how the transform is applied:

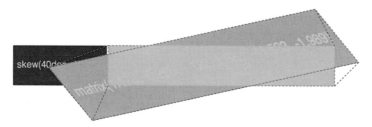

*Figure 11.14: Default transform-origin applied*

Now, if we adjust the `transform-origin` like this:

```
.matrix:hover {
  transform: matrix(1.678, -0.256, 1.522, 2.333, -51.533, -1.989);
  transform-origin: 270px 20px;
}
```

Then you can see the effect this has:

*Figure 11.15: You can amend the origin of transforms as needed*

The first value is the horizontal offset and the second value is the vertical offset. You can use keywords. For example, `left` is equal to 0% horizontal, `right` is equal to 100% horizontal, `top` is equal to 0% vertical, and `bottom` is equal to 100% vertical. Alternatively, you can use a length, using any of the CSS length units.

If you use a percentage for the `transform-origin` values, then the horizontal/vertical offset is relative to the height/width of the element's bounding box. If you use a length, then the values are measured from the top-left corner of the element's bounding box.

The specification for CSS Transforms Module Level 1 can be found here: `https://www.w3.org/TR/css-transforms-1`.

 For more on the benefits of moving elements with `transform`, read this old but great post by Paul Irish, `https://www.paulirish.com/2012/why-moving-elements-with-translate-is-better-than-posabs-topleft/`, which provides some good data.

So far, we have dealt with transforming in two dimensions, the *x* and *y* axes. However, CSS can also handle elements in 3D space. Let's look at what extra fun we can have with 3D transforms.

# CSS 3D transformations

As you've probably already realized, a 3D transform allows us to manipulate an element in an imaginary 3D space. Let's look at our first example. All we have in our example are two elements that each flip in 3D when hovered over. I've used hover here to invoke the flip, as it's a simple mechanism to trigger the effect. However, the flipping action could just as easily be initiated with any other state change—a class change (via JavaScript) or when an element has received focus, for example.

The only difference between these two elements is that one flips horizontally and the other vertically. You can view them in a browser by opening example_11-05. Images fail to fully convey this technique, but the idea is that the element flips from the green "face" to the red "face," giving the illusion of doing so through 3D space with the aid of perspective. Here's a grab partway through the transition from green to red, which hopefully conveys some of the effect:

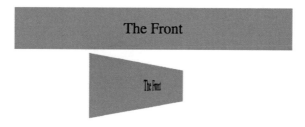

*Figure 11.16: Halfway through a 3D transform*

It's also worth knowing that while positioning an element absolutely with top/left/bottom/right values can only be calculated to whole pixels, a transform can interpolate at subpixel positions.

Here's the markup for the flipping element:

```
<div class="flipper">
  <span class="flipper-object flipper-vertical">
    <span class="panel front">The Front</span>
    <span class="panel back">The Back</span>
  </span>
</div>
```

The only difference with the horizontal one, markup wise, is that the flipper-vertical class is replaced with flipper-horizontal.

As the majority of the styles relate to aesthetics, we'll merely look at the essential ingredients in our styles to make the flipping effect possible. Refer to the full style sheet in the example file for the aesthetic styles.

When dealing with 3D transforms, the first essential ingredient is to define some kind of 3D space.

For our example, we need to set some perspective for .flipper-object, whether horizontal or vertical, to flip within. For that, we use the perspective property. This takes a length value, attempting to simulate the distance from the viewer's screen to the edge of the elements' 3D space. We set this on the outer-most element to provide the 3D context for our nested elements to move within.

The value you assign to perspective is arguably counter-intuitive—if you set a low number like 20 px for the perspective value, the 3D space of the element will extend right out to only 20 px from your screen, the result being a more pronounced 3D effect.

Setting a high number, on the other hand, will mean the edge of that imaginary 3D space will be further away, and therefore produce a less pronounced 3D effect. I recommend opening the example in the browser and playing with the perspective in the developer tools to get a feel for it:

```
.flipper {
  perspective: 400px;
  position: relative;
}
```

We use position: relative on the outer flipper element to provide a positioning context for flipper-object to be absolutely positioned within:

```
.flipper-object {
  position: absolute;
  width: 100%;
  height: 100%;
  transition: transform 1s;
  transform-style: preserve-3d;
}
```

Besides positioning .flipper-object absolutely, we set the height and width to 100% so that it fills the same space as the outer container. We have also set a transition for the transform. If you remember from earlier in this chapter, when we dealt with transitions, just setting the time for transition means the default timing function (ease) will be used.

The key thing here, 3D wise, is `transform-style: preserve-3d`. This declaration tells the browser that when we transform this element, we want any child elements to preserve any 3D effect.

If we didn't set `preserve-3d` on `.flipper-object`, we would never get to see the back (the red part) of the flipping element.

You can read the specification for this property here: `https://www.w3.org/TR/2009/WD-css3-3d-transforms-20090320/#transform-style-property`.

Each "panel" in our flipping element needs positioning at the top of its container, but we also want to make sure that, if rotated, we don't see the "rear" of it (otherwise we would never see the green panel as it sits "behind" the red one). To do that, we use the `backface-visibility` property. We set this to `hidden` so that the back face of the element is, you guessed it, hidden:

```
.panel {
  top: 0;
  position: absolute;
  backface-visibility: hidden;
}
```

Next, we want to make our back panel flipped by default (so that when we flip the whole thing, it will actually be in the correct position). To do that, we apply a `rotate` transform. Hopefully, having covered these in the previous section, you'll understand what they are doing here:

```
.flipper-vertical .back {
  transform: rotateX(180deg);
}
.flipper-horizontal .back {
  transform: rotateY(180deg);
}
```

Now that everything is in place, all we want to do is flip the entire inner element when the outer one is hovered over:

```
.flipper:hover .flipper-vertical {
  transform: rotateX(180deg);
}
.flipper:hover .flipper-horizontal {
  transform: rotateY(180deg);
}
```

As you can imagine, there are a bazillion (by the way, bazillion is definitely not a real amount, I just checked) ways you can use these techniques. If you're wondering what a fancy navigation effect, or off-canvas menu, might look like with a spot of perspective, I highly recommend paying Codrops a visit: `https://tympanus.net/Development/PerspectivePageViewNavigation/index.html`.

 You can read the W3C specification for the CSS Transforms Module Level 1 at `https://www.w3.org/TR/css-transforms-1/`.

It turns out there is a very handy property when working with transforms that can do all your $x$, $y$, and $z$ movement in one go. Let's take a look at that next.

## The translate3d property

I've found great utility in the `translate3d` function. With this single function, it is possible to move an element in the $x$ (left/right), $y$ (up/down), and $z$ (forward/backward) axes.

Let's amend our previous example and make use of the `translate3d()` function. You can view this example at `example_11-06`.

Besides setting the elements into the page a little more with padding, the only changes from our previous example can be seen here:

```
.flipper:hover .flipper-vertical {
  transform: rotateX(180deg) translate3d(0, 0, -120px);
}
.flipper:hover .flipper-horizontal {
  transform: rotateY(180deg) translate3d(0, 0, 120px);
}
```

We're still applying a transform, but this time, in addition to our rotate, we have also made use of `translate3d()`. The syntax for the comma-separated arguments you can pass into `translate3d` are $x$-axis movement, $y$-axis movement, and $z$-axis movement.

In our two examples, I'm not moving the element on the $x$ or $y$ axis (left to right and up and down); instead, I'm moving it toward or further away from you as you look at it.

If you look at the top example, you will see it flip behind the bottom button and end 120 px closer to the screen (minus values effectively pull it back toward you):

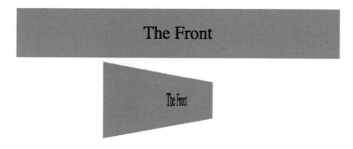

*Figure 11.17: Elements can be moved forward and backward in the Z plane*

On the other hand, the bottom button flips around horizontally and ends with the button 120 px further away from you:

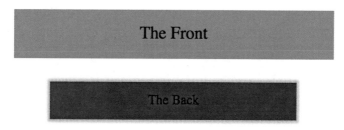

*Figure 11.18: Here, the element ends "further away"*

Although translate3d( ), like the other transforms, is very well supported, it actually got pushed into the later CSS Transforms Module Level 2 specification. You can read about that here: https://www.w3.org/TR/css-transforms-2/.

## A progressive enhancement example using translate3d

An area I have found using translate3d useful in is sliding panels on and off the screen, particularly "off-canvas" navigation patterns. If you open example_11-07, you'll see I have created a basic, progressively enhanced, off-canvas pattern.

Whenever you create interaction with JavaScript and modern CSS features like transforms, it makes sense to consider things from the lowest possible device you want to support. What about the two people that don't have JavaScript (yes, those guys), or if there is a problem with the JavaScript loading or executing? What if somebody prefers reduced motion? Don't worry. It's possible, with a little effort, to ensure a working interface for every eventuality.

When building these kinds of interface patterns, I find it most useful to start with the lowest set of features and enhance from there. First, establish what someone sees if they don't have JavaScript available. After all, it's no use parking a menu off-screen when JavaScript isn't available, if the method for displaying the menu relies on JavaScript. Instead, in this case, we are relying on markup to place the navigation area in the normal document flow. Worst case, whatever the viewport width, they can merely scroll down the page and click a link:

# A basic off-canvas menu

Lorem ipsum dolor sit amet, consectetur adipisicing elit, sed do eiusmod tempor incididunt ut labore et dolore magna aliqua. Ut enim ad minim veniam, quis nostrud exercitation ullamco laboris nisi ut aliquip ex ea commodo consequat. Duis aute irure dolor in reprehenderit in voluptate velit esse cillum dolore eu fugiat nulla pariatur. Excepteur sint occaecat cupidatat non proident, sunt in culpa qui officia deserunt mollit anim id est laborum.

Lorem ipsum dolor sit amet, consectetur adipisicing elit, sed do eiusmod tempor incididunt ut labore et dolore magna aliqua. Ut enim ad minim veniam, quis nostrud exercitation ullamco laboris nisi ut aliquip ex ea commodo consequat. Duis aute irure dolor in reprehenderit in voluptate velit esse cillum dolore eu fugiat nulla pariatur. Excepteur sint occaecat cupidatat non proident, sunt in culpa qui officia deserunt mollit anim id est laborum.

Lorem ipsum dolor sit amet, consectetur adipisicing elit, sed do eiusmod tempor incididunt ut labore et dolore magna aliqua. Ut enim ad minim veniam, quis nostrud exercitation ullamco laboris nisi ut aliquip ex ea commodo consequat. Duis aute irure dolor in reprehenderit in voluptate velit esse cillum dolore eu fugiat nulla pariatur. Excepteur sint occaecat cupidatat non proident, sunt in culpa qui officia deserunt mollit anim id est laborum.

Link 1
Link 2
Link 3
Link 4
Link 5

*Figure 11.19: A basic but usable default layout*

If JavaScript is available, for smaller screens, we "pull" the menu off to the left. When the menu button is clicked, we add a class to the body tag (with JavaScript) and use this class as a hook to move the navigation back into view with CSS `transform3d()`.

This will provide the best visual performance, as it's a process typically offloaded to the graphics processor, which excels at such tasks:

*Figure 11.20: With a click, we slide over our menu*

For larger viewports, we hide the menu buttons and merely position the navigation to the left and move the main content over to accommodate:

*Figure 11.21: Where screen size allows, we can show the menu by default*

Finally, to cater to anyone that prefers reduced motion, we use a media query to prevent movement when the menu is opened and closed:

```
@media (prefers-reduced-motion) {
    .navigation-menu {
        transition: none;
    }
}
```

If you open the example in the browser, you can simulate the different eventualities with the developer tools by changing the js class on the html element to no-js to see how it would look without JavaScript. Also, you can emulate the prefers-reduced-motion in Chrome by opening the Dev Tools Command Palette and typing prefers-reduced-motion, and then clicking the option to emulate it.

This is a simplified example, but hopefully it's apparent that embracing a progressive enhancement approach ensures the widest possible audience will get a workable experience from your design. Remember, your users don't need visual parity, but they might appreciate functional parity.

# Animating with CSS

If you've worked with applications like Final Cut Pro or After Effects, you'll have an instant advantage when working with CSS animations. CSS employs animation keyframing conventions found in timeline-based applications.

If you have never worked with keyframes or even come across the term, here is all you need to know. When you are devising an animation, you will choose key moments where things need to be in a certain position. Imagine a bouncing ball. At first, it is in the air, which would be one **keyframe**, and then it is on the floor, another keyframe. When you specify keyframes, the animation knows how to fill in the blanks between them and create the animation.

There are two components to a CSS animation; first, writing a set of keyframes inside an @keyframes at-rule declaration, and then employing that keyframe animation with the animation property and associated values. Let's take a look.

In a previous example, we made a simple flip effect on elements that combined transforms and transitions. Let's bring together all the techniques we have learned in this chapter and add an animation to the previous example. In the following example, example_11-08, let's add a pulsing animation effect around our element once it has flipped.

Firstly, we will create a keyframes at-rule:

```
@keyframes pulse {
  100% {
    text-shadow: 0 0 5px #bbb;
    box-shadow: 0 0 3px 4px #bbb;
  }
}
```

As you can see, after writing @keyframes to define a new keyframes at-rule, we name this particular animation (pulse, in this instance). The @keyframes at-rule describes what you want to happen for each cycle of your animation loop.

It's generally best to use a name that represents what the animation does, not where you intend to use the animation, as a single @keyframes rule can be used as many times as you need throughout a project.

We have used a single **keyframe selector** here: 100%. However, you can set as many keyframes (defined as percentage points) as you like within a @keyframes at-rule. Think of these as points along a timeline. For example, at 10%, make the background blue, at 30%, make the background purple, and at 60%, make the element semi-opaque. On and on as you need.

There is also the keyword from, which is equivalent to 0%, and to, which is equivalent to 100%. You can use the keywords like this:

```
@keyframes pulse {
  to {
    text-shadow: 0 0 5px #bbb;
    box-shadow: 0 0 3px 4px #bbb;
  }
}
```

You'll notice here that we haven't bothered to define a starting point. That's because the starting point is the state each of those properties is already at. Here's the part of the specification that explains that (https://www.w3.org/TR/css3-animations/#keyframes):

*If a '0%' or 'from' keyframe is not specified, then the user agent constructs a '0%' keyframe using the computed values of the properties being animated. If a '100%' or 'to' keyframe is not specified, then the user agent constructs a '100%' keyframe using the computed values of the properties being animated.*

In this @keyframes at-rule, we've added a text-shadow and box-shadow at 100%. We can then expect the keyframes, when applied to an element, to animate the text shadow and box shadow to the defined amount. But how long does the animation last? How do we make it repeat, reverse, and more? This is how we actually apply a keyframes animation to an element:

```
.flipper:hover .flipper-horizontal {
  transform: rotateY(180deg);
  animation: pulse 1s 1s infinite alternate both;
}
```

The animation property here is a shorthand for several animation-related properties. In this example, we are declaring (in order):

1. The name of the keyframes declaration to use (pulse).
2. The animation-duration (1 second).
3. The animation-delay before the animation begins (1 second, to allow time for our button to first flip).
4. The number of times the animation will run (infinitely).
5. The direction of the animation (alternate, so it animates first one way and then back the other).
6. That we want the animation-fill-mode, which we will cover in detail momentarily, to retain the values that are defined in the keyframes, whether going forward or backward (both).

The shorthand property can actually accept all seven animation properties. In addition to those used in the preceding example, it's also possible to specify animation-play-state. This can be set to running or paused to effectively play and pause an animation. Of course, you don't need to use the shorthand property; sometimes, it can make more sense (and help when you revisit the code in the future) to set each property separately. The following are the individual properties and example values. Where appropriate, alternate values have been listed with a comment:

```
.animation-properties {
  animation-name: warning;
  animation-duration: 1.5s;
  animation-timing-function: ease-in-out;
  animation-iteration-count: infinite;
  animation-play-state: running; /* could also be 'paused' */
```

```
    animation-delay: 0s;
    animation-fill-mode: none;
    /* could also be 'forwards', 'backwards' or 'both' */
    animation-direction: normal;
    /* could also be set to 'reverse', 'alternate' or 'alternate-reverse' */
}
```

You can read the full definition for each of these animation properties in the CSS Animations Level 1 specification at https://www.w3.org/TR/css-animations-1/.

You can run multiple animations on an element with the shorthand property by comma separating them. For example:

```
animation: animOne 1s alternate both, animTwo 0.3s forwards
```

As mentioned previously, it's simple to reuse a declared keyframes on other elements and with completely different settings:

```
.flipper:hover .flipper-vertical {
  transform: rotateX(180deg);
  animation: pulse 2s 1s cubic-bezier(0.68, -0.55, 0.265, 1.55) 5
  alternate both;
}
```

Here, the pulse animation would run over 2 seconds and uses an ease-in-out-back timing function (defined as a cubic-bezier curve). It runs five times in both directions. This declaration has been applied to the vertically flipping element in the example_11-08/styles.css file.

## The animation-fill-mode property

The animation-fill-mode property is worthy of a special mention. Consider an animation that starts with a yellow background and animates to a red background over 3 seconds. You can view this in example_11-09.

We apply the animation like this:

```
.background-change {
  animation: fillBg 3s;
  height: 200px;
  width: 400px;
  border: 1px solid #ccc;
}
```

```
@keyframes fillBg {
  0% {
    background-color: yellow;
  }
  100% {
    background-color: red;
  }
}
```

However, once the animation completes, the background of the div will return to nothing. That's because, by default, when an animation ends, the element goes back to exactly how it was before the animation ran. In order to override this behavior, we have the animation-fill-mode property. In this instance, we could apply this:

```
animation-fill-mode: forwards;
```

This makes the item retain any values that have been applied by the animation end. In our case, the div would retain the red background color that the animation ended on. More on the animation-fill-mode property here: https://www.w3.org/TR/css-animations-1/#animation-fill-mode.

**Without animation-fill-mode**

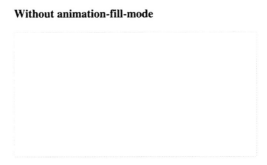

**With animation-fill-mode forwards**

*Figure 11.22: Without animation-fill-mode set to forwards, animations run and then imme-diately reset*

# Exercises and training

At this point, you might find it useful to find a site using transitions, transforms, and animations and try playing with the settings in the developer tools. Inspect any moving elements and then tweak the relevant values and properties. Can you send elements in the opposite direction? Can you make transitions take longer or shorter? Are there any 2D transforms you can amend to use the `transform3d()` function?

You can make a start on `https://rwd.education`—I won't mind!

# Summary

It would be entirely possible to fill multiple books covering the possibilities of CSS transforms, transitions, and animations. Hopefully, by dipping your toe in the water with this chapter, you've been able to pick up the basics and run with them.

In this chapter, we've learned what CSS transitions are and how to write them. We got a handle on timing functions like `ease` and `linear`, and then used them to create simple but fun effects. We then learned all about 2D transforms like `scale` and `skew`, and how to use them in tandem with transitions. We also looked briefly at 3D transformations before learning all about the power and relative simplicity of CSS animations. You'd better believe our CSS muscles are growing!

In the next chapter, we are going to look in depth at CSS custom properties and functions. These are recent additions to CSS, in comparison to things like media queries, and we will see how in many responsive situations, functions like `clamp()` provide better responsive solutions.

# 12

# Custom Properties and CSS Functions

Some years ago, I wrote a book about Sass, a superset language for CSS. One of the main selling points of Sass, alongside things like nesting – which we will look at later in the book – was that it allowed you to store oft-used values as **variables**. Things like colors could be named more simply as words rather than hex or RGB values, and that allowed for far easier reuse of those values.

Some years later, CSS got custom properties, which at first glance seemed like nothing more than a way to have variables in CSS, without needing a superset language like Sass. It turns out that CSS custom properties are far more powerful than Sass variables. So powerful, in fact, that a good share of this chapter is largely dedicated to them.

Another, newer, CSS addition that goes hand in hand with custom properties is the ability to manipulate values, including custom properties, with mathematical functions. Exploring these functions will also form a substantial part of this chapter.

As we will see, alongside viewport-related length values like vh and vw, these capabilities enable us to solve a multitude of responsive problems that would otherwise remain, well, problems!

We will begin by understanding custom properties, and then learn how to manipulate them, and other values with CSS functions.

Here are the main areas we will cover in this chapter:

- What a custom property is
- Special env() custom properties

- Setting a custom property with CSS and JavaScript
- Using a custom property with CSS and JavaScript
- Understanding CSS functions
- Reducing the need for media queries
- `calc()`, `clamp()`, and `min()`
- Examples of using custom properties with CSS functions

# Working with custom properties

Let's start with a simple use case, storing a font-family name that we can then reference more simply later in the style sheet. This is what a custom property definition looks like:

```
:root {
    --MainFont: "Helvetica Neue", Helvetica, Arial, sans-serif;
}
```

Here, we are using the :root pseudo-class to store the custom property in the document root. You don't have to store them in the root, but storing them here means that any descendent element has access to them.

But custom properties respect the cascade. As we will see shortly, being able to reassign custom properties in different scopes is one of their superpowers.

 The :root pseudo-class always references the topmost parent element in a document structure. In an HTML document, this would always be the HTML tag, but for an SVG document (we looked at SVG in *Chapter 10*, *SVG*), it would reference a different element.

When we set a custom property, the syntax is that it should always begin with two dashes, then the custom name, like this: --MainFont. After the end of the property, just like a normal CSS property, we terminate the property with a colon. Then we just assign whatever value we want to it in the normal manner.

 It is case-sensitive, so --MainFont would be a different custom property than --mainFont.

We can reference that value elsewhere in our style sheet with the var() notation, like so:

```
.Title {
    font-family: var(--MainFont);
}
```

And the browser would effectively read that as an instruction to do this:

```
.Title {
    font-family: "Helvetica Neue", Helvetica, Arial, sans-serif;
}
```

You can store as many custom properties as you need in this manner.

Even though in this example we are saving some characters using the custom property, making use of them isn't merely an exercise in convenience when authoring; it's an approach that pays you back time and again when you want to change things.

Imagine that you have defined and referenced colors and font declarations throughout your project in this manner, and then sometime later you want to change a color or font-family. It's now just a single change in one place and the values effectively get changed everywhere. Every rule that makes use of the variable gets the new value, without having to amend the rules directly.

## Simple theming

The ability to set a value in one place to be used in many other places makes custom properties a great candidate for theming. And we are not limited to CSS as a means of interacting with them, as there is a JavaScript API to get and set the values of custom properties.

Let's look at a simple example of using and switching custom properties with JavaScript. You can find this in example_12-01. We will make a page with the poem "If," by Rudyard Kipling. At the bottom is a simple light/dark mode toggle button. All the button will do is toggle the value of two CSS custom properties, --background and --foreground.

Here is our CSS:

```
body {
    background-color: var(--background);
    color: var(--foreground);
}
```

Below is the snippet of JavaScript we are using. Essentially, it just says that when someone clicks the toggle button, if the foreground variable is currently #eee (nearly white), then set it to #333 (a dark gray); otherwise, set it to #eee. And, if the background variable is #333, set it to #eee; otherwise, set it to #333:

```
var root = document.documentElement;
var btn = document.getElementById("colorToggle");
btn.addEventListener("click", (e) => {
    root.style.setProperty(
        "--background",
        getComputedStyle(root).getPropertyValue("--background") === "#333"
            ? "#eee"
            : "#333"
    );
    root.style.setProperty(
        "--foreground",
        getComputedStyle(root).getPropertyValue("--foreground") === "#eee"
            ? "#333"
            : "#eee"
    );
});
```

And here is a screenshot showing each state:

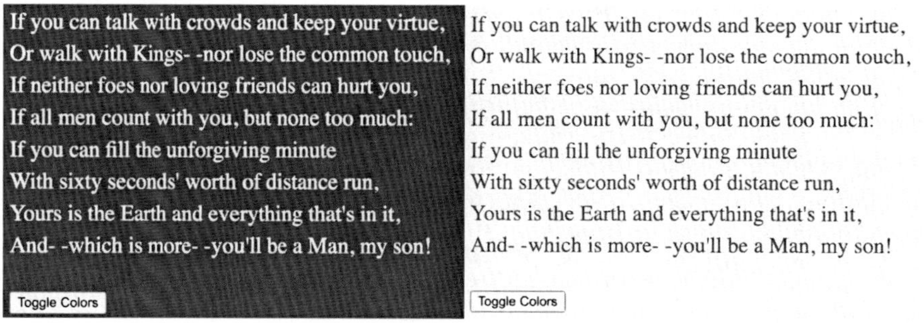

*Figure 12.1: An example of each state side by side, colors easily swapped with custom properties*

# Setting and getting custom property values with JavaScript

If you only take two things from that prior JavaScript snippet, it should be the manner in which you can both **get** and **set** custom properties. At first glance, it looks like you should be able to set a custom property to any string value you like. But it is a little stricter than that.

Suppose we have an element with a class of heading-information. We could try and set a custom property on that element with JavaScript like this:

```
const headerInfo = document.querySelector(".heading-information");

headerInfo.style.setProperty("--doILikeScones", "You bet I do!");

console.log(getComputedStyle(headerInfo).getPropertyValue("--
doILikeScones")); // hoping it will log out "You bet I do!"
```

But that won't work. Why? Well, custom properties must have their value set to a valid CSS value, so you can't use them to pass around any arbitrary snippet of data. If we amended our code and set the value to, say, "100px", we would then get that value logged out correctly.

So, that's the only real rule to be aware of. You *set* and *get* values in JavaScript as strings, but in order for those strings to "work," they must be valid CSS values.

Then, assuming you have set the property to something valid, when we *get* a value, using the getPropertyValue() method like this:

```
const headerInfo = document.querySelector(".heading-information");
const doILikeSconesValue =
getComputedStyle(headerInfo).getPropertyValue("--doILikeScones");
console.log(doILikeSconesValue); // would log out value of custom property
```

Everything will work as expected.

# Custom properties and specificity

Custom properties also behave like other properties in terms of the cascade and specificity. And that can be incredibly useful. For example, we set our custom properties at the root level, but if they are redeclared closer to the element in question, the more specific value will override the first, as they inherit values from the closest ancestor. Consider this CSS:

```
:root {
    --backgroundColor: red;
}


header {
    --backgroundColor: goldenrod;
}
```

The header and any elements within it that make use of the --backgroundColor custom property will have a "goldenrod" background color, whereas other elements will have a red background.

In our example we have just set a background color, but it is possible to set all manner of defaults in one place for items to inherit, and then override as necessary.

You could do something like this:

```
:root {
    --fontSize: 1.2em;
    --lineHeight: 1.4;
    --col1: #333;
    --col2: #f9f9f9;
    --fontFam: -apple-system, BlinkMacSystemFont, Helvetica Neue, Segoe
    UI, Tahoma, Roboto, Oxygen, Ubuntu, Cantarell, Fira Sans, Open Sans,
    sans-serif;
    --padInline: clamp(10px, 3vw, 25px);
    --padBlock: clamp(10px, 2vh, 20px);
}
```

And then anywhere you want a visual component that uses those properties, you can pick and choose them:

```
.component {
    font-size: var(--fontSize);
    font-family: var(--fontFam);
```

```
    line-height: var(--lineHeight);
    color: var(--col1);
    background-color: var(--col2, #000);
    --padInline: 15px;
}
```

Remember that you can also reassign them for any child elements.

Some things to note from those code blocks. You may have noticed `clamp()` in there. We haven't looked at that yet, but we will later in the chapter. We have also done something a little different on that `background-color`, and that's setting a fallback value. Let's talk about that a little more next.

## Setting a fallback value

There may be a situation where you want to protect against a custom property being unavailable. Perhaps the values are set with JavaScript, and that has failed to load, or hasn't been initialized yet. Whatever the reason, you can safeguard against the eventuality by providing a fallback value. The syntax is straightforward: simply provide your fallback value after the custom property name and a comma.

For example, suppose I wanted to use the `--backgroundColor` custom property, but default to a dark gray color if that variable was unavailable. I could write it like this:

```
.my-Item {
    background-color: var(--backgroundColor, #555);
}
```

If you are ever unsure whether a custom property will be set, it makes a lot of sense to get into the habit of supplying fallback values whenever you use custom properties. That way, if the visual component you are building finds itself in an area where the custom property is not set, it will still render with the sensible default you provided.

## env() environment variables

In addition to custom properties we might make for ourselves, there are also some system-level properties that can be read in from the environment we are operating in. These are called **environment variables**. The idea here is that there are certain values that only the host environment knows. This gives us the ability to factor in that unknown when we build, so regardless of the environment, our responsive designs can respond.

The only solid example of these I'm currently aware of are the `safe-area-inset-*` properties applicable to notched mobile phones. Made famous by the iPhone X, the "safe-areas" relate to the sections at the top and bottom of the screen where areas of UI or physical hardware, such as cameras, impinge upon the viewing area.

Environment variables are defined with the `env()` function, rather than the `var()` function for custom properties. Values are passed into this function just like you would any other CSS function. For example, if we wanted to add padding to the top of our element equal to the height of the environment's "safe area inset top," we could do this:

```
padding-top: env(safe-area-inset-top);
```

If the browser has that value available and it understands the `env()` function, it will apply the value; otherwise, it will skip over it to the next declaration.

Unlike custom properties, we are not able to set environment variables for ourselves; these are values set by the environment alone.

> You can read the current specification for environment variables here: `https://drafts.csswg.org/css-env-1/#env-function`.
>
> There are a few extra peculiarities to the iPhone notched screens. If you want a full walk-through of dealing with the iPhone notches, read `https://benfrain.com/css-environment-variables-iphonex/`.

## Custom properties and web components

Web components provide the web platform with native encapsulated components. This means the styles within them are contained, unable to access styles above them in the DOM. However, one thing that can penetrate this boundary is – you guessed it – custom properties.

This makes custom properties the perfect mechanism for passing around values that you want to share among nested components.

You can set a custom property on the outermost part of a web component using the `:host` pseudo-class, like this:

```
:host {
    --myCustomProperty: 100%;
}
```

And then that host component, and any nested components, can access that custom property.

 As interesting and useful as they are, we won't delve further into web components in this book as they are a little out of scope. For a good primer on web components, I'd recommend taking a look at https://developer.mozilla.org/en-US/docs/Web/Web_Components.

So now we are at a point where we know about custom properties, what they look like, and how we can set them at different places and use specificity to override them. We have also looked at setting defaults, just in case a custom property isn't set elsewhere. We have also looked at environment variables and where they may be a consideration.

It's time now to start manipulating these values with functions. Manipulating values provides a whole slew of additional capability and flexibility. Let's take a look.

# CSS functions

When it comes to solving the challenges of responsive web design, CSS functions are starting to replace and better media queries in some instances.

Want to have text that is no smaller than 16 px, but then scales with the size of the viewport, yet never gets bigger than 30 px?

With media queries, you would have to try to solve that problem something like this:

```
.headline {
    font-size: 16px;
}

@media (min-width: 400px) {
    font-size: 6vw;
}

@media (min-width: 1000px) {
    font-size: 30px;
}
```

But the reality is, that's quite brittle. You'll find yourself adding lots of little "tweak points" where you need to add another media query. For example, when the viewport is 950 px wide, that 6 vw is looking a little comically big.

Now we have a better tool for the job. You can do this instead:

```
.headline {
    font-size: clamp(16px, 4vw, 30px);
}
```

That's pretty powerful, right? The clamp() function is just one of many CSS functions we now have at our disposal. But hang on. I got a little excited then and jumped ahead. Before we look in detail at functions like clamp(), let's start by looking at a function you may have already looked at, calc().

## calc()

The calc() function allows us to do basic arithmetic in CSS. I purposefully said basic because it only allows addition, subtraction, division, and multiplication.

It's essential to put whitespace around the plus and minus symbols; otherwise, the calc() won't, err... calc! It isn't necessary to have whitespace around the division or multiplication symbols, but I always add it there too just for consistency.

So, to illustrate, this is good:

```
.thing {
    width: calc(100vw - 30px);
}
```

But this is bad:

```
.thing {
    width: calc(100vw -30px);
}
```

As you can see in the example above, you can mix and match units in the calculations. This is particularly useful in our responsive challenges. Suppose we are building some piece of user interface, and we want something the full height of the viewport but minus a fixed-height header that is 50 px. We can solve this with ease with calc:

```
.thing {
    height: calc(100vh - 50px);
}
```

Actually, that is not so dissimilar to the first example. So, how about we up the ante and factor in environment variables? That would look like this:

```
.thing {
    height: calc(
        100vh - env(safe-area-inset-top) - env(safe-area-inset-bottom) -
        50px
    );
}
```

And now our UI is the full height of viewport (`100vh`), minus any safe area the device has set, minus the height of our fixed height header. Now that is a responsive piece of interface!

And as you might imagine, you can use custom properties inside a `calc()` too.

 There are plenty of other mathematical expressions in the latest CSS Values specification, including trigonometry and exponential functions: `https://drafts.csswg.org/css-values/#trig-funcs`.

Now, as we go ahead and look at some of the "comparison" functions of CSS, notice that they have the `calc()` capability baked in. You don't need to use `calc()` in them explicitly; you can just use the basic math operations (addition, subtraction, multiplication, and division) in there directly. We will make use of this capability as we look at each function in turn. First up, `min()`.

# min()

The `min()` function accepts any number of comma-separated arguments, and resolves to the minimum.

Consider this:

```
.my-responsive-component {
    width: min(100vw, 700px);
}
```

Let's suppose we have our browser window 800 px wide. Looking at the code above, can you guess how wide our element will be? In that scenario, it will be 700 px because 100 vw would be 800 px. However, if we reduced our browser window width to say 600 px, it would resolve to 600 px (100 vw) as that would now be the minimum value of the two.

Remember we have basic math functionality in `min()` too, so if we wanted to make allowance for some responsive part, we can do that too. Here is the example amended to use a combination of hard and dynamic values:

```
.my-responsive-component {
    width: min(100vw, 700px - 5%);
}
```

And remember, we are not limited to just two arguments:

```
.thing {
    width: min(50vw, 400px, 100% - 10px);
}
```

## max()

Having just looked at `min()`, I'm sure you have a fair idea of how `max()` works. It takes any number of arguments and resolves to the largest.

Much like `clamp()`, which we will look at in more detail next, I find it most useful when I want text to smoothly scale in a responsive scenario but still have a minimum size for accessibility. For example, if I never want the text in a `label` to be less than 18 px:

```
label {
    font-size: max(4vw, 18px);
}
```

It can be confusing using these functions at first, as often you are using the math function that seems to have a name that is the opposite of what you are using it for! Here we are using `max()` to set a minimum size for something.

If the same happens for you, you'll just have to trust me that it gets less confusing the more you use them.

 If it's still making your brain hurt, just make sure that whatever value you want as a minimum is chucked inside a `max()` function, as the value is never going to resolve to less than that.

## clamp()

Beside `calc()`, the CSS function I tend to reach for the most in responsive work is `clamp()`.

It came to browsers slightly later than `min()` or `max()` but made up for its tardy arrival by solving a classic design conundrum. You know, the "I want the headline text to be flexible in size, but it can't go too small. And it can't go too big either." Yes, that "Goldilocks" one!

The `clamp()` function lets us specify, in the order we pass them into the function, a minimum, variable, and maximum size for any length. For example, we can address our Goldilocks text sizing problem with `clamp` like this:

```
.hero-text {
    font-size: clamp(32px, 40vw, 80px);
}
```

And while our headline text might vary in size, depending on the viewport, it will never be less than 32 px or larger than 80 px. Beautiful!

And like all the mathematical functions we have looked at, you can use custom properties in there too. Something like this would allow you to have a site-wide min and max text size set with a custom property, with any kind of responsive friendly unit in the middle:

```
.hero-text {
    font-size: clamp(var(--textMin), 40vw, var(--textMax));
}
```

And we can nest some calculations in there too if needed:

```
.hero-text {
    font-size: clamp(var(--textMin), 40vw + 5rem, var(--textMax));
}
```

And keep in mind that `clamp()` isn't just for text; you can use it any place that accepts a length value.

 You can read the specification for `clamp()` here: `https://www.w3.org/TR/css-values-4/#funcdef-clamp`.

# Putting it all together

Let's make a fun example, bringing together some of the things we have looked at in previous chapters.

With just a couple of elements, let's simulate the basics of a basketball court, and the ball bouncing and being passed around.

Here is the markup. Probably the least important part of this example:

```
<div class="court">
    <div class="ball"></div>
</div>
```

Let's make a vague court shape and give it a background color something like a basketball court:

```
.court {
    width: 400px;
    height: 200px;
    background-color: rgb(197, 150, 86);
    position: relative;
}
```

Now we want to add a ball to our court. This ball will simulate a bounce with an animation and transition its position, which we will set with custom properties. Now, if for some reason you haven't read *Chapter 11, Transitions, Transformations, and Animations*, yet (shame on you), all you need to know is that this animation makes a circle appear as if it is bouncing by making it scale up in size and then back down:

```
.ball {
    --ballSize: 18px;
    --ball-border: #fff;
    --ball-color: #df4a23;
    position: absolute;
    left: calc(var(--x) - var(--ballSize));
    top: calc(var(--y) - var(--ballSize));
    width: var(--ballSize);
    height: var(--ballSize);
    background-color: var(--ball-color);
    border-radius: 50%;
    transition: all 0.3s ease-in-out;
    border: 1px solid var(--ball-border);
    animation: 0.5s ease infinite alternate forwards bounce;
}

@keyframes bounce {
    0% {
        transform: scale(1);
    }
```

```
    100% {
        transform: scale(1.3);
    }
}
```

You can see that we are setting some custom properties on the ball. Particularly useful is --ballSize. We reference that a few times, which means that tweaking that value automatically changes both the width and height of the ball, and also factors in to the calculations being made to the left and top positions. In those calc() functions, you can also see there is a custom property for --x and --y, which we are setting every so often with JavaScript. Here is the snippet of JavaScript that powers our ball movement:

```
// Get the ball from the DOM
const ball = document.querySelector(".ball");
// Get a random number between the Min and the Max
const getRand = (min, max) => Math.floor(Math.random() * (max - min + 1) +
min);
// Set the values into the custom property
const setCoords = () => {
    ball.style.setProperty("--x", '${getRand(0, 100)}%');
    ball.style.setProperty("--y", '${getRand(0, 100)}%');
};

setCoords();
// Every so often, set the position of the ball
setInterval(() => {
    setCoords();
}, getRand(1000, 3000));
```

If you look at the DOM in example_12-02, you can see that the value is updated every 1-3 seconds. Because we have a transition set on all, when the ball gets its left and top position updated, we see the ball move to its new position.

Now, that's where I have parked the example. What about you? Perhaps you could take it further and use background-image to set and position a basketball court? Or use an image of a basketball for the ball?

If you are confident adding more JavaScript and markup, perhaps add some sliders to interactively resize the court with custom properties? Or perhaps a color picker to change the court or ball? Or perhaps tweak the animation to use custom properties based on screen width to alter the scale of the ball? Be creative; see what fun you can have!

# Summary

We've had a good look at custom properties in this chapter, and considered ways in which they can be set and read. We have learned how custom properties respect the cascade, inheriting values from their parents, a feature that can be leveraged to our advantage. We have also considered the fact that if we find ourselves working with web components, custom properties provide a means of crossing the usually impenetrable style boundary inside a component. We also looked at environment variables, a specific kind of custom property that lets us deal with the (clears throat) "practicalities" of notches and other peculiarities of specific hardware.

In the second half of the chapter, we also looked at CSS mathematical functions. From ones you have perhaps looked at before, such as `calc()`, to real time-saving functions like `clamp()`, a function that is tailor-made to solve responsive sizing challenges.

We've spent a bit of time together at this point so I feel safe enough to confess something. It's about forms. If there's one area of site design that I always avoid where possible, it's making forms. I don't know why; I've just always found making them a tedious and largely frustrating task. Imagine my joy when I learned that HTML5 and CSS can make the whole form building, styling, and even validating (yes, validating!) process easier than ever before. I was quite joyous. As joyous as you can be about building web forms, that is. In the next chapter, I'd like to share this knowledge with you.

# Join our book's Discord space

Still struggling with custom properties or CSS functions? Join the book's Discord workspace to discuss all your responsive web design concerns directly with the author and interact with other readers:

https://packt.link/RWD4e

# 13

# Forms

Before HTML5, adding things like date pickers, placeholder text, and range sliders into forms had always needed JavaScript. Similarly, there had been no easy way to signpost to users the kind of data we expect them to input into certain fields. For example, whether we expect telephone numbers, email addresses, or URLs.

The good news is that HTML5 largely solves these common problems.

We have two main aims in this chapter. Firstly, to understand HTML5 form features and, secondly, to understand how we can lay out forms more simply for multiple devices with the latest CSS features. In this chapter, we will learn how to:

- Easily add placeholder text into relevant form input fields
- Disable autocompletion of form fields where necessary
- Set certain fields to be required before submission
- Specify different input types such as email, telephone number, and URL
- Create number range sliders for easy value selection
- Place date and color pickers into a form
- Use a regular expression to define an allowed form value
- Style forms using Flexbox
- Change caret color

# HTML5 forms

I think the easiest way to get to grips with HTML5 forms is to work our way through an example form. Just like in daytime TV cooking shows, I have one I made earlier! A minor introduction is needed. Two facts: firstly, I love films. Secondly, I'm very opinionated about what is a good film and what is not.

Every year, when the Oscar nominations are announced, I can't help feeling the wrong films have got "the nod" from the Academy. Therefore, we will start with an HTML5 form that enables fellow cinephiles to vent their frustrations at the continual travesties of the Oscar nominations.

It's made up of a few `fieldset` elements, within which we are including a raft of the HTML5 form input types and attributes. Besides standard form input fields and text areas, we have a number spinner, a range slider, and placeholder text for many of the fields.

The HTML for this form can be found in the `example_13-01` code. Here's how it looks, with no styles applied, in Chrome:

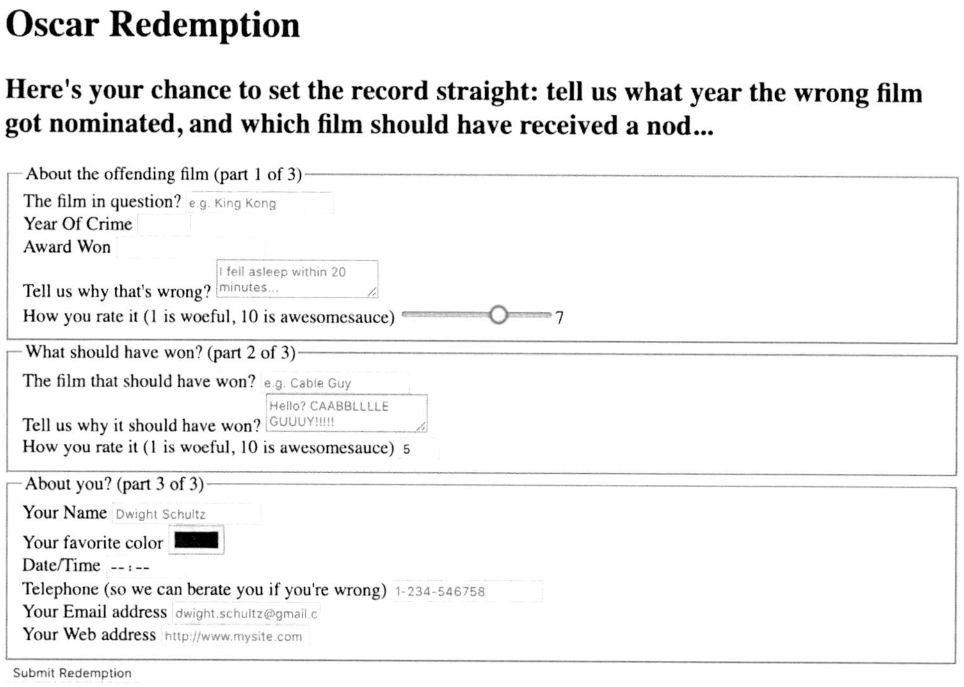

## Oscar Redemption

### Here's your chance to set the record straight: tell us what year the wrong film got nominated, and which film should have received a nod...

About the offending film (part 1 of 3)
The film in question? e.g. King Kong
Year Of Crime
Award Won

Tell us why that's wrong? I fell asleep within 20 minutes...
How you rate it (1 is woeful, 10 is awesomesauce) 7

What should have won? (part 2 of 3)
The film that should have won? e.g. Cable Guy
Tell us why it should have won? Hello? CAABBLLLLE GUUUY!!!!!
How you rate it (1 is woeful, 10 is awesomesauce) 5

About you? (part 3 of 3)
Your Name Dwight Schultz
Your favorite color
Date/Time --:--
Telephone (so we can berate you if you're wrong) 1-234-546758
Your Email address dwight.schultz@gmail.c
Your Web address http://www.mysite.com

Submit Redemption

*Figure 13.1: A basic form with no styling*

If we "focus" on the first field and start inputting text, the placeholder text is removed. If we blur focus without entering anything (by clicking outside of the input box again), the placeholder text reappears. If we submit the form (without entering anything), the following happens:

*Figure 13.2: A standard browser warning from a required field*

The great news is that all these user interface elements, including the aforementioned slider, placeholder text, spinner, and the input validation, are being handled natively by the browser via HTML5, and no JavaScript.

Let's begin by getting a handle on all the capabilities of HTML5 that relate to forms and make all this possible. Once we understand all the mechanics, we can get to work styling it up.

## Understanding the component parts of HTML5 forms

There's a lot going on in our HTML5-powered form, so let's break it down. The three sections of the form are each wrapped in a fieldset, which semantically groups the related sets of form fields, and a legend, which provides the textual explanation of what that fieldset is:

```
<fieldset>
  <legend>About the offending film (part 1 of 3)</legend>
  <div>
    <label for="film">The film in question?</label>
    <input
      id="film"
      name="film"
      type="text"
      placeholder="e.g. King Kong"
      required
      aria-required="true"
    />
  </div>
</fieldset>
```

You can see from the previous code snippet that each input element of the form is also wrapped in a div with a label associated with each input (we could have wrapped the input with the label element if we'd wanted to, too). So far, so normal. However, within this first input, we've just stumbled upon our first HTML5 form feature. After the common attributes of id, name, and type, we have placeholder.

## The placeholder attribute

As the name suggests, the placeholder attribute offers a means of providing a hint or some placeholder data to indicate the kind of input we are expecting. An obvious example would be the word **Search** in a search box.

Needing placeholder text within form fields is such a common requirement that the folks creating HTML5 decided it should be a standard feature of HTML. To add placeholder text for an input, simply add the placeholder attribute. Its value will be displayed in the input until the field gains focus. When it loses focus, if a value has not been entered, it will redisplay the placeholder text.

In our example, the placeholder attribute is filled in like this:

```
placeholder="e.g. King Kong"
```

## Styling the placeholder text

You can style the placeholder attribute with the :placeholder-shown pseudo-selector:

```
input:placeholder-shown {
  color: #333;
}
```

You can also change the text size of the placeholder text; it doesn't need to be the same as the values. As ever, be mindful of accessibility. Although it is only placeholder text, I still try to ensure the text is 16 px or greater.

 You shouldn't rely on the placeholder text to convey any essential informa-tion, as screen readers do not treat placeholder text as a label. Read more about that here: https://www.w3.org/WAI/tutorials/forms/instructions/ #placeholder-text.

When it comes to color accessibility, ensure you use appropriate contrast. If you don't already have a tool to check acceptable contrast levels, I'd recommend bookmarking https://webaim. org/resources/contrastchecker/.

## Styling the input caret with the caret-color CSS property

**Caret**, in our context here, refers to the insertion point in an input area. You might think of that typically blinking vertical line as a "cursor," but it is purposefully named differently in CSS to make the distinction from other cursors, such as the one produced by mouse input.

By the way, it's generally pronounced like your favorite orange vegetable, "carrot," but depending on your accent, you might need to alter your pronunciation to "carrit," such as we have to in the UK, which is fine as long as the Queen doesn't hear you!

The `caret-color` property is a fairly recent addition to CSS that allows us to change the color of the caret.

Suppose we wanted an orange input insert point; we could style it like this:

```
.my-Input {
  caret-color: #f90;
}
```

Sadly, apart from color, we don't get any real control over how the caret appears. We can't change the shape, thickness, or blink rate and style, for example. Hopefully, by the next edition of this book, all that will be possible!

 In case you weren't aware, there is an attribute called `contenteditable` that can make the contents of an everyday element, such as a `div` or `span`, editable. You can also make use of `:caret-color` in those situations too.

## The required attribute

`required` is a Boolean attribute, with "Boolean" meaning it has only two possibilities. In this case, you either include it or not.

When it is present, like this:

```
<input type="text" value="" placeholder="hal@2001.com" required />
```

It means that adding a value to this input will be required before the form can be submitted.

If the form submission is attempted without the input containing a requisite value, a warning message is displayed. The message itself differs both in content and styling depending on the browser and the input type used.

To be absolutely clear, the bad news here is that you can't change the message that the browser displays. But the good news is that it will provide the correct language version of the message for your users to match their language preference.

We've already seen what the required field browser message looks like in Chrome. The following screenshot shows the same message in Firefox:

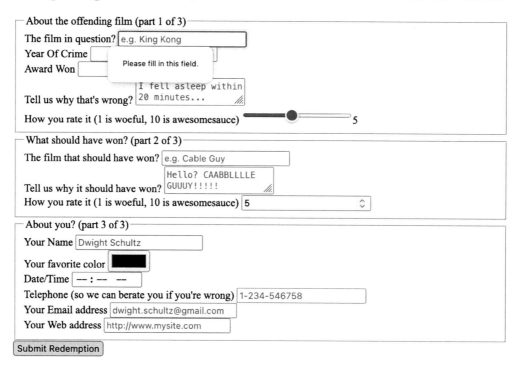

*Figure 13.3: Errors when submitting a form in Firefox without the required fields complete*

The required value can be used alongside many input types to ensure a value is entered. Notable exceptions are the range, color, button, and hidden input types, as they almost always have a default value.

# The autofocus attribute

The HTML5 autofocus attribute allows a form to have a field focused, ready for user input, as soon as the page loads. The following code is an example of an input field wrapped in a div with the autofocus attribute added at the end:

```
<div>
  <label for="search">Search the site...</label>
  <input
    id="search"
    name="search"
    type="search"
    placeholder="Wyatt Earp"
    autofocus
  />
</div>
```

Tread carefully with autofocus for a few reasons.

Firstly, if multiple fields have autofocus added, only the first autofocused field will be focused. It's not hard to imagine a scenario where you accidentally added autofocus to one field, and some time later added autofocus to another. Your user may not get the experience you expected, and you might have yourself a bug to troubleshoot.

Secondly, it's also worth considering that some users use the spacebar to quickly skip down the content of a web page. On a page where a form has an autofocused input field, this capability is negated; instead, a space is added to the focused input field. It's easy to see how that could be a source of frustration for users.

In addition, users of assistive technology will be instantly transported to a location on the page they have no control of—not exactly the best user experience!

If using the autofocus attribute, be certain it's only used once in a form and be sure you understand the implications.

# The autocomplete attribute

By default, most browsers aid user input by autocompleting the value of form fields where possible.

While the user can turn this preference on and off within the browser, we can now also indicate to the browser when we don't want a form or field to allow autocompletion with the `autocomplete` attribute. This is useful not just for sensitive data (bank account numbers, for example) but also if you want to ensure users pay attention and enter something by hand.

For example, for many forms I complete, if a telephone number is required, I enter a "spoof" telephone number. I know I'm not the only one that does that (doesn't everyone?), but I can ensure that users don't enter an autocompleted spoof number by setting the value of the `autocomplete` attribute to `off` on the relevant input field. The following is a code example of a field with the autocomplete attribute set to `off`:

```
<div>
  <label for="tel">Telephone (so we can berate you if you're wrong)
  </label>
  <input
    id="tel"
    name="tel"
    type="tel"
    placeholder="1-234-546758"
    autocomplete="off"
    required
  />
</div>
```

It's not possible to stop autocompletion on entire fieldsets in one go, but you can stop autocompletion on entire forms. Just add the `autocomplete` attribute to the `form` element itself. Here's an example:

```
<form id="redemption" method="post" autocomplete="off">
  <!-- content -->
</form>
```

# The list attribute and the associated datalist element

This `list` attribute and the associated `datalist` element allow a number of selections to be presented to a user once they start entering a value in the field.

The following is a code example of the `list` attribute in use with an associated `datalist`, all wrapped in a `div`:

```
<div>
  <label for="awardWon">Award Won</label>
  <input id="awardWon" name="awardWon" type="text" list="awards" />
  <datalist id="awards">
    <select>
      <option value="Best Picture"></option>
      <option value="Best Director"></option>
      <option value="Best Adapted Screenplay"></option>
      <option value="Best Original Screenplay"></option>
    </select>
  </datalist>
</div>
```

`datalist` contains the list of possible values for the `input`. To connect the `datalist` to the `input`, you have to set the value of the `list` attribute on the `input` to the `id` of the `datalist`.

In our example, we have added an `id` of `"awards"` to the `datalist` element and then set the value of the `list` attribute on the `input` to that.

Although wrapping the options with a `select` element isn't strictly necessary, it helps when applying scripts to add comparable functionality for browsers that haven't implemented the feature.

With our `list` and `datalist` wired up, the input field still appears initially to be just a normal text input field. However, when typing in the input, a selection box appears below it with matching results from the `datalist`. In the following screenshot, we can see the `list` in action (Firefox).

In this instance, as "B" is present in all options within the `datalist`, all the values are shown for the user to select from:

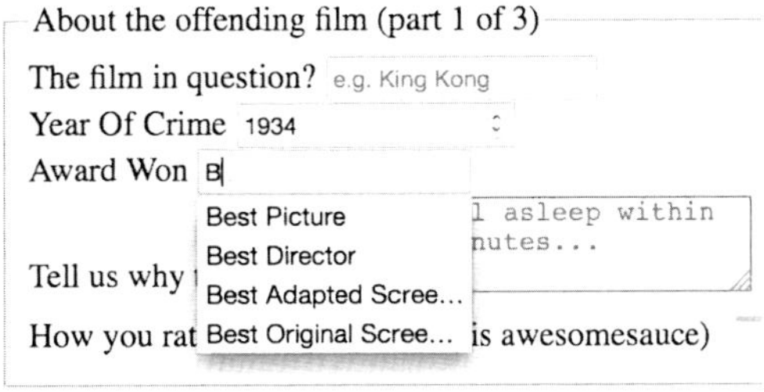

*Figure 13.4: The datalist element showing the matching possible choices*

However, when typing "D" instead, only the matching suggestions appear, as shown in the following screenshot:

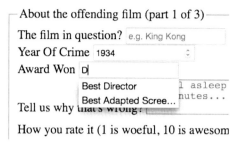

*Figure 13.5: The datalist narrows based on input*

list and datalist don't prevent a user from entering different text in the input box, but they do provide another great way of adding common functionality and user enhancement through HTML5 markup alone.

You can read the specification for datalist here: https://html.spec.whatwg.org/multipage/ form-elements.html#the-datalist-element.

When we started this chapter, I mentioned that there are ways of hinting to the user and, depending on the device, aiding the user in entering the appropriate data for the input at hand. We can do that with HTML5 input types. Let me show you how.

# HTML5 input types

HTML5 has a number of extra input types. These have been a great addition because when they are supported, they offer great additional functionality and, when not supported, they still behave like a standard text type input. Let's take a look at them.

## The email input type

You can set an input to the type of email like this:

```
type="email"
```

Supporting browsers will expect a user input that matches the syntax of an email address. In the following code example, type="email" is used alongside required and placeholder:

```
<div>
  <label for="email">Your Email address</label>
  <input
    type="email"
    id="email"
    name="email"
    placeholder="dwight.schultz@gmail.com"
    required
  />
</div>
```

When used in conjunction with required, trying to input a non-conforming value will generate a warning message:

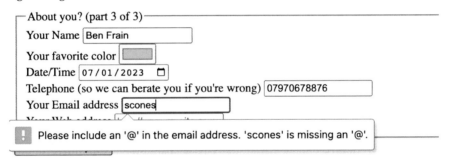

*Figure 13.6: An error shows when incorrect data is entered*

Perhaps most usefully, most touchscreen devices (Android, iPhone, and so on) change the software keyboard presented to the user based on this input type. The following screenshot shows how the software keyboard on an iPad is shown when focusing an input with type="email".

Notice the "@" symbol has been added for easy email address completion:

*Figure 13.7: Software keyboards will often adapt to the input type*

## The number input type

You can set an input field to expect a number like this:

```
type="number"
```

With the type of input set to number, browsers also sometimes add pieces of UI called "spinner" controls. These are tiny pieces of user interface that allow users to easily click up or down to alter the value input.

The following is a code example:

```
<div>
   <label for="yearOfCrime">Year Of Crime</label>
   <input
      id="yearOfCrime"
      name="yearOfCrime"
      type="number"
      min="1929"
      max="2015"
      required
   />
</div>
```

The following screenshot shows how it looks in Chrome, complete with spinners:

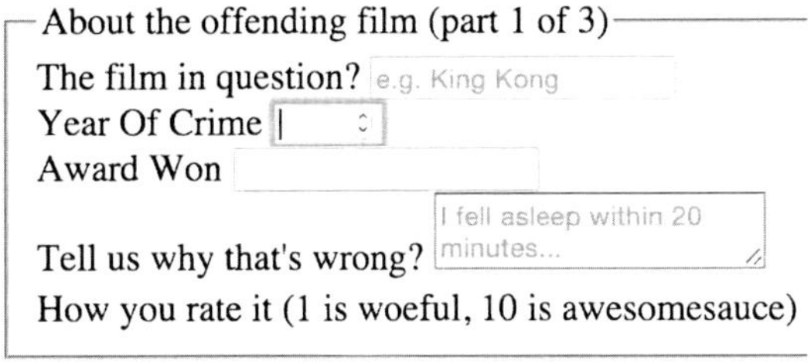

*Figure 13.8: On desktop browsers, "spinners" are shown for number inputs*

And here is how `type="number"` makes the software keyboard appear on an iPad. Notice how all the numerical keys display by default:

*Figure 13.9: Software keyboards default to showing numbers for number inputs*

What happens if you don't enter a number? This can vary subtly between browser implementations. For example, Firefox does nothing until the form is submitted, at which point it displays a warning, **Please enter a number**. Safari, on the other hand, gives the vaguer message of **Fill out this field**.

## Using min and max to create number ranges

You'll notice in the previous code example that we set a minimum and maximum allowed range:

```
type="number" min="1929" max="2015"
```

If you try to submit the form with numbers outside of this range, the browser will show a warning that the value should be within the specified range.

## Changing the step increments

You can alter the step increments (granularity) for the spinner controls of numerical input types with the use of the step attribute. For example, to step 10 units at a time:

```
<input type="number" step="10" />
```

# The url input type

You can set an input field to expect a URL like this:

```
type="url"
```

As you might expect, the url input type is for URL values. Similar to the tel and email input types, it behaves almost identically to a standard text input. However, some browsers add specific information to the warning message provided when submitted with incorrect values. The following is a code example that includes the placeholder attribute:

```
<div>
    <label for="web">Your Web address</label>
    <input id="web" name="web" type="url" placeholder="https://www.mysite.
    com" />
</div>
```

The following screenshot shows what happens when an incorrectly entered URL field is submitted in Chrome:

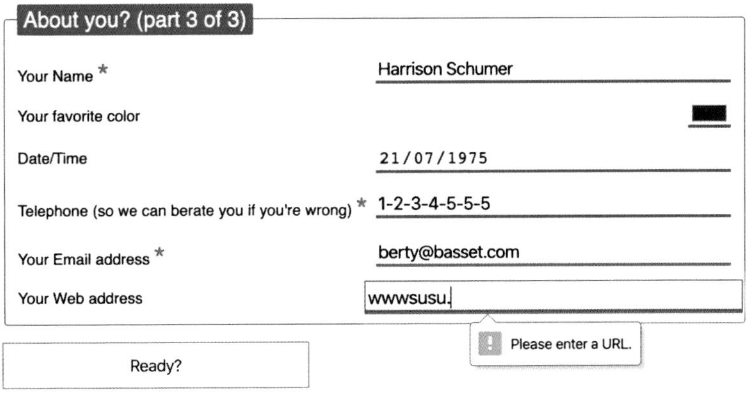

*Figure 13.10: Chrome will show a warning when the input doesn't match the type*

Like type="email", touchscreen devices often amend the software keyboard based on this input type. The following screenshot shows how the software keyboard of an iPad is changed with an input type set to url:

*Figure 13.11: Software keyboard adapting for url input*

Notice the ".com" key? Because we've used a url input type, the software keyboard provides a key for easy top-level domain completion.

On iOS, if you're not going to a `.com` site, you can press and hold that button for a few other popular top-level domains.

## The tel input type

You can set an input field to expect a telephone number type of value, like this:

```
type="tel"
```

Here's a more complete example:

```
<div>
  <label for="tel">Telephone (so we can berate you if you're wrong)
  </label>
  <input
    id="tel"
    name="tel"
    type="tel"
    placeholder="1-234-546758"
    autocomplete="off"
    required
  />
</div>
```

Browsers do little validation on the tel input type. When an incorrect value is input, they fail to provide a suitable warning message.

However, some better news is that, like the `email` and `url` input types, touchscreen devices often thoughtfully accommodate this kind of input with an amended software keyboard for easy completion; here's the `tel` input type when accessed with an iPad (running iOS 13.3):

*Figure 13.12: Software keyboard adapting to telephone input*

Notice the lack of alphabet characters in the keyboard area? This makes it much faster for users to enter a value in the correct format.

If the default blue color of telephone numbers in iOS Safari annoys you when you use a `tel` input, you can amend it with the following selector:

```
a[href^=tel] { color: inherit; }
```

That will set them to the color of the parent element.

# The search input type

You can set an input as a search type like this:

```
type="search"
```

The search input type works like a standard text input. Here's an example:

```
<div>
  <label for="search">Search the site...</label>
  <input id="search" name="search" type="search" placeholder="Wyatt Earp">
</div>
```

As with many of the prior input types, software keyboards (such as those found on mobile devices) often provide a more tailored keyboard. Note the "go" button in iOS 15.5 when focused in a search box:

*Figure 13.13: A keyboard subtly tailored for searching*

# The pattern input attribute

You can set an input to expect a certain pattern input like this:

```
pattern=""
```

Note that this isn't an input type. However, it is a means of communicating to the browser that we expect input of a certain pattern.

The pattern attribute allows you to specify, via a **regular expression**, the syntax of data that should be allowed in a given input field.

**Learn about regular expressions (regexes)**

If you've never encountered regular expressions before, I'd suggest starting here: https://en.wikipedia.org/wiki/Regular_expressions. Regular expressions are used across many programming languages as a means of matching strings. While the format is intimidating at first, they are incredibly powerful and flexible. For example, you could build a regular expression to match a password format or select a certain style of CSS class-naming convention. To help build up your own regex pattern and get a visual understanding of how they work, I'd recommend starting with a browser-based tool like https://www.regexr.com/.

The following code is an example:

```
<div>
  <label for="name">Your Name (first and last)</label>
  <input
    id="name"
    name="name"
    pattern="^([\D]{2,30}\s+)+([a-zA-Z]{2,30})$"
    placeholder="Dwight Schultz"
    required
  />
</div>
```

Such is my commitment to this book, I searched the internet for an entire 458 seconds to find a regular expression that would match a basic first and last name syntax (Western European languages only, sorry). This is by no means bulletproof but should ensure that the value entered is not a number (sorry, R2-D2, you will have to register your film complaints elsewhere) and is made of at least two space-separated values between 2 and 30 characters long.

By entering the regular expression value within the pattern attribute, it makes supporting browsers expect a matching input syntax. Then, when used in conjunction with the required attribute, incorrect entries get the following treatment in supporting browsers. In this instance, I tried submitting the form without providing a last name:

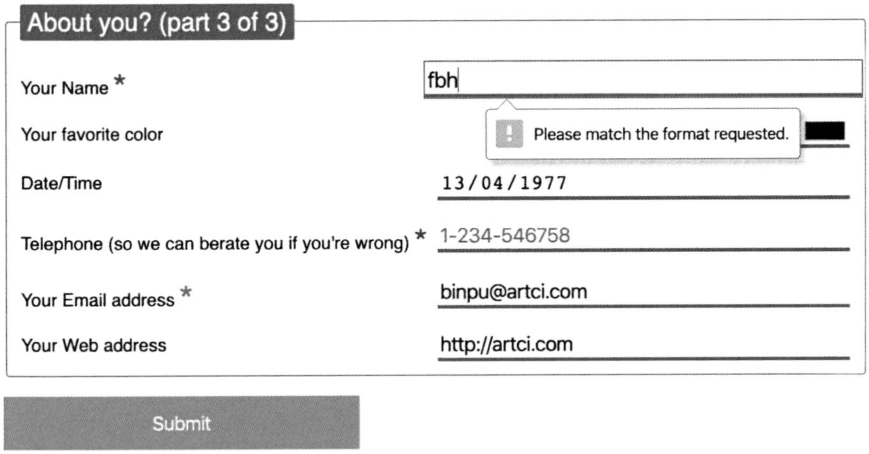

*Figure 13.14: The pattern type provides a vaguer warning but allows you to create bespoke requirements*

As with other browser-generated form messages, it's not possible to amend it, so depending on your use case, it may be beneficial to state in your label text the kind of input you require.

## The color type input

Want to set an input field to receive a color value?

```
input type="color"
```

The color input type invokes the host operating system's color picker, allowing users to select a color. The following code is an example:

```
<div>
    <label for="color">Your favorite color</label>
    <input id="color" name="color" type="color" />
</div>
```

I'll be honest, it's not a type I've yet to need in practice, but it's not hard to imagine scenarios where it would be very handy.

# Date and time

If you've ever bought tickets to an event online, chances are that you have used a date picker of one sort or another. The thinking behind the new date and time input types is so that the browser can provide a consistent piece of user interface for that situation.

Sadly, as I write this in 2022, it's hard to entirely recommend using the native date and time input types across the board, as compatibility is not consistent.

It's not a completely useless situation; as with all the HTML5 input types, without support the input will behave like a normal input box. However, it's worth checking https://caniuse.com/input-datetime first to avoid disappointment. This may be one of the few remaining types where you are going to need a JavaScript solution to provide an entirely consistent experience.

Regardless, in the hope that cross-browser compatibility is sorted soon, let's consider the core capabilities of the date and time input types.

## The date input type

The following code is an example:

```
<input id="date" type="date" name="date" value="2022-06-16"/>
```

Notice that it isn't just a matter of changing the type attribute; you might also want to use the value attribute to set the starting date for the picker. If you don't set your own date, the picker will default to today's date. If, however, you set a date in ISO8601 format (YYYY-MM-DD), inside the value, the start date will be set to that. Despite the value being written in code as YYYY-MM-DD, the browser will actually display the picker in a format better suited (arguably) to your own locale in the browser UI.

Here is the UI that is generated in a supporting browser. Note that as a UK user, I get that date displayed in a slightly more UK-friendly format (MM-DD-YYYY):

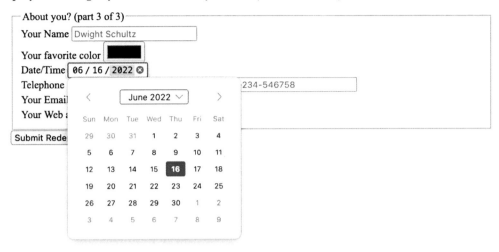

*Figure 13.15: A date-picking interface provided by the browser*

However, depending on your locale, this isn't ideal and may actually be a worse experience for users. In the UK, we write dates in the DD-MM-YYYY format, so this could be confusing if you have a date like 05-06-2024; a UK user would assume that was June 5, 2024. Your own locale may differ again. This discrepancy is what has led many institutions that deal with forms extensively to split the component parts of a date up into separate input fields. For example, the UK government's design system is well documented with examples, well worth a read if you encounter a form design heavy on the date side of things: `https://design-system.service.gov.uk/components/date-input/`

There are a variety of different date- and time-related input types available. What follows is a brief overview of the others.

## The month input type

The following code is an example:

```
<input id="month" type="month" name="month" />
```

The interface allows the user to select a single month and sets the value of the input to a year and month, should you want to access it via scripting; for example, "2023-06". Here is a grab of the user interface that iOS displays:

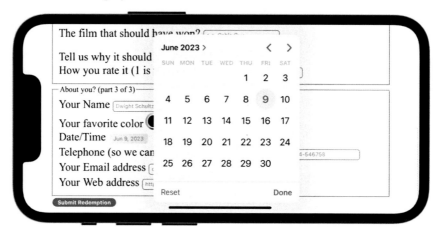

*Figure 13.16: Remember, different operating systems often have their own UIs to achieve the same goal*

## The week input type

The following code is an example:

```
<input id="week" type="week" name="week" />
```

When the week input type is used, the picker allows the user to select a single week within a year and sets the value of the input in "2025-W28" format.

This is currently only supported in Chromium-based browsers. The following screenshot shows how it looks in Chrome:

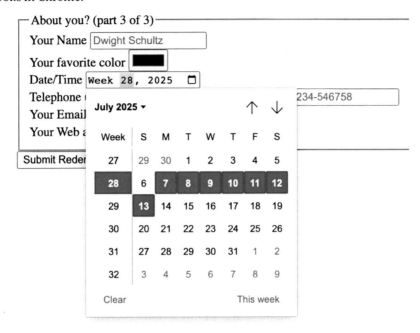

*Figure 13.17: The week input type gets its own data picker style in supporting browsers*

## The time input type

The following code is an example:

```
<input id="time" type="time" name="time" />
```

The time input type allows a value to be set to a 24-hour format; for example, "20:26".

It displays like a standard input in supporting browsers but with additional spinner controls, and it only allows relevant time values.

Touch devices show their own UIs. Here's how it looks on iOS:

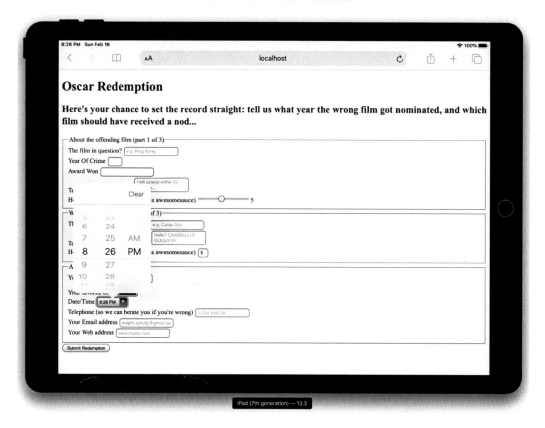

Figure 13.18: The time input type produces specific pieces of interface in supporting browsers

## The range input type

The range input type creates a slider interface element. Here's an example:

```
<input type="range" min="1" max="10" value="5" />
```

And the following screenshot shows how it looks in Firefox:

Figure 13.19: A range slider doesn't show numerical values by default

The default range is from 0 to 100. However, by specifying a min and max value, in our example, we have limited it to between 1 and 10.

One big problem I've encountered with the range input type is that the current value is never displayed to the user. Although the range slider is only intended for vague number selections, I've often wanted to display the value as it changes. Currently, there is no way to do this using HTML5. However, if you absolutely must display the current value of the slider, it can be achieved easily with some simple JavaScript. Amend the previous example to the following code:

```
<input
  id="howYouRateIt"
  name="howYouRateIt"
  type="range"
  min="1"
  max="10"
  value="5"
  onchange="showValue(this.value)"
/>
<span id="range">5</span>
```

We've added two things, an onchange attribute and also a span element with the id of "range". Now, we'll add the following tiny piece of JavaScript:

```
<script>
  function showValue(newValue)
  {
    document.getElementById("range").innerHTML=newValue;
  }
</script>
```

All this does is get the current value of the range slider and display it in the element with an id of "range" (our span tag). You can then use whatever CSS you deem appropriate to change the appearance of the value. We will do that ourselves in a moment once we start styling our form.

# Styling HTML5 forms with CSS

We have our HTML5-powered form built now, and understand the various input types and associated attributes. However, we need to make it a little more visually appealing across different viewport sizes. By applying some of the techniques we've learned throughout the previous chapters, I think we can improve the aesthetics of our form considerably.

I've taken my own stab at styling the form; you can check that version out at example_13-02, and remember, if you don't already have the example code, you can grab it at https://rwd.education.

Here's how the form looks in a small viewport with that basic styling applied:

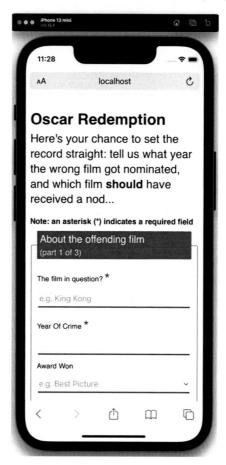

*Figure 13.20: Our form on mobile with basic styling applied*

And here it is with a larger viewport:

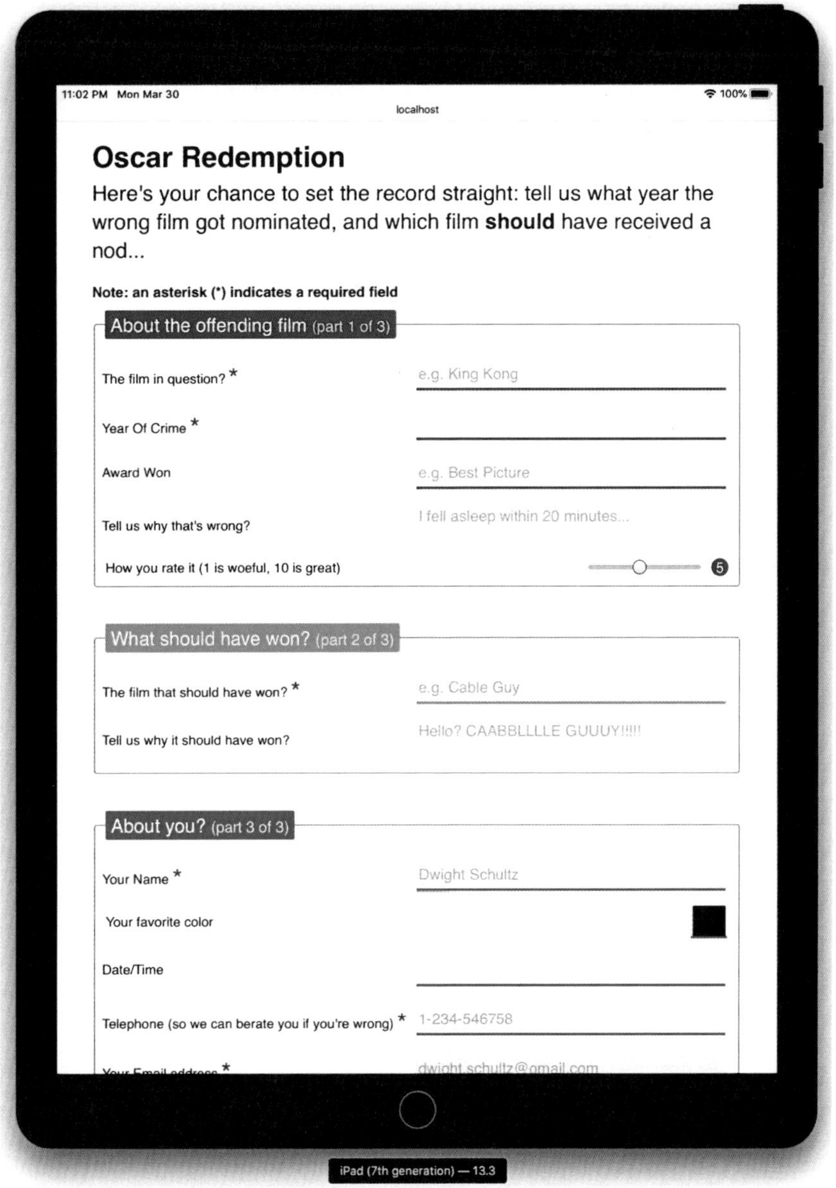

*Figure 13.21: Our same form styled for wider viewports*

If you look at the CSS in the example, you'll see many of the techniques we've looked at throughout previous chapters applied. For example, Flexbox (*Chapter 4*) is used to create uniform spacing and flexibility for elements.

Transforms and transitions (*Chapter 11*) are used so that the focused input fields grow and the ready/submit button flips vertically when it gains focus. Box shadows and gradients (*Chapter 8*) are used to emphasize different areas of the form. Media queries (*Chapter 3*) are used to switch the Flexbox direction for different viewport sizes, and more recent CSS selectors (*Chapter 6*) are used for selector negation.

But look, here's a thought. I'm no hotshot designer. How about you take the markup from example_13-01 and have a shot at styling it up yourself? If it all goes horribly wrong, you can always continue with the styled version, but this would be a solid exercise to put into practice the considerable styling skills you have learned so far.

With that in mind, I won't be going over the techniques I chose in detail here again. Instead, I just want to focus on a couple of form-specific peculiarities. Firstly, how to visually indicate required fields (and for bonus points, indicate a value has been entered) and, secondly, how to create a "fill" effect when a field gets user focus.

## Indicating required fields

We can indicate required input fields to a user using CSS alone. For example:

```
input:required {
  /* styles */
}
```

With that selector, we could add a border or outline to the required fields or add a background-image inside the field. Basically, the sky's the limit! We could also use a specific selector to target an input field that is required, but only when it gains focus. For example:

```
input:focus:required {
  /* styles */
}
```

However, that would apply styles to the input itself. What if we want to amend styles on the associated label element? I've decided I'd like to indicate required fields with a little asterisk symbol at the side of the label:

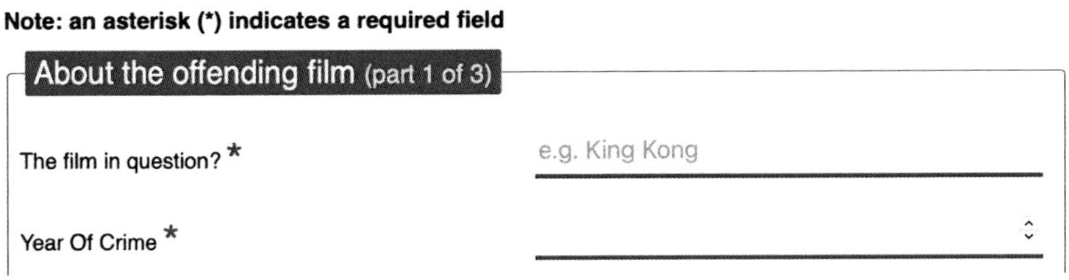

**Note: an asterisk (\*) indicates a required field**

About the offending film (part 1 of 3)

The film in question? **\***          e.g. King Kong

Year Of Crime **\***

*Figure 13.22: An asterisk to indicate a required field is a common pattern*

But this presents a problem. Generally, CSS only lets us effect a change on elements if they are children of an element, the element itself, or a general or adjacent sibling of an element that receives "state" (when I say state, I'm talking about hover, focus, active, checked, and so on). In the following examples, I'm using hover, but that would obviously be problematic for touch-based devices:

```
.item:hover .item-child {
}
```

With the preceding selector, styles are applied to item-child when the item is hovered over. Now consider:

```
.item:hover ~ .item-general-sibling {
}
```

With this selector, when the item is hovered over, styles are applied to item-general-sibling if it is at the same DOM level as item and follows it. Next up:

```
.item:hover + .item-adjacent-sibling {
}
```

Here, when the item is hovered over, styles are applied to item-adjacent-sibling if it is the adjacent sibling element of item (straight after it in the DOM).

So, back to our issue. If we have a form with labels and fields like this, with the `label` above the input (to give us the requisite basic layout), it leaves us a little stuck:

```
<div class="form-Input_Wrapper">
  <label for="film">The film in question?</label>
  <input
    id="film"
    name="film"
    type="text"
    placeholder="e.g. King Kong"
    required
  />
</div>
```

In this situation, until recently in CSS, there was no way to change the style of the `label` based on whether the `input` is required or not (as it comes after the `label` in the markup). So, let's look at two ways to solve the issue. The code for both is in the `example_13-02` files.

In recent browsers, which support the `:has` selector that we looked at in *Chapter 6, CSS Selectors, Typography, and More*, we can easily use a selector like this:

```
.form-Input_Wrapper:has(input:required) label::after {}
```

And then style the `::after` pseudo-element accordingly. This looks at the element that contains the label and the label and says, "If I have a required input in here, select the label inside."

But as support for that isn't great, let's consider how to work around the problem for older browsers.

We could switch the order of those two elements in the markup, but then we would end up with the label underneath the input.

However, have you remembered that both Flexbox and Grid give us the ability to visually reverse the order of elements (read all about them in *Chapter 4* and *Chapter 5* if you haven't done so already) with ease?

That allows us to use the following markup to create a direct sibling association we can use in CSS:

```
<div class="form-Input_Wrapper">
  <input
    id="film"
```

```
      name="film"
      type="text"
      placeholder="e.g. King Kong"
      required
    />
    <label for="film">The film in question?</label>
  </div>
```

And then simply apply `flex-direction: row-reverse` or `flex-direction: column-reverse` to the parent. These declarations reverse the visual order of their child elements, allowing the desired aesthetic of the label above (smaller viewports) or to the left (larger viewports) of the input.

Now, we can get on with actually providing some indication of required fields and when they have received input.

Thanks to our revised markup, the adjacent sibling selector now makes this possible:

```
input:required + label:after {
}
```

This selector essentially says, "For every label that follows an input with a `required` attribute, apply the enclosed rules." Here is the CSS for that section:

```
input:required + label:after {
  content: '*';
  font-size: 2.1em;
  position: relative;
  top: 6px;
  display: inline-flex;
  margin-left: 0.2ch;
  transition: color 1s;
}
input:required:invalid + label:after {
  color: red;
}
input:required:valid + label:after {
  color: green;
}
```

Then, if you focus on a required input and enter a relevant value, the asterisk changes color to green. It's a subtle but helpful touch.

At this point, it seems appropriate to tell you that the content value is not read out by all screen readers, which makes the point once more that using the right elements, labels, and attributes is always the best policy. In this case, the presence of the required attribute should provide a screen reader with the relevant prompt to communicate this need to the user.

## Creating a background fill effect

Back in *Chapter 8, Stunning Aesthetics with CSS*, we learned how to generate linear and radial gradients as background images. Sadly, it isn't possible to transition between two background images (which makes sense, as the browser effectively rasterizes the declaration into an image). However, we can transition between values of associated properties like background-position and background-size. We'll use this capability to create a fill effect when an input or textarea receives focus.

Here are the properties and values added to the input:

```
input:not([type='range']),
textarea {
  min-height: 40px;
  padding: 2px;
  font-size: 17px;
  border: 1px solid #ebebeb;
  outline: none;
  transition: transform 0.4s, box-shadow 0.4s, background-position 0.2s;
  background: radial-gradient(400px circle, #fff 99%, transparent 99%),
  #f1f1f1;
  background-position: -400px 90px, 0 0;
  background-repeat: no-repeat, no-repeat;
  border-radius: 0;
  position: relative;
}
input:not([type='range']):focus,
textarea:focus {
  background-position: 0 0, 0 0;
}
```

In the first rule, a solid white radial gradient is being generated but positioned out of view. The background color that sits behind (the hex value after `radial-gradient`) is not offset and so provides a default color. When `input` gains focus, `background-position` on `radial-gradient` is set back to the default and because we have a `transition` on `background-image` set, we get a nice transition between the two. The visual result of this is the appearance of the input being "filled" with a different color when it gains focus.

It's an effect better used than viewed as a screenshot, so be sure to try out the example code.

## Summary

In this chapter, we learned how to use a host of HTML5 form input types and attributes. They have enabled us to make forms more usable and helpful, and in turn, allow us to capture better quality information.

We've also made use of some techniques we have learned throughout this book to restyle our form and make its layout respond to the constraints of the device on which it is used.

We're nearing the end of our responsive HTML5 and CSS journey. But before we get to our final chapter of parting advice, there are a bunch of bleeding-edge features I'm excited to share with you. Some of these have just shipped in browsers as I write this; others are specified and potentially game changers. So much so that I think they are worth looking at, even without an actual browser implementation to test them on.

Got 5 minutes? Let me tell you about CSS cascade layers and nesting.

# Section III

# Latest Platform Features and Parting Advice

In the first section of the book, we covered the essentials of responsive web design. We didn't just cover the principles; we took deep dives into media queries and the latest layout systems like Flexbox and Grid.

In *Section 2*, we concentrated on the CSS features I believe are essential for solving all manner of day-to-day styling challenges. We covered selecting items, typography, new color features, SVG, animations, and heaps more; the sort of tools that you will be using day-in and day-out if your work involves CSS. And frankly, if your work doesn't involve CSS, I'm not sure why you are here! Mom, is that you?

In the next two chapters, which comprise the final section of this book, I want to cover a couple of broader topics; a bunch of tips, tricks, and techniques that didn't necessarily fit elsewhere, and firstly, in this chapter, some of the latest platform features.

# 14

# Cutting-Edge CSS Features

Depending on when you are reading this, the contents of this chapter may seem commonplace and less cutting-edge in your daily CSS writing. However, as these words are written, these are some of the latest additions to the CSS language.

So, here is what we will take a look at in this chapter:

- What cascade layers are and the problems they solve
- The syntax and typical applications of cascade layers
- The rules for layer ordering
- Adding imported style sheets to a layer
- Understanding the importance of `!important`
- CSS nesting and its origins
- Examples of syntax and its use cases
- The `@nest` at-rule
- Nesting media queries
- How to write CSS nesting today
- How to tell browser vendors you want nesting!

In the case of CSS nesting, which we will cover shortly, there are no browser implementations, merely a specification. However, it is an update to the language that I am genuinely excited about – an addition I believe will fundamentally change the way we all write CSS. Therefore, I feel it is worth covering ahead of time.

But before we get to CSS nesting, I want to cover something that is both new to the language and is actually available for use in all modern browsers: CSS cascade layers.

# Cascade layers

Cascade layers exist as a high-level tool to manage the grouping, and priority, of style rules. When writing CSS, I make a point of only using classes as the styling hooks to make my changes. To exemplify, if I need to style a button, I won't use an isolated element selector as a styling hook like this:

```
button {
    /* styles */
}
```

This is because, when using element selectors, it isn't possible to create a specificity equality across all the selectors. As soon as I want a different style button elsewhere, I will need to create a more specific selector to override the styles I have already created. Instead, I would add a class to the button and do this:

```
.btn {
    /* styles */
}
```

 If the nuance of why this is important when authoring projects is lost on you, I'd recommend reading my shorter book, *Enduring CSS*, free online at https://ecss. benfrain.com (or buy yourself an eBook/hardcopy).

However, there may be scenarios where things aren't entirely within your control. To give you a common scenario where this situation plays out, consider the following.

Imagine that, despite this author's advice against using frameworks in the next chapter, you decide you want to include a CSS framework called "Shoe Lace" in your project. This framework has rules set for the display of common elements such as buttons, lists, and the like.

You include the framework CSS and get working on your project. However, when looking at the buttons on the page, you decide you'd like to tweak the styling a little. Maybe that border needs to be a little thinner?

You look at your markup:

```
<button class="btn">Buy Scone</button>
```

And you do the sensible thing and apply the lightest possible selector in your own style sheet to make a change:

```
.btn {
    border: 1px dotted goldenrod;
}
```

Then you check the change in the browser and... nothing has happened. What is going on?

Eventually, you look inside the "Shoe Lace" framework files and uncover the problem. They have a selector like this:

```
/* CSS framework code */
button.btn {
    font-size: 1.3em;
    border: 2px solid #333;
}
```

This means that every time you want to override this set of styles, you need to use a more specific selector. That's far from ideal, as now your own styles and selectors have become more specific, which is sure to lead to more issues in the future.

Cascade layers exist to solve these kinds of problems. They can also be a useful tool in organizing your own groups of styles. But before we consider that, let's take our first look at cascade layers by seeing how we could solve our prior issue:

```
@layer framework {
    /* CSS framework code */
    button.btn {
        font-size: 1.3em;
        border: 2px solid #333;
    }
}

.btn {
    border: 1px dotted goldenrod;
}
```

And just like that, our problem has been solved. Using the @layer at-rule establishes a cascade layer, meaning that the styles inside the layer are immediately deemed subordinate to those outside the layer. And we will get into the nitty-gritty of how layers do that momentarily.

The syntax should be relatively familiar to you. In much the same way that styles inside a media query are encapsulated by a condition, the @layer encompasses the styles within a layer. Cascade layers can also be applied on file imports too, allowing you to import a style sheet into a layer. This is something quite likely to be useful if we are dealing with a third-party library. Importing a style sheet into a cascade layer is done like this:

```
@layer framework;
@import url("shoelace-framework.css") layer(framework);
```

In that instance, we still make our layer first, and then import our style sheet into it with the layer() function.

Right. At this point, it's time we go through some ground rules when working with cascade layers.

## Naming cascade layers

Naming a cascade layer is just like naming a set of keyframes. Within reason, name your layers however it suits your project. If you like grouping code by area, you can do that. If naming by types of styles, like "reset", "utilities", or "colors" is more your thing, then that is fine too. There is no right or wrong; it's a case of doing whatever best suits the way you work.

You can also have anonymous layers, and they will work just the same. I can't really recommend doing that, though. For how little it takes to name a layer, it will make it far easier to work with, and think about, if it is named.

## Where to declare layers

Declare your layers near the start of your style sheet. As you can't put layers between @import statements, I ensure that layers get defined at the top, then any @import statements, and then the styles. As we will see in a moment, that doesn't mean all the styles for a layer need to be nested there too. It's just for the initial setup.

When you declare layers, they work top to bottom, with the last one declared being a higher priority than the first. So, suppose we had layers declared like this:

```
@layer reset,
framework,
layout,
components;
```

The reset would get the lowest priority, followed by the framework, then layout, with the components layer having the highest priority. Whitespace isn't important, so you can write them vertically or on one line.

This would work equally well:

```
@layer reset, framework, layout, components;
```

Personally, I think it's easier to reason about them listed vertically, as it enforces the order of priority, but you do you!

It is also important to remember that the first instance of a layer defines its priority for perpetuity. Anywhere you subsequently add to, or re-declare that layer, it will remain in its current priority order.

## Adding rules to layers

Because you don't have to add styles to a layer when you define it, you can add rules to a layer any number of times from any location. After a few hundred lines of CSS, if you decide you need to add a rule to layout, you can simply do this:

```
@layer layout {
    .my-Thing {
        display: grid;
        grid-auto-flow: column;
    }
}
```

The rule will be added to the relevant layer and obey the priority assigned to that layer when it was defined.

## The priority of rules in and outside of layers

A helpful feature of cascade layers is that any styles outside of a layer are always a greater priority than styles in one. This makes it helpful if you want to, effectively, quarantine styles. This is exactly the procedure we followed at the outset, moving our mythical "Shoe Lace" framework CSS into its own layer, allowing us to write styles for our button easily without needing to battle specificity.

The great thing with cascade layers is that you know that what is left outside any layers will be unaffected. So perhaps another helpful way to think of cascade layers is as a way to de-emphasize styles by grouping rules into tiers.

## Nesting layers inside other layers

If you find yourself in a suitably complicated scenario, you can even nest layers inside other layers. Let's suppose we have layouts split into areas like header, sidebars, content, and modals. You might decide these concerns would be better organized under a layout layer. We could set that up like this:

```
@layer framework;
@layer layout {
    @layer header,
    sidebars,
    content,
    modals;
}
@layer components;
```

And then we use a dot notation to add styles to the nested layers like this:

```
@layer layout.header {
    header {
        display: flex;
    }
}
```

We give the outer layer name, then a period character, and then the nested layer name.

Or if we wanted to @import into a nested layer, it would look like this:

```
@import url("header.css") layer(layout.header);
```

The top-to-bottom prioritizing of layers is applied to the nested layers too, so in this instance, layout.modals would have a higher priority than layout.sidebars, for example. It isn't any more "specific," though, just because it is nested. So something in layout.modals wouldn't have greater priority than something in components, for example.

# The importance of !important

I feel the use of !important has been a little vilified over the years. Like all of the best villains, that's perhaps because it is a little misunderstood. I'll exemplify. Can you explain to me what !important does here?

```css
/* Author stylesheet */
body {
    font-size: 1.1em !important;
}
```

I mean, sure, we probably all know that if you are having trouble getting a rule to have a certain declaration applied, slapping an !important on there usually fixes it. But how and why does it actually do that?

Confession. I've been writing CSS for over 20 years, and it was only when reading the specification for cascade layers that I think I fully, truly, understood the mechanics of !important. Want to bore fellow developers next time you are sharing a coffee? Pay attention to this next bit; it will be !important (see what I did there?).

When styles are applied by the browser, onto the page, there is an order of priority:

- Firstly, the browser applies its own set of styles; you often see these marked in your dev tools as **User Agent Style Sheet**.

- Then, user style sheets are applied. You may have none set, but if you were to set a minimum font size in your browser preferences, that setting would go into your user style sheet.

- Finally, at the greatest priority of the three are the author style sheets; the sheets you and I write day-to-day.

With that initial order of precedence established, we can envisage that if the font-size for the body was set by the browser, the user, and the author, the author styles (that we as developers write) would "win" and take precedence. This works well enough for the most part, but what if a user needs a large minimum font-size for accessibility or preference? And, in our ignorance, we thought that 12 px was absolutely fine for all? That would be a problem for many! The solution to this issue is the !important declaration.

The !important declaration inverts the established order. So, not only will an !important declaration take precedence over a normal declaration in the same style sheet, but if an !important declaration is added to a user style sheet, such as for our aforementioned font-size preference, this will take precedence over any author style sheet declaration.

This way, users have a guaranteed mechanism to ensure their needs are applied.

In addition, any user-agent (e.g. browser) !important declarations trump even the user !important styles. There is further nuance if needing to factor in encapsulation contexts such as shadow trees, but for our purposes, this mental model will suffice.

> The specification for cascade layers offers additional information regarding encapsulation: https://www.w3.org/TR/css-cascade-5/#cascade-context.
>
> In addition, Level 6 of the CSS Cascade specification also introduces the notion of scoped styles, which are sure to make isolating groups of rules even more flexible. You can read that draft specification here: https://www.w3.org/TR/css-cascade-6/#scoped-styles.

So, what does this have to do with cascade layers?

## !important in cascade layers

Let's extend our earlier, simplistic example:

```
@layer reset,
framework,
layout,
components;
```

In this instance, as we have established, in terms of the layers, reset will have the least priority, and components the most. However, should we add an !important to one of the declarations in the reset layer, this is what would effectively happen:

```
reset,
framework,
layout,
components;
!components
!layout
!framework,
!reset,
```

The browser effectively makes important "versions" of each layer, crucially in reverse order. The outcome of this, practically, is that an !important rule in the reset becomes the highest priority, despite normal rules being the least priority in the "normal" reset layer.

So, all this is to help you understand that when using cascade layers, you need to be even more vigilant in your use of !important. If you can avoid it in your layers, so much the better and the more predictable they will be.

As an exercise, take a look at the CSS of example_14-01:

```
@layer reset,
type;

@layer reset {
    .para {
        font-size: 2rem;
        color: hotpink !important;
        text-decoration-style: dotted;
        text-decoration: line-through orange !important;
    }
}

@layer type {
    .para {
        font-size: 1.2rem !important;
        color: goldenrod !important;
        text-decoration: solid overline lime !important;
    }
}

.para {
    font-size: 1rem;
    color: brown;
    text-decoration: wavy underline lime !important;
}
```

Before you open up this page in a browser and see which styles get applied, consider what you have just learned. What do you think will be the applied font-size, color, and text-decoration?

## Old browsers

All modern browsers have shipped cascade layers but, depending on the browsers you need to support, it may be some time before you can make use of them in production. Remember, you can always check support at https://caniuse.com/css-cascade-layers.

Unfortunately, there is no way of providing any kind of fallback for cascade layers in older browsers; the layers will simply be ignored. You can test for cascade layers with @supports, which we covered in *Chapter 6*, *CSS Selectors, Typography, and More*. That would look like this:

```
@supports not at-rule(@layer) {
    /* Styles added here for browsers that don't support layers */
}
```

That concludes our overview of cascade layers.

Now onto something that, at this time, is a little more conceptual. Regardless, a feature that will hopefully be with us soon: CSS nesting.

## CSS nesting

If you have done any work with CSS in the last 10–15 years, you will have come across CSS pre-processors, the most enduring of which is Sass.

When Sass first appeared, there was nothing like variables, color functions, or nesting in CSS. I don't think it's even debatable that had it not been for the popularity and ultimate ubiquity of Sass and other pre-processors like LESS, we wouldn't now have CSS custom properties, color manipulation functions, and hopefully soon, the topic of this section: native CSS nesting.

CSS nesting does not provide anything new in the browser. It's purely a developer experience improvement; syntactic improvements, if you will. It's also subtly different than how Sass implements nesting; just different enough that it might catch you out at first.

Let's consider how CSS nesting works and you can decide whether it's something you feel will improve your development experience or not.

 I was so enamored with Sass that back in 2013 I wrote a book on it, *Sass and Compass for Designers*. Despite being nearly a decade old, it's still largely relevant today. You can find out more about it here: https://sassandcompass.com.

If you have never used Sass before, and the concept of nesting is entirely lost on you, consider CSS like this:

```
.parent {
    font-size: 16px;
}

.parent .child {
    font-size: 1em;
}

.ancestor .parent {
    font-size: 1.5rem;
}
```

In those three rules, the common selector is the `.parent` class, which is repeated in each of the rules. With nesting, we could compact those three selectors like this:

```
.parent {
    font-size: 16px;
    & .child {
        font-size: 1em;
    }
    @nest .ancestor & {
        font-size: 1.5rem;
    }
}
```

Let's unpack what's going on here. Firstly, by putting a selector inside the first set of braces, prefixed by an ampersand &, we establish a parent-child relationship. The & symbol is used in nesting to represent the context, or selector, of the rule it is nested within.

To make something a child of something else, you must use the & as the first non-whitespace character of the nested selector. While a direct child doesn't require anything further than the initial ampersand, expressing other relationships does require additional syntax.

For example, in the second nested rule in the example above, we express the relationship between the parent selector and ancestor selector above it with the @nest keyword and the ampersand & selector after the selector.

The @nest at-rule is used to make explicit to both the author and the browser that some nesting context, indicated by the &, is going to be present on that line, even though it isn't the first character. Remember, the ampersand, &, is a symbolic reference to the outer, parent selector of the rule. By placing the & after the selector, we are making the nested selector be "printed" first, and then the outer selector. Just remember that whenever you see the &, that will be replaced by the outer selector in the eyes of the browser.

With @nest and &, the full gamut of selector relationships is possible to express. For example, here is an adjacent sibling relationship and a selector where a data attribute and class are combined:

```css
.item + .item {
    /* styles */
}


[data-scones].item {
    /* styles */
}
```

That could be written nested like this:

```css
.item {
    @nest & + .item {
        /* styles */
    }
    @nest &[data-scones] {
        /* styles */
    }
}
```

You do need to be aware that every selector in a list needs an &. So, for example, this would not work:

```css
.item {
    color: #fff;
    & .child,
    .child-2 {
        color: #ddd;
    }
}
```

It's subtle, but notice that the `.child-2` selector is nested but doesn't have an & as the first character. What we actually need would be:

```
.item {
    color: #fff;
    & .child,
    & .child-2 {
        color: #ddd;
    }
}
```

## Nesting conditionals such as media queries

You can also nest media queries inside a selector. We mentioned this technique briefly in *Chapter 3*, *Media Queries and Container Queries*, as it is a great way to encapsulate all the variations that happen to a selector.

Consider this:

```
.item {
    width: 100%;
    @media (min-width: 40em) {
        width: 90%;
        margin-inline: auto;
    }
}
```

Notice that with the conditional/media query, we don't need to use the & symbol; we can just directly nest it.

Whether an element needs to have styles changed due to changes above it in the DOM tree, different media situations, or we need to express new styles in the situation where it has certain sibling selectors present, with CSS nesting we can contain it all within a single nesting rule. Here is an example:

```
.item {
    color: #333;
    @media (prefers-color-scheme: dark) {
        color: #e8e8e8;
```

```
        }
    @nest .container-big & {
        width: 100%;
    }
    & + & {
        margin-left: 10px;
    }
}
```

Here, we have created "one rule to, err..., rule them all." The entire life of `.item` is inside a set of curly braces, so you only need to find that one string in your CSS codebase to be able to understand and control everything that ever happens to that element.

## Trying CSS nesting syntax today

If you are used to using Sass in your projects, there is probably little need to do anything right now. However, if you are using PostCSS in your setup, which often comes built-in with modern build tools like Vite (`https://vitejs.dev`), you can try the CSS nesting way of writing nested styles right now with the aptly named "PostCSS Nesting" plugin: `https://github.com/csstools/postcss-plugins/tree/main/plugins/postcss-nesting`.

## Giving your feedback on the proposal

As I write this, the CSS nesting proposal is in flux. You can look at the issues and discussions around the specification at `https://github.com/w3c/csswg-drafts/issues?q=is%3Aissue+is%3Aopen+label%3Acss-nesting+c`, so if there is something you particularly want to see in the specification, there is nothing to stop you from making your voice heard.

## Asking browser vendors to implement CSS nesting

I would welcome CSS nesting, but as there are currently no browser implementations, you can voice your interest in the feature at the following browser support tickets:

- Chrome: `https://bugs.chromium.org/p/chromium/issues/detail?id=1095675`
- WebKit/Safari: `https://bugs.webkit.org/show_bug.cgi?id=223497`
- Firefox: `https://bugzilla.mozilla.org/show_bug.cgi?id=1648037`

The more interest in the feature that browser vendors see, the more likely it is we will see it in browsers sooner rather than later.

# Summary

In this chapter, we have looked in detail at two big changes to CSS. The first, cascade layers, gives us a fundamentally different set of tools to organize our code, and we can use it in browsers today. It's the perfect way of keeping third-party code from causing unwanted side effects.

We then looked at CSS nesting, new functionality still in the mere specification stage that promises to offer us new ways to write more compact and expressive code. There are tools to write it today, and hopefully, in the not-too-distant future, it will be something we can write without thinking whenever we write CSS.

CSS has moved at an incredible pace in the last few years, and it seems that never a week goes by without me coming across some new functionality I have missed or that is coming to browsers soon. It's certainly easy to feel overwhelmed with the pace of changes in front-end development. However, you shouldn't. With some common sense and a basic interest in what's going on, I feel it is easy enough to stay in the game.

Anyway, the more philosophical musings on how to deal with modern front-end development, and many of the other new things coming to CSS and HTML, could be a chapter all of its own.

Which is handy, because that's exactly what our last chapter is all about.

You've made it this far; walk this last mile with me, will you?

# 15

# Bonus Techniques and Parting Advice

In my favorite stories and films, there's usually a scene where a mentor passes on valuable advice and some magical items to the hero. You know those items will prove useful; you just don't know when or how.

Well, I'd like to assume the role of mentor in this final chapter—besides, my hair has waned, and I don't have the looks for the hero role. I would like you, my fine apprentice, to spare me just a few more moments of your time while I offer up some final words of advice before you set forth on your responsive quest.

This chapter will be half philosophical musings and guidance, and half a grab-bag of unrelated tips and techniques. I hope, at some point in your responsive adventures, these tips will prove useful.

Here's the grab-bag of tips we'll cover:

- Truncating text; single-line and multi-line
- Creating horizontal scrolling panels
- Customizing scrollbars
- Using CSS Scroll Snap
- Smooth scrolling with CSS `scroll-behavior`

And here are the topics I will suggest guidance on:

- Getting designs in the browser
- Testing on real devices

- Embracing progressive enhancement
- Defining a browser support matrix
- Avoiding CSS frameworks in production
- Hiding, showing, and loading content at different viewports
- Validators and linting tools
- Performance
- The next big things

Right, now pay attention, 007...

In my day-to-day work, I've found that I use some CSS features constantly and others hardly ever. I thought it might be useful to share those I've used most often, especially those that pop up time and again with responsive projects.

These are in no particular order. None are more important than any other. Just dip in if and when you need them.

# Truncating text

Sometimes, you encounter a situation where space is limited and you would prefer to see text truncated rather than wrapped. We've been trained to spot truncated text on websites for years with the ellipsis symbol "...".

## Single-line truncation

This is straightforward in CSS. Consider this markup (you can view this example in example_15-01):

```
<p class="truncate">
  OK, listen up, I've figured out the key to eternal happiness. All you
  need to do is eat lots of scones.
</p>
```

However, we actually want to truncate the text at 530 px wide, so it looks like this:

> OK, listen up, I've figured out the key to eternal happiness. All you need to do is...

*Figure 15.1: Truncation is handy when keeping dimensions constant is of paramount importance*

Here is the CSS to make that happen:

```css
.truncate {
  width: 530px;
  overflow: hidden;
  text-overflow: ellipsis;
  white-space: nowrap;
}
```

Each one of those properties is needed to make the truncation occur.

 You can read the specification for the `text-overflow` property here: `https://drafts.csswg.org/css-overflow-3/#text-overflow`.

Whenever the width of the content exceeds the `width` defined, it will be truncated. The `width` can just as happily be set as a percentage, such as 100% if it's inside a flexible container.

We set `overflow: hidden` to ensure that anything that overruns the box is hidden.

When the content does overrun, `text-overflow: ellipsis` creates the ellipsis symbol in the correct place to indicate the overrunning content. This could be set to `clip` if preferred. In that instance, the content just gets clipped where it overflows, possibly mid-character.

The `white-space: nowrap` property/value pair is needed to ensure that the content doesn't wrap inside the surrounding element, which is what it would do by default.

## Multi-line truncation

There still isn't a perfect way to do multi-line truncation despite there being a specification: `https://drafts.csswg.org/css-overflow-3/#propdef--webkit-line-clamp`.

This is based on a proprietary WebKit way of doing things that has been around for so long now that browser providers have actually implemented it in their own browsers, with `-webkit-` prefix and all!

Right now, you can use `-webkit-line-clamp` like this, which you can view in `example_15-02`:

```
.multi-line-truncate {
    width: 250px;
    text-overflow: ellipsis;
    overflow: hidden;
    -webkit-line-clamp: 2;
    -webkit-box-orient: vertical;
    display: -webkit-box;
}
```

And that produces an effect like this:

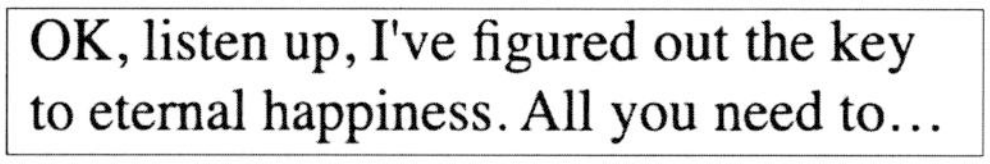

> OK, listen up, I've figured out the key
> to eternal happiness. All you need to…

*Figure 15.2: Multi-line truncation is possible with caveats*

This seems like exactly what we want. However, be advised that the implementation is brittle. Here are some reasons why. Firstly, if you happen to omit the `overflow: hidden` declaration, you still get the ellipsis at the line length you specified, but the text continues. Worse, even with those declarations all added, if you happen to add padding inside the box you get a similar effect of an ellipsis at the specified line but with additional text still visible.

It can certainly help you out in a pinch, but be aware of the caveats.

# Creating horizontal scrolling panels

When I say horizontal scrolling panel, hopefully you know the kind of thing I mean.

Horizontal scrolling panels are common on the iOS App Store and Google Play Store for showing panels of related content (movies, albums, and more). Where there is enough horizontal space, all of the items are viewable. However, when space is limited (think mobile devices), the panel is scrollable from side to side.

We made a horizontal scrolling panel together in `example_05-10` from *Chapter 5, Layout with CSS Grid*. That will be the start for the finished `example_15-03`, which we are going to move toward in the next sections. It was already perfectly functional, but there are some new, scrolling-related, treats we can add with CSS that will really elevate the experience of using it.

Our horizontal slider looks like this on an iPhone 13 mini, running iOS 15.5:

*Figure 15.3: A horizontal scrolling panel*

The markup pattern looks like this; note that I'm just showing the first item in the list for brevity:

```
<div class="Scroll_Wrapper">
<figure class="Item">
<img src="Sun.jpg" alt="Our Sun in space" />
    <figcaption class="Caption">The Sun</figcaption>
        <p>
            The Sun ...
        </p>
</figure>
```

To get the scrolling working, we just need a wrapper that is narrower than the sum of its contents and to set it to overflow automatically in the *x* axis. That way, it won't scroll if there is enough space, but it will if there isn't.

With Grid, the main scroller is set like this:

```
.Scroll_Wrapper {
    display: grid;
    width: 100%;
    overflow-y: hidden;
    overflow-x: auto;
    gap: 0 20px;
    grid-template-rows: auto auto;
    grid-auto-columns: auto;
    grid-auto-flow: column;
}
```

No matter how many items are added to the grid, it will continue to add them as columns. Skip back to *Chapter 5, Layout with CSS Grid*, if you need a refresher on any of the properties and values used.

One thing you might not be very happy about is the default scrollbar. This is typically quite elegant on touch devices but a little more unrefined on desktop.

Here it is on Chrome:

*Figure 15.4: Default scrollbars in Chrome*

And here it is in Firefox (both browsers on macOS):

*Figure 15.5: Default scrollbar on Firefox (macOS)*

I actually think the default appearance on Firefox is very nice and I'm not sure I would do much to change it. However, the Chrome one could maybe do with a little work.

## Styling scrollbars

Nowadays, we can make visual changes to the way scrollbars look. Safari and Chrome use a non-standard approach, while good old Firefox, which steadfastly refused to allow its scrollbars to be changed (since the year 2000!) until there was a specification, now follows the CSS Scrollbars Styling Module Level 1: https://www.w3.org/TR/css-scrollbars-1/.

Let's start with the specification and see what that gives us. It's important to note that the specification is purposefully more limiting than some of the non-standard scrollbar controls. This is because it is not possible to know exactly what constituent parts a scrollbar will have on any given system. As such, the specification limits us to the color of the scroll track and **thumb** (that's the term for the part you click/touch and drag), and the width of the scrollbar itself. Here it is applied:

```
.Scroll_Wrapper {
    display: grid;
    width: 100%;
    overflow-y: hidden;
```

```
    overflow-x: scroll;
    gap: 0 20px;
    grid-template-rows: auto auto;
    grid-auto-columns: auto;
    grid-auto-flow: column;
    /* standards way, currently only implemented by Firefox */
    scrollbar-color: #b5b5b5 #616161;
    scrollbar-width: thin;
}
```

With scrollbar-color, you give it two values; the first the color for the scrollbar "thumb," the second for the track of the scrollbar. For scrollbar-width, you have only three choices: auto, thin, or none. I've opted for thin, but as you can see in my case, in Firefox, that has made very little difference:

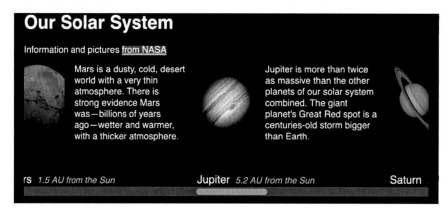

*Figure 15.6: scrollbar-width has a vague effect in Firefox (macOS)*

Now, here comes the real problem with the official way of doing things. It has not yet been implemented in Chromium or WebKit browsers.

 If, by some cruel twist of fate, you find yourself needing to style scrollbars for the much older legacy browser Internet Explorer, be aware it has its own -ms- prefixed rules for styling and removing the scrollbar.

It's unsurprising then, that most people turn to using the non-standards way of styling them, as that typically covers the overwhelming majority of users.

However, before we get into the non-standards, proprietary way that Safari and Chrome-based browsers use, an important point. If you are going down the route of altering scrollbars in any significant manner, ensure you consider accessibility. In the example above, I went for a 3:1 color contrast ratio of track to background, and thumb to track. That should be the minimum you opt for, despite the fact that, often, the host operating system's own scrollbars do not adhere to those contrast ratios!

 If you want a deeper dive into the considerations when styling scrollbars, I recommend the following: `https://adrianroselli.com/2019/01/baseline-rules-for-scrollbar-usability.html`.

Here is what I have added to deal with WebKit and Chrome browsers:

```
.Scroll_Wrapper::-webkit-scrollbar {
    width: 25px;
    background-color: #616161;
}

.Scroll_Wrapper::-webkit-scrollbar-thumb {
    background-color: #b5b5b5;
    border-radius: 12px;
}
```

And in Chrome, this is the effect that has:

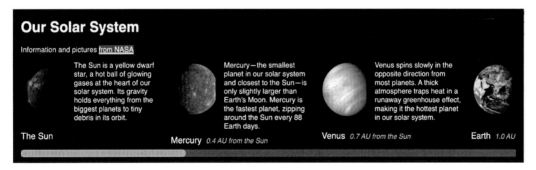

*Figure 15.7: Using non-standards scrollbar styling in Chrome*

There are other `-webkit-` prefixed scrollbar properties; the aim here is merely to get us some equivalence to the "official" declarations we set. Remember, regardless of what you set, mobile browsers tend to do their own things.

For desktop browsers, you could also opt to only show the scrollbar when the parent element is hovered over. However, remember that if you stray from the standard scrollbars, you are liable to make all the accessibility considerations and affordances needed for them to be usable.

Well, with these minor tweaks, our example is in decent shape and fairly consistent. We have a nice simple grid layout, with subgrid in there for browsers that support it, and some custom scrollbar work in there too. Now I want to show you another lovely little scrolling-based extra that is simple to add but produces a very polished result.

# CSS Scroll Snap

CSS Scroll Snap snaps the scrolling of content to predefined points in the container. Again, it is a user interface pattern that is commonplace in the interfaces of native applications, app stores, and things like carousels. However, historically, such functionality required JavaScript to implement to get anything approaching a near comparable experience.

 You can read the official specification for CSS Scroll Snap at `https://www.w3.org/TR/css-scroll-snap-1/`.

Let's use CSS Scroll Snap to add scroll snap functionality to our horizontal "Solar System" container.

## The scroll-snap-type property

First of all, we define the `scroll-snap-type` for our scrolling container. This is where we can decide whether we want the container to scroll snap in the x, y, or both, axes.

This property also allows us to define the strictness of the scroll snapping that is applied. The `mandatory` value is the one I always opt for unless I'm resetting scroll snapping, at which point you can use `none`. `none` will revert scroll snap to behave like a standard scroll container.

What `mandatory` does is ensure that if an item is partially scrolled within the container (for example, the left-hand side is off the viewport by a certain amount), then it will be "snapped" into or out of view.

There is also a `proximity` value. What this does is leave the snapping to the discretion of the browser.

It is important to understand why you may occasionally want and need to use proximity. Suppose you had items in a carousel that were always bigger than the viewport. Because, with mandatory, it would always snap, you may have trouble advancing the scroll panel. Setting it to proximity means that content will remain accessible as the browser will determine how much room should be left to accommodate scrolling.

Despite that, in our instance, since we know the width of our cells won't exceed the width of the viewport, we will apply mandatory for a consistent experience.

So, our container will be amended with this extra line:

```
.Scroll_Wrapper {
    /* other styles */
    scroll-snap-type: x mandatory;
}
```

Now, if you refresh the browser and try the scroll panel, you will likely be disappointed. That, by itself, doesn't do anything. We now need to apply the scroll-snap-align property to the child items.

## The scroll-snap-align property

The scroll-snap-align property controls where an item inside a scroll-snap container will snap to. The options are:

- none to reset an item.
- start to snap the item to the beginning of a scroll snap area.
- end to snap the item to the end of a scroll snap area.
- center to snap the item to the center of the scroll snap area.

So, let's add .Item and set it to snap to the start:

```
.Item {
    /* other styles */
    scroll-snap-align: start;
}
```

Now, if you scroll, you'll see that the items snap within their container.

## The scroll-snap-stop property

By default, an excessive scroll action can send several items past the scroll snap point. With `scroll-snap-stop`, it is possible to make the browser stop at each snap point with each scroll action. There are just two values to choose from:

- `normal`, which is what the browser does by default; or
- `always`, which ensures that no scroll snap points are skipped.

You add this declaration onto the items inside the scroll container.

The only slight annoyance is that, as I write this, `scroll-snap-stop` is not supported in Firefox. However, if this is functionality you want, there is no need to add a fallback; Firefox will skip over it and the browsers that understand it will make use of it.

CSS Scroll Snap is a hugely satisfying piece of functionality to use! In just a few lines, we are able to achieve in CSS what used to take whole libraries of JavaScript to achieve. All this talk of scrolling brings me to another, simple but effective, feature I need to relate.

## Smooth scrolling with CSS scroll-behavior

One of the oldest capabilities of HTML is the ability to anchor to different points in a document. You set a link on the page, and rather than it sending the user to another webpage, the user is instead instantly taken to a different point on the same page.

Typically, such functionality is in the $y$ axis, or down a page. However, it works just as well horizontally in the $x$ axis.

Historically, jumping to an anchor link has always been a little jarring. As the user is instantly transported to the new point on the page, there is no affordance to communicate to the user what just occurred. People have solved this common issue over the years with the help of JavaScript, by effectively animating the scroll action.

Now the Web Platform has provided us with a simple API to achieve this effect, which can be used by either JavaScript or CSS. For CSS, it is the `scroll-behavior` property.

I'm going to add "start" and "end" anchor points to each end of the scroll panel we just made and add two links below the scrolling panel.

So, on the first scrolling item we add this id:

```
<figure id="start" class="Item">
```

And on the last this:

```
<figure id="end" class="Item">
```

And our two links look like this:

```
<a class="ScrollBtn" href="#start">Start</a>
<a class="ScrollBtn" href="#end">End</a>
```

Now, our mechanism is set up as traditional anchor points: as you might imagine, by default, clicking on **End** instantly scrolls the panel to the end. However, if we add `scroll-behavior: smooth` to our scroll panel, we get a silky-smooth scroll behavior instead:

```
.Scroll_Wrapper {
    display: grid;
    width: 100%;
    overflow-y: hidden;
    overflow-x: scroll;
    gap: 0 20px;
    grid-template-rows: auto auto;
    grid-auto-columns: auto;
    grid-auto-flow: column;
    /* standards way, currently only implemented by Firefox */
    scrollbar-color: #b5b5b5 #616161;
    scrollbar-width: thin;
    scroll-snap-type: x mandatory;
    scroll-behavior: smooth;
}
```

Nice! Sadly, this is something that images just don't convey. However, if you open example_15-03, then you can have a play with it for yourself.

We've taken a basic scrolling panel and, with some choice CSS, managed to add custom-colored scrollbars, smooth scrolling, and snap points for a very impressive and robust user experience.

We've reached the end of the bonus techniques section. Hopefully, you have a few more handy tricks in your arsenal for the next project you embark on.

# Parting advice

All that is left, in the remainder of the chapter, and indeed the book (please, don't cry—you'll start me off), is for me to offer what I feel are the most important considerations for any responsive web project. Here goes.

## Getting designs in the browser as soon as possible

The more responsive web work I have done, the more important I have found it to get designs up and running in a browser environment as soon as possible. If you are a designer as well as a developer, then that simplifies matters. As soon as you have enough of a feel, visually, for what you need, you can get it prototyped and develop the idea further in a browser environment.

If you are primarily a developer, then this can aid the design process hugely in order to get the design living and breathing in the browser. Without fail, every project that I work on gets revised in some way as a result of the designs being built in the browser. That isn't a failure of the original flat designs; it's a consequence of realizing that the design is just a step towards realizing an idea. And seeing it working in a browser is one step closer.

There is a slew of problems that can only be solved by seeing the design in a browser. What about all those device and browser window sizes? What about the interactivity that occurs when the user opens a menu? How long should that introductory animation run for? And is it too much anyway? These are the kind of design decisions that can only be made when the design is realized in a browser.

## Testing on real devices

If you can, start to build up a "device lab" of older devices (phones/tablets) to view your work on. Having a number of varied devices is hugely beneficial. Not only does it let you feel how a design actually works across different devices, but it also exposes layout/rendering peculiarities earlier in the process. After all, no one enjoys believing that they have finished a project only to be told it doesn't work properly in a certain environment. Test early, and test often! Buying extra devices need not cost the earth. For example, you can pick up older phone and tablet models on eBay, or buy them from friends/relatives as they upgrade.

## Embracing progressive enhancement

In previous chapters, we have considered the notion of progressive enhancement. It's an approach to development that I have found so useful in practice that I think it bears repeating.

The fundamental idea of progressive enhancement is that you begin all your frontend code (HTML, CSS, or JavaScript) with the lowest common denominator in mind. Then, you progressively enhance the code for more capable devices and browsers. That may seem simplistic, and it is, but if you are used to working the other way around, then by designing the optimum experience and then figuring out a way of making that thing work on lesser devices/browsers, you'll find progressive enhancement an easier approach.

Imagine a low-powered, poorly featured device. It has no JavaScript, no Grid support—the most basic of devices you can imagine. In that scenario, what can you do to provide a usable experience? Most importantly, you should write meaningful HTML5 markup that accurately describes the content. This is an easier task if you're building text- and content-based websites. In that instance, concentrate on using elements like `main`, `header`, `footer`, `article`, `section`, and `aside` correctly. Not only will it help you discern different sections of your code, but it will also provide greater accessibility for your users at no extra cost.

If you're building something like a web-based application or visual UI components (carousels, tabs, accordions, and the like), you'll need to think about how to distill the visual pattern down into accessible markup.

The reason good markup is so crucial is that it provides a base-level experience for all users. The more you can achieve with HTML, the less you have to do in CSS and JavaScript to support older browsers. And nobody, and I really mean nobody, likes writing the code to support older browsers.

It's by no means a simple feat to think in this manner. However, it is an approach that is likely to serve you well in your quest to do as little as possible to support ailing browsers. Now, about those browsers...

## Defining a browser support matrix

Knowing the browsers and devices a web project needs to support upfront can be crucial to developing a successful responsive web design. We've already considered why progressive enhancement is so useful in this respect. If done correctly, it means that the vast majority of your site will be functional on even the oldest browsers.

However, there may also be times when you need to start your experience with a higher set of prerequisites. Perhaps you are working on a project where JavaScript is essential, which is not an uncommon scenario. In that instance, you can still progressively enhance, but you are merely enhancing from a different starting point.

Whatever your scenario, the key thing is to establish what your starting point is. Then, and only then, can you define and agree on what visual and functional experiences the different browsers and devices that you intend to support will get.

## Functional parity, not visual parity

It's both unrealistic and undesirable to get any website looking and working the same in every browser. Besides quirks that are specific to certain browsers, there are essential functional considerations. For example, we have to consider things like touch targets for buttons and links on touchscreens that aren't relevant to mouse-based devices.

Therefore, some part of your role as a responsive web developer is to educate whoever you are answerable to (your boss, client, or shareholders) that "supporting older browsers" does not mean "looking the same in older browsers." The line I tend to run with is that all browsers in the support matrix will get functional parity, not visual parity. This means that if you have a checkout to build, all users will be able to go through the checkout and purchase goods. There may be visual and interaction flourishes afforded to the users of more modern browsers, but the core task will be achievable by all.

Plus, we are in somewhat of a golden era when it comes to support for CSS features. There are still some features you can only get in one browser, but the overwhelming majority of important features nowadays enjoy broad support.

 Browser vendors themselves have even had programs to ensure greater interoperability. Read more about that here: https://web.dev/interop-2022/.

## Choosing the browsers to support

Typically, when we talk about which browsers to support, we're talking about how far back we need to look. Here are a couple of possibilities to consider, depending on the situation.

If it's an existing website, take a look at the visitor statistics (for example, Google Analytics or similar). Armed with some figures, you can do some rough calculations. For example, if the cost of supporting browser X is less than the value produced by supporting browser X, then support browser X!

Also, consider that if there are browsers in the statistics that represent less than 10% of users, look further back and consider any trends. How has usage changed over the last 3, 6, and 12 months? If it's currently 6% and that value has halved over the last 12 months, then you have a more compelling argument to consider ruling that browser out for specific enhancements.

If it's a new project and statistics are unavailable, I usually opt for a "previous 2" policy. This would be the current version, plus the previous two versions of each browser. For example, if Safari 16 was the current version, look to offer your enhancements for that version plus Safari 15 and Safari 14 (the previous two). This choice is easier with the "evergreen" browsers, which is the term given to browsers that continually update on a rapid release cycle (Firefox, Chrome, and Microsoft Edge, for example).

## Tiering the user experience

Let's assume your shareholders are educated and on board. Let's also assume you have a clear set of browsers that you would like, and need, to add enhanced experiences for. We can now set about tiering the experience. I like to keep things simple, so, where possible, I opt to define a simple "base" tier and a more "enhanced" tier.

Here, the base experience is the minimum viable version of the site, and the enhanced version is the most fully featured and aesthetically pleasing version. You might need to accommodate more granularity in your tiers, but regardless of how the tiers are defined, ensure you define them and what you expect to deliver with each. Then you can go about coding those tiers. That's where techniques like feature queries, which we covered in *Chapter 6, CSS Selectors, Typography, and More*, will come in handy.

## Avoiding CSS frameworks in production

There are a plethora of free CSS frameworks available that aim to aid in the rapid prototyping and building of responsive websites. The two most common examples are Bootstrap (`https://getbootstrap.com`) and Foundation (`https://get.foundation/`). While they are great projects, particularly for learning how to build responsive visual patterns, I think they should be avoided in production.

I've spoken to plenty of developers who start all of their projects with one of these frameworks and then amend them to fit their needs. This approach can be incredibly advantageous for rapid prototyping (for example, to illustrate some interaction with clients), but I think it's the wrong thing to do for projects you intend to take through to production.

Firstly, from a technical perspective, it's likely that starting with a framework will result in your project having more code than it actually needs. Secondly, from an aesthetic perspective, due to the popularity of these frameworks, it's likely your project will end up looking very similar to countless others.

Finally, if you only copy and paste code into your project and tweak it to your needs, you're unlikely to fully appreciate what's going on "under the hood." It's only by defining and solving the problems you have that you can master the code you place into your projects.

## Hiding, showing, and loading content across viewports

One of the commonly touted maxims regarding responsive web design is that if you don't have something on the screen in smaller viewports, you shouldn't have it there in larger ones either.

This means users should be able to accomplish all the same goals (such as buying a product, reading an article, or accomplishing an interface task) at every viewport size. This is common sense. After all, as users ourselves, we've all felt the frustration of going to a website to accomplish a goal and being unable to, because we're using a smaller screen.

This also means that as screen real estate is more plentiful, we shouldn't feel compelled to add extra things just to fill the space (widgets, adverts, or links, for example). If the user could live without those extras on smaller screen sizes, they'll manage just fine on bigger ones.

In broad terms, I think the preceding maxim is sound advice. If nothing else, it makes designers and developers question more thoroughly the content they display onscreen. However, as ever in web design, there will be exceptions.

As far as possible, I resist loading in new markup for different viewports, but, very occasionally, it's a necessity. Some complex user interfaces might simply work better with different markup and designs at wider viewports. In that instance, JavaScript is typically used to replace one area of markup with another. It isn't the ideal scenario, but it is sometimes the most pragmatic.

By the same token, I think it's perfectly reasonable to have sections of markup hidden in CSS until they are appropriate. I'm thinking about things like headers. On more than one occasion, before Grid was well supported, I wasted an inordinate amount of time trying to figure out how to convert one header layout for mobile into a different layout for larger screens, all while using the same markup. It was folly! The pragmatic solution is to have both pieces of markup and just hide each as appropriate with a media query. When the difference is a handful of elements and the associated styles, there are almost always more sensible savings to make elsewhere.

These are the choices you will probably face as you code more and more complex responsive web designs, and you'll need to use your own judgment as to what the best choice is in any given scenario. However, it's not a cardinal sin if you toggle the visibility of the odd bit of markup with display: none to achieve your goal.

## Validators and linting tools

Generally speaking, writing HTML and CSS is pretty forgiving. You can nest the odd thing incorrectly, miss the occasional quotation mark or self-closing tag, and not always notice a problem. Despite this, on an almost weekly basis, I manage to befuddle myself with incorrect markup. Sometimes, it's a slip-up, like accidentally typing an errant character. Other times, it's schoolboy errors like nesting a div inside a span (invalid markup as a span is an inline element and a div is a block-level element, which leads to unpredictable results).

Thankfully, there are great tools to help out. At worst, if you're encountering a weird issue, head over to https://validator.w3.org/ and paste your markup in there. It will point out any errors along with line numbers, helping you to easily fix things up:

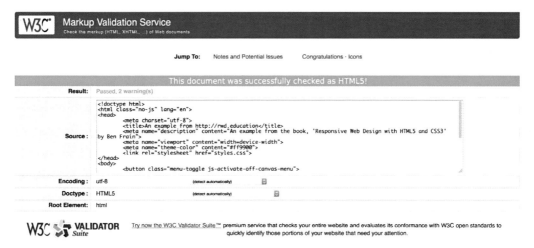

*Figure 15.8: Skip the validation of HTML at your peril!*

Better still, install and configure **linting** tools for your HTML, CSS, and JavaScript. Or, choose a text editor with some sanity checking built in. Then, problem areas are flagged up in your code as you go.

Here's an example of a simple spelling error in CSS flagged up by the LSP (Language Server Protocol) in the Neovim editor:

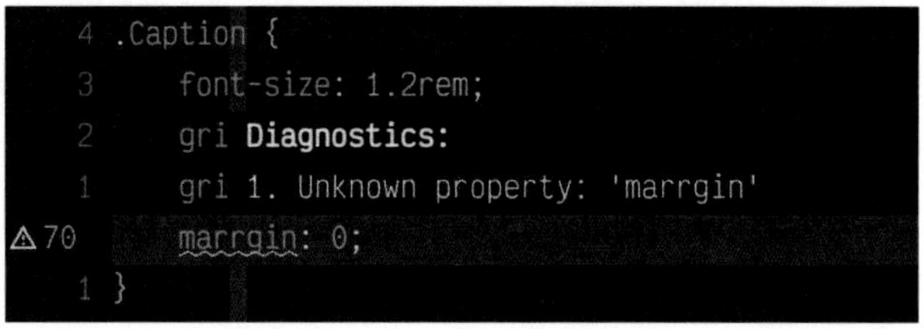

*Figure 15.9: Embrace tooling that saves you from basic mistakes*

Like a clown, I've clumsily typed "marrgin" instead of "margin". The editor has spotted this fact and pointed out the error of my ways. Embrace these tools where possible. There are better uses of your time than tracking down simple syntax errors in your code.

## Performance

Considering the performance of your responsive web designs is as important as the aesthetics. However, performance presents something of a moving target. For example, browsers update and improve the way they handle assets, new techniques are discovered that supersede existing "best practices," and technologies eventually get enough browser support that they become viable for widespread adoption. The list goes on.

There are, however, some basic implementation details that are pretty solid advice. These are:

- Minimize the page weight. If you can compress images to a fraction of their original size, you should. This should always be your first task with optimizing. It's possible to double the file size savings by compressing one image compared to compressing and minifying all of your CSS and JavaScript. We looked at image optimization more fully in *Chapter 9, Responsive Images*.
- Defer non-essential assets. If you can load any additional CSS and JavaScript after the page has initially rendered, it can greatly reduce the perceived load time.
- Ensure the page is usable as soon as possible, which is often a byproduct of doing all the preceding points.

## Performance tools

There are great tools available to measure and optimize performance. My personal favorite is `https://webpagetest.org`. At its simplest, you can pick a URL and click on **START TEST**.

It will show you a complete analysis of the page, but even more usefully, if you choose the visual comparison option, it shows a "filmstrip" view of the loaded page, allowing you to concentrate on getting the rendered page completed sooner. Here's an example of the "filmstrip" view of the previous version of the `https://rwd.education` home page:

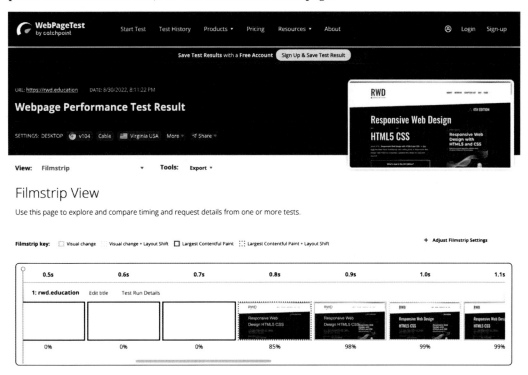

*Figure 15.10: Seeing the page load as a filmstrip can really tell the story of performance*

Even the free tier of this service will offer practical advice on what to do to make your website load faster and be more accessible. I learn something new almost every time I test a site there!

There are also increasingly powerful performance tools built into browser developer tools. Although, you should be aware these can be a little intimidating at first use. It can feel a little like opening something like After Effects for the first time and wondering what on earth you are supposed to do!

Delving into the developer tools in any detail is beyond our discussion scope here, but let's consider some of the kinds of information you can get at to improve the performance of your site.

If you're working on something that uses a lot of JavaScript or video, which is sure to negatively affect the device battery, then the CPU timeline feature of Safari (macOS only, unfortunately) may be of interest: `https://webkit.org/blog/8993/cpu-timeline-in-web-inspector/`.

Firefox has the Profiler tool, which mercifully has a full guide here: `https://profiler.firefox.com/docs/#/`. It can give you incredibly detailed information, including the same kind of filmstrip feedback we saw in Web Page Test. I'll confess to finding it a little unapproachable, especially when we are typically looking for the "low-hanging fruit" when it comes to fixing up our sites.

*Figure 15.11: Firefox Profiler is powerful but perhaps overkill*

Typically, I tend to use Lighthouse, which has its own tab in the Google Chrome developer tools. Point it at a site and it will give you a breakdown of where improvements can be made:

## Accessibility

These checks highlight opportunities to improve the accessibility of your web app. Only a subset of accessibility issues can be automatically detected so manual testing is also encouraged.

ARIA

▲  `[aria-hidden="true"]` elements contain focusable descendents                                          ⌄

These are opportunities to improve the usage of ARIA in your application which may enhance the experience for users of assistive technology, like a screen reader.

*Figure 15.12: The Lighthouse tools not only tell you what you can improve, but they tell you how to do it*

It's such a great tool, as every piece of advice has links to additional documentation, so you read more about the problem and potential ways of addressing it.

If you are new to looking at the performance of the sites you are making, my advice would be to start with Lighthouse and go deeper only if you feel you need or want to. If you have four scores close to 100 in Lighthouse, you've done a decent job.

Whenever you try to optimize performance, ensure you take measurements before you begin (otherwise, you will not understand how effective your performance work has been). Then make amendments, test, and repeat.

# The next big things

One of the interesting things about front-end web development is that things change rapidly. There is always something new to learn and the web community is always figuring out better, faster, and more effective ways of solving problems.

For example, when writing the first edition of this book, over ten years ago, responsive images (`srcset` and the `picture` element, which are detailed in *Chapter 9, Responsive Images*) simply didn't exist. Back then, we had to use clever third-party workarounds to serve up more appropriate images to different viewport sizes. Now, that common need has been rationalized into a W3C standard, which has been implemented across browsers.

Similarly, only a few years ago, Flexbox was just a twinkle in a specification writer's eyes. Even when the specification evolved, it was still difficult to implement until a super-smart developer called Andrey Sitnik, along with his colleagues at Evil Martians (`https://evilmartians.com/`) created Autoprefixer. This was a tool that allowed us to write a single syntax and have our CSS be processed into code that could work across multiple implementations as if by magic. Skip forward a few more years and prefixing CSS values is a practice few even need to concern themselves with.

Progress on the web shows little sign of abating. Even now, things like WebAssembly, or WASM, as it is often referred to, are gaining more and more traction. WebAssembly is a means of having web code that runs far more akin to the speed of a compiled language. In short, it will make things on the web feel a whole lot faster. Lin Clark, a developer at the browser-maker Mozilla, has a very accessible series on WebAssembly here: `https://hacks.mozilla.org/2017/02/a-cartoon-intro-to-webassembly/`. Design tools you may be familiar with, such as Figma, make extensive use of WebAssembly: `https://www.figma.com/blog/webassembly-cut-figmas-load-time-by-3x/`.

And due to the current infancy and few implementations, in this book, we didn't even look at things like scroll-linked animations, `@when/else` for "logic" in CSS, scoped styles to isolate styles to a particular section of the DOM, or the `@property` CSS at-rule for creating your own properties.

In short – expect change, and embrace it!

# Summary

As we reach the end of our time together, your humble author hopes to have related all the essential techniques and tools you'll need to start building your next website or web application responsively.

It's my conviction that, by approaching web projects with a little forethought, and by potentially making a few modifications to existing workflows and practices, it's possible to embrace modern techniques that provide fast, flexible, accessible, and maintainable websites that can look incredible, regardless of the device used to visit them.

We've covered a wealth of information in our time together: techniques, technologies, performance optimizations, specifications, workflow, tooling, and more. I wouldn't expect anybody to absorb it all in one read.

Therefore, the next time you need to remember this or that syntax, or to refresh your mind about one of the responsive-related subjects we've covered, I hope you'll dip back into these pages; I'll be right here waiting for you.

Until then, I wish you good fortune in your responsive web design quests.

See you again sometime.

# Join our book's Discord space

Before you embark on your responsive journey, join the book's Discord workspace to discuss all your responsive web design concerns directly with the author and interact with other readers:

https://packt.link/RWD4e

packt.com

Subscribe to our online digital library for full access to over 7,000 books and videos, as well as industry leading tools to help you plan your personal development and advance your career. For more information, please visit our website.

## Why subscribe?

- Spend less time learning and more time coding with practical eBooks and Videos from over 4,000 industry professionals
- Improve your learning with Skill Plans built especially for you
- Get a free eBook or video every month
- Fully searchable for easy access to vital information
- Copy and paste, print, and bookmark content

At www.packt.com, you can also read a collection of free technical articles, sign up for a range of free newsletters, and receive exclusive discounts and offers on Packt books and eBooks.

# Other Books You May Enjoy

If you enjoyed this book, you may be interested in these other books by Packt:

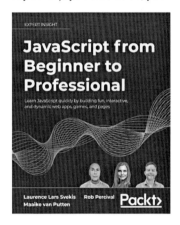

**JavaScript from Beginner to Professional**

Laurence Lars Svekis

Maaike van Putten

Rob Percival

ISBN: 9781800562523

- Use logic statements to make decisions within your code
- Save time with JavaScript loops by avoiding writing the same code repeatedly
- Use JavaScript functions and methods to selectively execute code
- Connect to HTML5 elements and bring your own web pages to life with interactive content

- Make your search patterns more effective with regular expressions
- Explore concurrency and asynchronous programming to process events efficiently and improve performance
- Get a head start on your next steps with primers on key libraries, frameworks, and APIs

**Node.js Design Patterns, Third Edition**

Mario Casciaro

Luciano Mammino

ISBN: 9781839214110

- Become comfortable with writing asynchronous code by leveraging callbacks, promises, and the async/await syntax
- Leverage Node.js streams to create data-driven asynchronous processing pipelines
- Implement well-known software design patterns to create production grade applications
- Share code between Node.js and the browser and take advantage of full-stack JavaScript
- Build and scale microservices and distributed systems powered by Node.js
- Use Node.js in conjunction with other powerful technologies such as Redis, RabbitMQ, ZeroMQ, and LevelDB

**Mastering TypeScript, Fourth Edition**

Nathan Rozentals

ISBN: 9781800564732

- Gain insights into core and advanced TypeScript language features

- Integrate with existing JavaScript libraries and third-party frameworks

- Build full working applications using JavaScript frameworks, such as Angular, React, Vue, and more

- Create test suites for your application with Jest and Selenium

- Apply industry-standard design patterns to build modular code

- Develop web server solutions using NodeJS and Express

- Design and implement serverless API solutions

- Explore micro front-end technologies and techniques

# Packt is searching for authors like you

If you're interested in becoming an author for Packt, please visit authors.packtpub.com and apply today. We have worked with thousands of developers and tech professionals, just like you, to help them share their insight with the global tech community. You can make a general application, apply for a specific hot topic that we are recruiting an author for, or submit your own idea.

# Share your thoughts

Now you've finished *Responsive Web Design with HTML5 and CSS, Fourth Edition*, we'd love to hear your thoughts! Scan the QR code below to go straight to the Amazon review page for this book and share your feedback or leave a review on the site that you purchased it from.

*https://packt.link/r/180324271X*

Your review is important to us and the tech community and will help us make sure we're delivering excellent quality content.

# Index

# Download a free PDF copy of this book

Thanks for purchasing this book!

Do you like to read on the go but are unable to carry your print books everywhere?

Is your eBook purchase not compatible with the device of your choice?

Don't worry, now with every Packt book you get a DRM-free PDF version of that book at no cost.

Read anywhere, any place, on any device. Search, copy, and paste code from your favorite technical books directly into your application.

The perks don't stop there, you can get exclusive access to discounts, newsletters, and great free content in your inbox daily

Follow these simple steps to get the benefits:

1.  Scan the QR code or visit the link below

https://packt.link/free-ebook/9781803242712

2.  Submit your proof of purchase
3.  That's it! We'll send your free PDF and other benefits to your email directly